ERIC GIULIANI

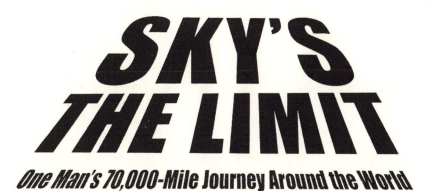

SKY'S THE LIMIT

One Man's 70,000-Mile Journey Around the World

Sky's the Limit: One Man's 70,000-Mile Journey Around the World
Copyright © 2021 by Eric Giuliani
All rights reserved.
First Edition: 2021

Editors: Kristen Tate & Christina Boys
Cover Design: Kathryn Maus
Interior Formatting: Streetlight Graphics

Print ISBN: 978-0-57882058-3
eBook ISBN: 978-0-578-82059-0

For Annika

AUTHOR'S NOTE

I changed the names of most of the people in my book, as well as the Miami middle schools and a few of the hotels I write about. I used the stories I wrote on my blog while traveling as the backbone for this book. I hope you enjoy the ride.

PROLOGUE

UNITED STATES

NORTH AMERICA

"One's mind, once stretched by a new idea,
never regains its original dimensions."

— *Oliver Wendell Holmes*

I LOOK OUT ACROSS THE ROOM and see fifteen faces wearing indifferent expressions staring back at me. They match mine.

"Hello, everyone, my name is Eric, and I'm so happy to be here today at . . ."

Shit! Where am I?

Even though I pulled in and parked not more than ten minutes ago, I've already forgotten which Miami middle school I'm at. They all share the same 1970s cookie-cutter architecture—clusters of classroom buildings connected by covered breezeways.

I clear my throat, look down at my notes, and pull the name out of the morass of details. "I'm happy to be here today at your school, PR Clark Middle School."

Truth is, I'm not happy to be here. I can't stand what I do for a living. In fact, I wouldn't even call it living. I'm the implementation manager for Miami-Dade County, working for a New Jersey–based company that sells educational software. That's just a glorified way of saying I show teachers—all of them frustrated, hostile or disinterested—how to push a few buttons on their computers. I'm just one of many interchangeable cogs in the corporate wheel.

After I take roll, I slink behind the warped wooden desk at the front of the computer lab. "Okay, everyone, step one. Please type in your username and password, like so."

I switch to autopilot as I go through the same presentation I've given at every single one of the eighty schools I'm responsible for. I can no longer differentiate one day from another. I'm Bill Murray's character in *Groundhog Day*.

Is this all my life will ever amount to?

I'm brought back to earth by a few snickering teachers in the front row. I do a double take because I can't decide if what I'm seeing is serious or not.

A sixth-grade teacher around my grandmother's age has her mouse pressed up against the computer's monitor, and she's moving it from side to side like Mr. Miyagi is teaching her wax on, wax off. I stare in disbelief; she can't possibly think that's how computers work? It's 2013, for God's sake. Surely she's joking. I play along and offer an Oscar-worthy fake laugh as I get up and stride toward her. She looks up at me with a helpless expression, and my stomach sinks. She actually thinks computers work this way. I'd thought I'd seen it all by now, but this is a new low. Trying not to embarrass her, I move the mouse back onto the mouse pad beside her and point to the arrow on the screen as I move the mouse back and forth, but I can tell she doesn't get it.

It's only 8:45 a.m., and it's already one of those days. Then again, every day lately has been one of those days. While I feel bad for her, selfishly I feel worse for myself. I'm going to have to stop after each step and walk over to her and literally put my hand on hers so I can push her finger down on the mouse until it clicks. It's the only way she'll be able follow along, and it's going to take me twice as long to get through my Punxsutawney presentation today because of it.

At thirty-two years old, I've done everything like I'm supposed to. I've gone to college, gotten a "good" job, and moved to my dream city of Miami Beach. I live in a stunning one-bedroom condo overlooking the part of the ocean that cradles the sunset each night. I drive a sleek BMW, go to rooftop pool parties each weekend, and see the sun almost 365 days a year. And while I'm incredibly grateful for those things, I can't stand my life.

#

Two years ago, after a particularly awful day covering for a sick coworker, I called up my manager and pleaded for a three-month leave of absence. I needed not just a vacation, but a reassessment of the life I was living. I knew it would take her longer to hire and train someone else than just wait for me to return. She begrudgingly accepted, and I sublet my apartment to my buddy Daniel. The day before my flight, my manager reneged and told me she couldn't guarantee my job would be there when I came back. But a teeny tiny voice inside me kept whispering, "The world has something it needs to tell you."

So I let that teeny tiny voice propel all six feet ten inches of me forward and boarded the flight to Hong Kong anyway. I traveled with just a carry-on bag and a beat-up laptop in my backpack, which I used to pull up Google Earth and Kayak.com. I'd pore over what cities were nearby, buying cheap one-way tickets as I bucket-listed my way around the globe. Even the planning and purchasing were intoxicating.

I spent a wild weekend in Patong Beach, went scuba diving at the Great Barrier Reef, got my first taste of Paris, watched the sun rise over Machu Picchu, and drank a glass of homemade red wine in the Italian apple field my great-great-grandfather used to plow.

I gobbled up as many books as I could fit into the front pocket of my carry-on by authors like Paulo Coelho, Eckhart Tolle, Joseph Campbell, and Dr. Wayne Dyer. I collected more books during my travels: the *Bhagavad Gita* in Malaysia; the *Teachings of Buddha* in Thailand; the *Thoughtful Guide to Islam* in the Middle East; and Deepak Chopra's *Jesus* at an airport in Europe. My suitcase held more books than shirts, which is strange because I've always hated to read. Suddenly I couldn't stop. Each book was a chance to learn something new. Each author handed me a different piece of my puzzle.

During these three months, I transformed from tourist to traveler and I know the exact moment it happened.

"If you could be anyone else in the world, who would you be?" I asked Rajinder as he eased his foot off the gas. He slowed down, as he did every time he spoke in English—understandable since he'd translate my

English to his Hindi, then his Hindi back to my English, all while dodging the cattle, chickens, humans, motorbikes, rickshaws, and elephants that filled New Delhi's lawless streets.

"Let me think about this one, Mister Eric."

I'd gotten to know Rajinder pretty well in the week I'd spent crammed inside the rolling sauna he calls a taxi. He grew up in a quiet farming village eight hours north and sends most of his earnings to support his family back home. He lives in a tent, where he keeps his only belongings—his other shirt, a sleeping bag, and a few books in English. He told me, "I really want to learn English, so I try to read it as much as I can."

He'd spoken highly of Barack Obama, but in India cricket is like a religion—so I was expecting him to name either the US president or India's greatest batsman, Sachin Tendulkar. Rajinder's eyes take on a different shade of blue whenever Tendulkar's name comes up in conversation.

"Okay, Rajinder, so who's it going to be?"

Incessant honking and dust filled the air. Rajinder wove through a crowded roundabout and swerved dangerously close to an empty oxcart. "Just one more minute, Mister Eric."

Two days before, he had driven me to the Taj Mahal. I asked him to come inside and see it with me, offering to pay for his ticket. But he said, "Mister Eric, I have been waiting my whole life to go inside, but every time I'm here I restrain myself from going past this point. Since the Taj Mahal is a tomb built to honor Shah Jahan's favorite wife, I want the first time I see it to be alongside my wife."

Rajinder had come to the parking lot of the Taj Mahal over a hundred times, but he'd only recently entered into an arranged marriage with a woman in the village he grew up in. He'd resisted going inside all those times without knowing if he would ever actually marry.

"Okay, I know my choice, Mister Eric. I know who I would be," Rajinder said as he slowed down to let a stray brown-haired dog scamper past the front bumper. He looked over at me. "I would be water."

I couldn't stop my laughter from bursting out. "You must have misunderstood the question." In typical ignorant American fashion, I spoke slower and louder: "IF YOU COULD BE ANYONE ELSE IN THE WORLD, WHO WOULD YOU BE?"

"I would choose to be water, Mister Eric."

"But, Rajinder, that doesn't make sense."

"Sure it does, Mister Eric. Everyone needs water to survive, and if I was water then I could help the most people."

Those words have stayed with me ever since.

When I walked off the plane in Miami at the end of my trip, I felt as if I had lightning in my limbs. Life was exploding in all directions, and the possibilities for what I might become seemed endless. I actually smiled when I saw the email notifying me I had been terminated. I felt free, and I was so sure that the previous three months were going to springboard me toward my deepest dreams.

However, the euphoria wore off a few weeks later, and reality quickly set in. I had spent fifteen thousand dollars in three months—every single dime I had, plus two thousand dollars I didn't have on my credit cards. Bills piled up, and the rent felt like it was due every other day.

Worst of all, I couldn't piece together what I wanted to do. The job of my dreams wasn't waiting for me in the want ads like I'd hoped. So I got scared and settled—for the same safe, predictable job I'd had before. I'll never forget the feeling of failure that washed over me when I put on the only suit I owned on the morning I'd interviewed for my current job. I had to force my legs forward as I walked toward my future.

#

Now I leave this school like I do every other, racing down the halls with the company-issued Lenovo computer curled up under my arm like a football. With my car in sight a teacher with a question approaches me in the parking lot, but I juke past him like I'm Barry Sanders. I slide into my car and rest my head on the steering wheel, exhausted.

Ten minutes later, I'm trapped in a steady stream of red rush hour taillights. As I creep forward, my eyes are drawn to the airport, and my desire for the richness I found at the height of my travels returns with a vengeance. I need to find a way back to that time in my life. I reach for my blinker and then curl around exit 969 and head north on Milam Dairy Road. After a quick right and a sharp left, I'm parked up against the chain-link fence that borders the west end of the airport runway.

The service road is all but empty, and when a plane takes off just a few feet above me, the rumble from its engine rattles my teeth. The hair on the back of my neck stands up, and I crack my first faint smile of the day. I hop out of my car and lock my fingers around the fence so I can feel the tail wind whip by when a British Airways flight lands just a few hundred yards in front of me. I lean back on the hood of my car and wave to an Aeroméxico flight as it hurtles down the runway and lifts into the air. Then I pull out my iPhone and snap a picture of the underbelly of a Boeing 797 as it sails by. I've never seen an airplane from this angle before, and I'm amazed by the creative composition of the photo. As I watch a few more flights take off and touch down, I feel something slowly being restored in me.

I'm not leaving this spot until I figure things out once and for all. I'm sick of feeling trapped in this life. There has to be more. It feels like there's an important part of myself that I've yet to discover. I don't know what it is, but I can feel it just below the surface of my skin. My three-month trip around the world was supposed to be a catalyst for change, yet I haven't changed.

I take a deep breath and ask myself the same question I once asked Rajinder: "If you could be anyone else in the world, who would you be?"

The answer doesn't come.

I try again. "What do I really want to do with my life? What are my deepest dreams? If I could do anything in the world, what would I want to do?"

I begin to feel a humming inside my spine. The answer is so close I can taste it. My dream is dangling like a word I can't quite remember. It's at the tip of my tongue, but as I try to put all the syllables in order, I still can't string it together.

I recall all the things I enjoyed doing when it didn't matter if I did them well: the creative writing elective I took my junior year of high school; the short horror film I shot with one of those bulky VHS video camcorders in a multimedia class; the travel blog I wrote on TravelPod.com during my three-month sabbatical. I remember how much I loved traveling with my AAU basketball team during high school, my conversations with Rajinder in India, the enthusiasm of my Buddha-bellied Italian uncle Luciano as he leapt through his apple fields, and the sweet-and-salty smells of Singapore's back streets. I begin to yearn for the rush I'd get when I was chasing my curiosity from city to city.

All my senses seem to sync, and my dreams shoot out of a dark tunnel and straight into the honeycombs of my heart. Suddenly I know exactly what I need to do!

Just taking a leave of absence and going on a three-month trip isn't going to be enough. I want more. I need to go on a long journey. And I want something more challenging than just flying from city to city. I want to survive by my wits and see every inch of dirt and sand this world has to offer.

After a deep breath, I work up the courage to tell the empty air around me, "I want to travel across Africa, Europe, Asia, Australia, North and South America—and even the oceans in between. And I want to do it all over land and sea. I want to travel using just buses, boats, and trains—no airplanes this time!"

But that's just the outward journey. I don't want to go around the world only to come back to Florida and return to the same job—again. I want to transform my life once and for all. And I need to make it stick this time. I want to live a life that taps into the creativity I've been too insecure to express, and I want it to converge with my love of traveling.

I've never been courageous enough to pursue anything that required even so much as an ounce of creativity. But there's something about traveling, taking in other cultures, that sends my senses spilling out of my soul. Everything is that much more vivid and vibrant abroad.

I want an everlasting adventure, which is not only travel-related, but also a soul-deep experience. Creativity at its core is a connection to something unseen and often described as a spiritual affair. I've experienced only brief flashes of that feeling, but I want it to become my norm. I will find the creative self I've ignored for far too long. I will write, film, and photograph every moment, every discovery. I will merge work and play. I will live one life, not two. I will become a globe-trotting writer, filmmaker, and photographer.

There's just one problem. This idea is impossible. There's no way in hell I can pull all that off. I have no experience in any of these artistic endeavors. I failed just about every high school English class I ever took, and the only camera I own is the one inside my iPhone 4. I'm also almost completely broke. And yet, I suddenly can't see myself doing anything other than at least attempting this Impossible Idea.

As the sun rises high above Biscayne Bay's turquoise waters the following morning and Saturday begins to take shape, so too does my plan. I decide to turn my dreams into goals and then break down the goals into (very long) to-do lists. I take down the generic canvas prints I got at TJ

Maxx and wallpaper almost all of my living room wall with chart paper. Next I center the world map that has gathered as much dust as my dreams on top of the chart paper and tack it into place.

Just to the left of North America, I write, "Step one, sign up for a beginner photography class. Step two, buy a camera." The space beside Asia becomes home to all the things I need to learn about if I want to become a filmmaker; the list runs all the way from Japan to Jakarta. My black Sharpie squeaks as I outline all the aspects of travel writing I'll need to learn underneath South America. The area west of Africa agrees to keep track of all the steps I'll have to follow in order to build my own travel blog.

I've always been a visual learner, and when I step back and see all that I'll need to do, the project, while still Herculean, feels just a bit more manageable. I riffle through the travel magazines I keep in my front closet and cut out pictures of all the places I still want to see and tape them atop the map. Then I add a few favorite quotes to the wall so that they'll prod me forward:

"Your inner vision trumps your innate talent every time." – Wayne Dyer

"The secret of change is to focus all your energy, not on fighting the old, but on building the new." – Socrates

The second quote leads me to the final thing I need to address: money. I'll need to build a bank account that can keep pace with long-term travel. It's time I finally get my finances in order and set a goal. I write $25,000 and underline it several times. Then I open every bill in the stack on my kitchen counter and figure out how much I owe in total: $8,458.06. I check my bank account and see I have exactly $8,902.14. I decide to get this monkey off my back once and for all and pay off all my bills on the spot.

I write the amount that's left on the chart paper so that I can see exactly how much money I'm starting with: $444.08. There's something about the symmetry of seeing three fours lined up together that is oddly encouraging. Four has always been my favorite number, the one I insisted on for my first-ever basketball jersey way back in second grade.

I decide to give myself exactly one year to meet my savings goal and learn all the things scribbled on my gigantic vision board. I write March 9, 2014, at the very top of the chart paper using a bright orange Sharpie.

As I back away from the wall, it looks like an incredible collage of hopes and dreams.

I don't see obstacles and excuses anymore; instead, I see the blueprint for a better life.

* * *

I start making changes right away—first little things, then bigger and bigger things. I shrink my circle of friends, sell my TV, and become a bookworm. I stop going out, quit complaining about money, and work at my soul-sucking job with defiant determination. Every move I make and dollar I spend has a purpose now, and that purpose quickly becomes the most powerful force I've ever felt.

Step one is that beginning photography class. Even though the course is just around a hundred and fifty bucks, I have to wait until my next two paychecks come in before I can register. In addition to Beginner Digital Photography, I also sign up for Better Writing 1 and Introduction to Adobe Photoshop. They're just your basic continuing education courses offered by Miami-Dade Community College, but this is how I've decided to spend my nights now. I'll be here from 6:30 to 9:30 p.m. on Monday, Wednesday, and Thursday nights for the foreseeable future.

As I walk down the hallway to my first class, I shake my head, surprised that I'm here. I always hated school. If I hadn't gotten a basketball scholarship, I never would have gotten into college—not just the college I went to, Binghamton University, but any college. My grades were that bad, and I've always struggled when it comes to schoolwork. However, today feels different. I'm optimistic. This digital photography class is the first class I've ever signed up for out of interest.

I push open the door of room 1652 and see a sterile classroom filled mostly with soccer moms. At the front of the classroom is the teacher, a Haitian man with bloodshot eyes. "Hi, I'm Johnny," he says and asks for my name so he can check it against the roster on his clipboard.

It isn't long until I'm back to being the scared student I was in middle school, the one that tried to avoid eye contact when the teacher asked a question or needed a volunteer to read the next paragraph out loud. The trigger this time, though, is my own stupidity. Johnny's first order of business is to walk around the room so he can see what type of DSLR camera everyone will be shooting with for the next six weeks.

Johnny stops at my desk and asks, "Where's your camera, Eric?"

I shy my eyes away and say, "Well, I didn't know we needed one."

"It's in the course description. Did you read the course description?"

I lie and say yes. Then I swivel my head around the room and see that every single person in the class has a shiny new DSLR camera out on top of their desk. Some people have Nikons, some have Canons, and a few have Sonys. All I can think to do is to pull my iPhone 4 out of my pocket and say, "I'm going to use this."

Johnny laughs and tells me that I need to get a real camera by the next class, but before I can tell him that I can't afford one, he's already moved on to the middle-aged man in front of me who looks like he's come straight from selling insurance all afternoon.

After a lecture about the history of photography, Johnny tells us to look through our viewfinders and adjust our shutter speed to $1/100^{th}$. Everyone picks up their cameras and follows along, but I just look down hopelessly at my iPhone. Johnny sees me and condescendingly calls over, "See, Eric, this class is going to be pretty tough without a camera."

As the whole class laughs at his remark, I begin to plot my escape. I think I'll be able to make myself small and sneak out when Johnny gives us a break.

A few minutes later while I'm shuffling my notes into my backpack, Johnny says, "Before our break, I want to say one last thing." Johnny saunters over to an empty desk at the front of the room and puts his calloused hands on its backrest. He leans forward and whispers, "You see a desk, but a photographer sees possibilities."

Huh? What?

"Okay, everyone, be back in fifteen minutes so we can talk about ISO and white balance."

As everyone files out and the classroom empties, a light inside me slowly illuminates.

I'm caught completely off guard by what Johnny just said. Honestly, I'd already given up on wanting to become a photographer and had been thinking about the kind of pizza I was going to order on the way home, but suddenly I've been sucked back into this space.

I get up and slowly walk toward the desk Johnny has just referenced. Each step allows me study the desk from a different direction. As I do, something blooms inside my eyes. What Johnny said reminds me of the photo I took the day I decided on my dreams. I think of how unique the underbelly of the airplane looked when I snapped it at the edge of the airport. I remember how my body tingled when I took it.

I return to my desk and take my notes back out.

\#

Much to Johnny's chagrin, I complete not just beginning photography but also the intermediate course without a camera. Just like Rocky when he's using old school training methods in snowy Russia for his fight against Drago, I figure out that not owning the best equipment actually gives me an advantage. Using my little old iPhone 4 forces me to tap into my creativity and figure out what photography is all about, which I quickly realize has very little to do with the type of camera the photographer uses.

Since the camera in my iPhone is so limited compared to my class-mates' state-of-the-art DSLRs, I have to approach each assignment from a completely different angle, both literally and metaphorically. I start getting sucked deep into each moment and quickly discover the still, small place where my creative composition thrives. During one practice session at the beach, it feels like I am just riding the wind's coattails, letting it push and pull me across the sand. One of the photos from that session actually makes it into the *Sun Sentinel* one Sunday.

Once I complete both photography courses, I decide to grit my teeth and get a second job as an economics teacher for an online high school, which helps me scrape together enough money to buy a refurbished Canon 7D camera and a used lens to go with it. I spend a few hours each night grading assignments and contacting students and their parents. My performance is based on how quickly I can get the students to complete the course. The quicker a student finishes all the assignments and exits the course, the quicker that roster spot opens up for someone else. While the school is federally funded, it's also a for-profit venture. When I've actu-ally done my job correctly and slowed a student down or asked them to redo an assignment, it's raised red flags—not on the student, but on me. After the fifth angry phone call from my boss, Andrea, asking me why I don't understand my role within the company, I decide to stick to copy-and-pasting in the responses another teacher had given me so I can keep the kids moving along and myself under the radar.

In order to fit practicing my photography into my days, I start waking up early and getting to the beach as the sun rises each morning. Every single day of my life, I hit the snooze button and often oversleep, but I've finally found a goal that is bigger than keeping my eyes closed.

* * *

Based on all the inspiring autobiographies I've read, it seems to be a universal truth that dreams are great dancers. They love to tango: two steps forward then one step back. As my one year deadline approaches, my financial goal is in reach, but I'm not making progress fast enough. So I drag my sectional couch and all the rest of my belongings out of my one-bedroom apartment and down the hall into a studio apartment. Just two weeks later, while reviewing my paperwork for the apartment switch, the building management team uncovers the fact that I had sublet my apartment to Daniel while I was traveling two years ago and stick a notice on my door saying that I have two weeks to be out.

This works in my favor because it allows me to break my lease without penalty, and I move into an even smaller studio apartment on the corner of Seventh and Washington. It's a pretty ratty place, about the size of a jail cell, but this Impossible Idea is beating so hard inside me that my comfort has become the least of my concerns. At least until I start waking up with bright red rashes on my arms and legs. When I peel back the faux leather of my headboard a few inches, hundreds of tiny brown bedbugs scurry out like the cops have just showed up at the world's biggest underage house party.

Infestation is an understatement and I choke back the urge to vomit.

I find a cheap exterminator, but when I arrive home from work, my heart sinks. The room reeks of chemicals, and all my things have been pushed in a pile and sprayed down with something gooey. There is a filmy white residue covering every single thing I own. My head falls into my hands. I've thought all the hard work I'd been putting in showed the Universe my seriousness, but I guess I was wrong. I don't even know where to begin.

A soft voice cuts through my thoughts and catches me off guard. "Hey, I thought you could use some help." I turn around and, much to my surprise, I see Naomi standing in the doorway.

"How did you even know I was home?"

She smiles wide and holds up a pair of yellow rubber gloves, a plastic bucket, and a bag full of cleaning supplies. "I just had a feeling."

My heart melts.

I met Naomi about seven months ago. She was on her way back from Cambodia and stopped in Miami Beach for the holidays to see our mutual friend, Brian. They've had a sibling-like relationship for the past twenty years, and Brian predicted that she and I would hit it off. We did, but first as friends. A freer spirit I have not met. The first time we talked, she said she was off to wherever the wind took her next. Which she meant, literally. She's thirty-one and left her boring desk job years ago to float (often penniless) across the world. She made didgeridoos in Australia, helped the homeless in Nepal, and motorbiked through Kazakhstan. Somewhere during her solo travels she developed a cosmic connection to the Universe that I can't help but be consumed by.

Our first date was on New Year's Eve. She wore the only dress she owns—a yellow sundress she'd bought at the floating market in Chiang Mai, Thailand—and it was the first time I'd seen her with her long dark hair down. She was striking, and my feelings for her shot through my shoes. Since then, she's extended her stay in Miami Beach, and we've gone on walks, stayed up late playing gin rummy, given the birds that fly by funny little names, and read in bed to one another. I've been trying to teach her simple things like how to swim and the subtleties of backgammon, and she's been trying to teach me important things like how to slow down and let love in. Not only have I never dated a girl like her, but I've never even met anyone like her. She loves everything with her whole heart, including herself.

Although I haven't told her yet, I officially fell in love with Naomi last week. She's not much of a morning person, but she woke up early so we could share a sunrise. She read a book on the sand while I took photos of the sea. Then, while I went for a jog and did push-ups and sit-ups on the harder sand, she unrolled her yoga mat and balanced and blissed across it. We kept sneaking smiley glances at one another as we each did our own thing, and afterward we rented bikes and rode to the top of South Pointe Park together. When the trail narrowed and I turned around halfway up the hill to see if she was still behind me, the love that had been building between us reached out and wrapped its arms around me. I don't know if it was the way she was smiling back from underneath the brim of the baseball cap she'd borrowed from me or the way she giggled when our eyes met, but whatever it was, I was hers.

Sometimes I'll watch her in awe and wonder if she's just a figment of my imagination, but the thing that makes me pinch myself the most is just how understanding she's been of my dreams. As I've continued to grind down my goals one by one, she's given me the space and solitude I need to pursue them. But at the same time she has this uncanny knack for showing up exactly when I need her most, like right now.

"Where should we start?" she says optimistically.

"I have no clue." I pick up a stack of books that the exterminator ruined. "It looks like one of those Nickelodeon slime bombs exploded in here."

"I think you just need to throw everything out. This will be good practice for you anyway. You're going to need to live with less if you want to travel around the world."

She's right, nothing is salvageable. After moving twice already this year, my place was pretty Spartan, but by the time we make our last trip to the dumpster all that remains is the floor, the walls, and the gigantic vision board I'd created when I first decided on my dreams. Once we take it down and deem that there are no bedbugs hiding on or behind the chart paper, we hang it back up together. As we do this, it suddenly feels like the three of us become one. Naomi, my dreams, and I merge.

When I initially hatched this plan to travel around the world without flying, I saw myself as a lone wolf on a kind of vision quest, loving every minute of it. I'm an only child, a solitary soul, and happier to be alone than among friends most of the time. I've always been content in the company of my own thoughts. To some extent, Naomi's a lot like me in that regard. It's almost like we're both in pursuit of an indefinable shared solitude.

I watch her attack the residue on the floors with soap, water, and an extra helping of elbow grease, a smile radiating across her face. *She's the perfect partner.* Everything that's been slowly building inside me since we met is once again confirmed.

I love this woman.

That night, lying side by side on the air mattresses we bought at Walmart in my empty apartment like we're camping under the stars, I roll over and reach out for Naomi's hand. Once our fingers lace, I look through the darkness until I find her soft hazel eyes.

"I want you to be a part of this. Will you come and travel around the world with me?" I say.

Naomi looks deep into my eyes and without blinking says, "Yes, of course I will."

* * *

I'm thrilled that Naomi said yes, but it means that travel expenses have now doubled. I continue working both jobs, but by mid-August, months past my deadline, I still have nowhere near enough money.

Then one day, as I drive home after enduring hours of tedious training and knowing there are hours of mindless mouse-clicking ahead that night, I put my foot down. Not on the gas, but on my excuses. I'm not going to let my bank account derail my dreams any longer. I hatch an absurd plan, one even more ridiculous than my already Impossible Idea.

While waiting for the stoplight to change on Alton Road, I adjust the rearview mirror until I can see my mouth in it. I clear my throat and say, "We're going to travel around the world for free."

I can't help but laugh maniacally at myself as the light changes and I pull away. It's outlandish. But it was Walt Disney that said, "If you can dream it, you can do it."

I spend the evening pacing my tiny studio apartment. The biggest travel expense will undoubtedly be lodging. Even if Naomi and I were to stay in cheap hotels or hostels, it would add up quickly and break the bank. *Surely some of them would be willing to work off the barter system, wouldn't they?* When I finally stop pacing and sit down at my desk, I start thinking about all the things I can offer hotels in exchange for a room.

Around 8:00 p.m., I start drafting a short letter on my computer. My offer is simple and straight to the point. I propose to take photos of the entire hotel, from the rooms to the restaurant, the exterior and every amenity, which they can then use on their website or any way they see fit. I also offer to make a two-minute film of the property. In exchange, I ask for a week's worth of room and board. In the email I include a link to my newly built travel blog (TravelTall.com) and social media accounts (@ TravelTall). The blog itself is pretty sparse, I'm planning on sharing my photos, films and stories there as I go, but at the moment it only has a few photos of Miami Beach sunrises, one five-minute film I put together and two short stories I'd written.

After revising the letter several times and emailing it to Naomi so she can look it over for grammar mistakes, I email it to fifty hotels and hostels in and around Cape Town, South Africa. As the southernmost major city in Africa, it seems like a logical starting point for the journey.

After all, fortune favors the bold, or so I hope. And this is about as bold as it gets because I've never taken a single photo of a hotel room or made a film for anyone, let alone a hotel. But I think with all the practice that I've been putting in lately that I just might be able to pull it off should one of these places take me up on my whimsical offer.

I decide to keep going. My chances are only going to increase the more hotels and hostels I contact. By the time I send out my hundredth email, it's well past midnight. I close my laptop and set it on the ground next to me and then I rub my bleary eyes. I set my alarm for 5:30 a.m. so I can get to the beach for sunrise as usual, and then I roll over onto my right side in the darkness. My air mattress squeaks when my shoulder plies into it. Just before I close my eyes, I try to manifest a miracle.

All I need is one yes. Just one.

The next thing I know I'm reaching out from the warmth of my covers to fumble through the darkness for my phone. Once I stop my morning alarm from blaring, I slide my groggy fingers across the smooth surface and open my inbox. South Africa is six time zones ahead, so it's unlikely but possible that some of the hotels or hostels have replied to my offer. I can't help but imagine the appalled and confused looks on the faces of those reading my ridiculous request for free room and board.

Junk emails ping through and populate my screen, and then a slew of deflating work-related emails start to download. Just as I'm about to put my phone down and head for the shower, one more message slides through. It's got the same subject line I sent to all the hotels in Cape Town last night.

Holy shit! Someone wrote me back! Someone wrote me back!

My fingers can't get to it fast enough.

It's from Leslie, the manager of Ashanti Lodge. As I quietly read her words aloud to my darkened apartment, I can't stop the tears from squirting out of the sides of my eyes.

Your travel blog looks amazing, Eric! I have made a provisional booking for you at ASHANTI LODGE in a double en-suite room, please see attachment. The room will be free of charge. Please confirm that you'd like this complimentary booking.

It worked! Oh my God, it worked!

Turns out Plato was right: necessity *is* the mother of invention.

My hands shake with excitement, and my heart beats harder than ever before. When I see that two more emails have come through from Kalk Bay, a suburb of Cape Town, and that two chic bed-and-breakfasts have also accepted my offer, the shock of sudden success is almost too much for me to handle. After a year and a half of giving every single ounce of myself to this Impossible Idea, I've finally found my route out.

The world is mine for the taking, finally.

CHAPTER 1
SOUTH AFRICA
AFRICA

*"Two roads diverged in a wood, and I—
I took the one less traveled by, And that has made all the difference."*

— *Robert Frost*

I N ORDER TO GET AROUND the earth you've got to start at the edge of it, and that's what brought me to Cape Town. The entire African continent lies in front of me, and the only way across it is up. Now that I'm here, my attempt to travel around the world over land and sea is officially under way. I allowed myself to fly to get to my starting point, but it will be only buses, boats, and trains from here on out.

Even though today is my first day on the road, I still haven't planned anything. I don't even know where I'm headed after Cape Town.

For years I've had to go where the companies I worked for wanted me to go, wear what they wanted me to wear, and say what they wanted me to say. So naturally I want the opposite of that for my travels. I want to figure things out on the fly, and I don't want to place any expectations or demands on my journey. I want it to unfold one unexpected step at a time. To traipse down another traveler's trail would be pointless, and so I've also decided not to allow myself the use of guidebooks or Google for assistance. The goal is to cross six continents and all I have is a rough sketch of my route in my head. I know there are seven continents in total, but I'm not including Antarctica because, well, that would just be impossible to get to. But I am including the oceans in between. First I'm going to cross Africa from south to north, making my way from Cape Town to Cairo, then I'll cross Europe, heading toward London. If I can make it to London, I'll head east across Asia, then Australia, North America, and South America, and I'll keep going until I loop all the way back around to the same spot in London.

I have no clue what countries I'll need to cross in order to pull this off, and I have absolutely no idea how I'm going to get across the Atlantic and Pacific Oceans, but I'll worry about crossing those bridges when I get to them. There are no deadlines for my travel, I'm giving myself as long as it takes or as long as my life savings lasts to make it around the world.

I met my savings goal of $25,000 before I'd left, but money is still probably going to be the biggest issue. I've bartered a room with Ashanti Lodge and two bed-and-breakfasts in Kalk Bay for next week. But what if that's just beginner's luck and I can't barter with any other hotels after this? Let's say that this journey around the world, if I actually make it, takes three years. That means I'd have to book a hotel or hostel for Naomi (once she gets here) and I for 1,095 nights. Now let's assume that I'll be able to find and book the cheapest room each stop along the way, which I'll estimate at thirty-five dollars a night. After doing the math, that alone adds up to over thirty-eight thousand dollars. And that doesn't include money for transportation or food.

Still, right before I left, I told my parents that I'd rather end up broke in Bangkok than be a millionaire in Miami Beach, and I truly mean that. I'm pushing all my chips to the center of the table, and I'm going for broke this time. I'll be traveling as if my life depends on it, because quite frankly it does.

I've already had one major challenge. When I printed out my boarding pass at my parents' house, the printer's alignment was off and the arrival time mistakenly got printed under the departure time. So I showed up two hours late and missed my flight out of West Palm Beach. Luckily, I was able to reach my parents, who had just dropped me off, and they came back and picked me up. I admit, I was pretty dejected, but my parents wouldn't let me quit because they've never quit—never on each other and certainly never on me. Before the airport was even out of sight, they helped me find and book a cheap flight out of Orlando to JFK. My father pushed the gas pedal down without hesitating, and my mother offered up a shortcut that would get us to the other airport in just over two hours. They both had the same look in their eye. It's easy for me to spot because I've seen it a billion times before: it's that unconditional *I'll do anything I can for you* look. Thanks to them, I was able to make my original connection to Cape Town.

But now, as I walk up to the front gate of the Ashanti Lodge, I am completely on my own. I'm a bit anxious because I'm not exactly sure how this is going to work. I have the email from Lesley, the lodge's manager, that says that my room will be free of charge, but I don't know if there's an actual reservation under my name. I didn't want to ask questions once she emailed me back and have her think twice about the offer, so I just sheepishly replied, "I accept, see you then."

I press a white button on the intercom and say my name loudly. The metal gate buzzes, so I push it open and walk in. The lodge isn't what I was expecting. It's a beautifully refurbished Victorian mansion, and I follow a well-manicured path to its burnt-orange front door and the front desk.

When I meet Lesley, she squashes all my fears as she eagerly walks me back across the garden. She has fair skin and long, frizzy brown hair that looks like it has recently been untwisted from dreadlocks and a piercing on the right side of her nose.

"The lodge doubles as a backpackers' hostel, and most of the rooms inside are double rooms or dorm rooms," Lesley says. "I think you'll be more comfortable out here, plus you can see the top of Table Mountain from the window in your room. Oh, and your breakfast is included, and you can use the communal kitchen inside anytime."

She's given me the nicest room in the place; it's the only double en-suite room they have, and it looks like a cute little cottage from the outside. It's located in the front garden and shaded by two pretty date palm trees.

When Lesley hands me the key, I thank her profusely and ask her about the photos and film she wants me to make in exchange for the room.

"Oh, you don't have to do anything in exchange for the room," she says. "We actually don't need anything your email promised. How about you just mention us on your travel blog one day?"

I try to play it cool like I've actually done this before and say, "Easy enough," but meanwhile my heart is doing summersaults underneath my shirt. *I can't believe this is actually happening! I can't believe I get to stay here for a week for free! This is freaking perfect!*

Once Lesley heads back up to the front desk, I let myself in my room and set my bags down. Beneath the steepled roof there's a queen-sized bed with crisp white sheets and a tan blanket draped across the bottom of it. A TV hangs from the wall in the corner of the room, and a stainless steel teakettle and a set of white coffee cups rests on the waist-high bookshelf below. There's a tiny bathroom too.

I've been sleeping on an air mattress for the past four months, so I almost don't know what do with a real bed. I kick my shoes off, open the blinds as far as they'll go, and then climb atop the bed. I look out the window and lock eyes on Table Mountain. Then I let out the widest smile of my life and start jumping for joy.

After a few waves of euphoria work their way up and out of my body, I climb down off the bed and set my bag, Timberland, atop the ruffled sheets. I call it that not because it's musically inclined, but because the manufacturer decided to write its name across the side of it in block letters so big and bright that it's embarrassing. I'd rather get out in front of the jokes. I suspect that's the reason Timberland made it all the way to the lowly clearance aisle at the discount store, Ross.

It's a simple navy blue bag, not one of those fancy expedition backpacks. It does have a tiny interior pocket deep inside where I hid four crisp one hundred dollar bills, as well as a handle that extends from the top and two reinforced inline skate wheels at its base. I'm a big believer in the theory that it's easier to roll something than to carry it, plus the cushioned backpack I keep my photography equipment, GoPro, and my MacBook Retina computer in already takes up all my shoulder space.

As I begin to pull everything out, a strange feeling hits me. This is all I own now. I didn't squirrel anything away in a storage unit somewhere. Everything's either been donated or dumpstered. Yet I'm already feeling weighed down. I didn't quite realize how much I'd packed until I had to pay a fee at the airport because Timberland was over the fifty-pound limit.

I dig through the mountain of clothes and decide to remove seven of the fourteen T-shirts, one of the three pairs of jeans, the beige sweatshirt, the Real Madrid jersey, a pair of shorts, two pairs of underwear, and four of the sets of socks. I also decide that I don't need the Pacsafe antitheft bag protector, a bag made of wire rope I could put my camera bag inside, lock closed, then secure around something so it won't get stolen when I'm not watching it.

I stuff everything I'm no longer willing to lug around inside a garbage bag and offer it to Lesley as a donation. She accepts, then gives me directions to Lion's Head Mountain.

Three hours later, I'm nearly two thousand feet above the city and standing atop Lion's Head's highest lookout. To my left is Table Mountain's two-mile-long flat top, which runs perfectly parallel along today's cloudless sky. With the absence of high rises in much of the city, almost every street corner here gives way to a view that rises from sage to sandstone. I've always been in awe of how the city slinks up, down, and around this African icon, and Camps Bay is perfectly poised just below the both of us. Turquoise waves are slowly rolling in, and the bright color fades the farther out to sea I look. A few ships sail along the horizon, but they're moving so slowly it almost looks like they're anchored. On the rocky slope just in front of me there's a launch point for paragliders. They're taking just a few quick steps and then throwing themselves off the side of the mountain. I fall into a deep hypnosis as I watch the wind act as a puppeteer, gradually lifting them up just before they fall. They look as light as a feather as they go from the known into the unknown and glide out over the Atlantic. I hold my camera up to my eye as they drift toward a blood-orange sun that's just about to set. But just before I snap my first shot, I pause, shake my head, and smile. The first photo from my Impossible Idea is going to be one of people hurling themselves off a cliff and into the unknown.

On the way back from Lion's Head, I walk past the Debonairs Pizza shop on Kloof Street. The smell coming from its brick oven leads me to the menu in its window like a trail of bread crumbs. Names like the meaty triple-decker and tikka chicken have me salivating, but I pry myself away and opt for the Checkers grocery next to it. Since Ashanti Lodge has a communal kitchen, I figure a good way to save a couple bucks will be to cook all my meals instead of eating out.

I anxiously peruse the aisles inside Checkers looking for the cheapest dinner available, double-checking the price of everything using the currency converter on my iPhone before taking it off the shelf. I settle on a box of spaghetti for twenty-three rand (about two US dollars). When I look at the prices on the jars of tomato sauce one aisle over, I decide that paying thirty-four rand for a topping is too much of an indulgence so early in my travels.

After checking out with just my box of spaghetti, I walk into Debonairs Pizza and take a few packets of salt from one of the tables by the entrance. Then I head back to Ashanti Lodge and right to its communal kitchen. As I swish my salty spaghetti around my mouth, I can't help but begin to question my dreams. Now that I'm out here on the road, with no plan B, am I going to be able to pull off this Impossible Idea after all?

#

My concerns are calmed a few days later when I discover the scenic fishing village of Kalk Bay, a suburb of Cape Town. Wooden fishing boats covered in colorful peeling paint trawl in and out of the pea-sized harbor and, combined with the train tracks that run just between the beach and the town's bookstores, a more scenic spot I have not seen. It sets my creativity a blaze. I fill my days walking up and down the docks snapping shots and my evenings gorging myself on the fish those very boats had brought in. After dinner, I listen to grizzled men in worn wool caps fill the air with sounds from their harmonicas, and watch little boys cast and catch their first fish off the end of the docks while beached seals soak up the last few seconds of sunlight.

Feeling encouraged, I make my way southeast along the coast by taking the Baz Bus, a hop-on/hop-off service designed for backpackers, though I still have to hitch a ride to reach Hermanus Bay. I find a trinket-filled town center that ends abruptly where a steep cliff drops off to the lip of ocean. My destination, the Shark Lab, is at the bottom of that cliff, carved into the rock wall just a few feet from where the ocean's waves peter out. The South African Shark Conservancy (SASC) has agreed to provide room and board in exchange for a promotional film, and while SASC won't be paying me, this is exactly the kind of work I want to be doing. Even if I had Steven Spielberg's help, I couldn't have scripted a better opportunity.

The inside of the Shark Lab looks like a secret headquarters fit for Aquaman. My contact, Lisa, the director and lead scientist, is nine months pregnant and seems about to burst. Right after we shake hands she lights a cigarette, letting it dangle from her lips. Sandy, who is second in command, appears just as tough as nails as she grips my outstretched hand like a vise. But isn't that the case with anyone that works with the sea?

Sandy takes me on a quick tour and leads me into a room that has two small above-ground swimming pools. Inside them are baby sharks swimming in slow circles. The room just beyond that is the rest of the team's workspace. There are all kinds of scientific charts on the walls and measuring devices strewn about—I can't imagine the use of half of them. Eight industrial-style desks are lined up along the wall, and every chair but one is filled with a bright-eyed student. They're an eclectic group, undoubtedly from all over the world.

Sandy introduces me to the group as a filmmaker, which sends a nervous shiver across my shoulders because it's the first time anyone's ever called me that. I glance around the room, hoping a real filmmaker doesn't pop up to say, "He's only pretending to be a filmmaker—get him out of here!" I have to clear my throat before I can explain why I'm here. "I'm excited to work with everyone. This is my thirteenth day in South Africa, and I've always been interested in great white sharks, so I reached out to Lisa last week and asked her if I could come and stay with you guys for a little while. In exchange, I'll be making a short film for SASC. The film is going to cover all the research and cool things you do here."

Sandy adds, "We're going to put Eric's film on the SASC website once it's finished."

Joseph jumps up and shakes my hand as soon as Sandy leaves the room. He's the operations manager I've been coordinating with via email this past week. He's almost as tall as me, with long, shaggy hair and a Tom Selleck mustache. It takes me a second to adjust to his Zambian accent, which is slightly murkier than the South African one my ears have just started getting used to. I'll be staying with him and the seven SASC interns at the house they all share in Onrus Beach for the next two weeks.

I wheel Timberland over to the corner of the room and take a seat behind the only empty desk. The first thing that strikes me about the interns is how happy they are. As I'd guessed, they're from all over the world— France, Canada, and the Netherlands, just to name a few. Studying sharks is their passion, and it shows on all their exuberant faces, which is such a difference from the drab and depressed looks I'd grown used to seeing from the teachers who were forced to show up for my training sessions.

Joseph asks me to stand and sizes me up before leaving the room. A few moments later, he's back and tosses me a damp wet suit. "This is the biggest we have, mate."

"No worries," I say. "I'll squeeze into it. But what do I need this for?"

"We're gonna head to Gansbaai in a few minutes. Then we'll take the boat out to Dyer Island, chum the water, and get you inside the cage so you can get some underwater video of a few great whites. Should be epic, mate."

Holy shit! I think, but don't say.

Two hours later and true to his word, Joseph is throwing bloody tuna heads into the ocean like they're beanbags at a backyard barbeque. I'm distracting myself by stuffing my long limbs into the damp wetsuit. I can't tell if the goosebumps going up and down my back are from the freezing foamed neoprene that just hit my skin or the gigantic fin that I just saw skim the horizon.

When the interns hoist a coffin-sized cage over the starboard side, that's my cue. Joseph lifts the lid and I jump in with my GoPro before giving myself time to second guess things. The sea sways violently as I try to get my balance underwater. I steady myself against the bars and press record just as a school of silver fish swim by. It strikes me as odd when they scatter just seconds later. Camera shy, I think. Suddenly from the deepest shade of blue below me, a great white hurtles towards the cage. Its speed makes a bullet look slow and my heart stops. I let go of the cage and retreat to the center as the shark opens its massive mouth. Its barbwire teeth look like they're coming right at me because they are. At the last second, Joseph yanks the tuna head, tied to a rope, back into the boat. The great white crashes into the cage with the power of a steam engine. We're eye to eye for a split second before it flicks its tail and disappears.

Sometimes, happiness is something you feel in hindsight, after the joy has had time to settle and sink in, but this is not one of those times.

Right here, right now, I am as happy as I've ever been.

* * *

My alarm goes off at 1:30 a.m. the following morning, and I flail around in the dark, trying to shut it off. I drag myself out of bed, and quietly set off through the sketchy South African darkness. I stop in the empty parking lot of Moltenos, the soul food and pizza restaurant where I had dinner just hours ago with Joseph and two interns, Alexandre from France and

Thomas from Canada. Moltenos is, of course, closed. All the lights are off, and there isn't a soul in sight. I walk up to its big bay window and hold my phone as close as I can to it. *Come on, Moltenos, please tell me you've left your router on tonight.* When my phone eventually picks up the network, I let out a sigh of relief and then type in the same password our waiter gave us earlier.

I'm here for Naomi, and the charade we've come up with to allow her to earn some money. Rather than quit my online teaching job when I left, Naomi has taken it over and she's really done it well—too well, in fact. The students are soaring. Naomi's like that, though; she's the hardest worker I've ever met. She's been putting in fifty-hour workweeks for a job that requires only ten; it goes without saying, but I'll say it anyway—I'm really proud of her.

There are just two problems with this arrangement. The first is Naomi is only able to do about 90 percent of the job. The other 10 percent requires my actual voice and presence on the phone. So once a week, I have to call all the new students on my roster to welcome them to the class and then call the struggling ones to give them a little nudge in the right direction. Because I no longer have a data plan for my cell phone, I have to hunt down the nearest reliable Wi-Fi and then use a complicated combination of Google Voice and Skype to call the students' cell phones. Then I have to log into the school's system and write notes describing the conversations.

It's only my second week here, and I already resent this arrangement. I've risked everything to follow my heart here, and now that I'm here, I want to pursue my passions. I already feel at home. Not location-wise, but in the sense that this is the creative space I want to be living in. I've found indescribable joy when writing, filming, and taking photos for my travel blog. It feels as though I'm shedding more and more light on the best part of myself.

But these phone calls are the yin to that yang. It's much more than just a quick conversation; it's a potholed road that throws my creative suspension out of alignment. I can't just bounce back into the creative space after I finish making all the calls; they hang around for the rest of the day. The only reason I took this job I hated in the first place was to earn enough money to get where I am now and I couldn't wait to quit. All I've sacrificed to get here, all the risks I'm taking to push forward, was to break free from my old life and start something new. I feel like Michael Corleone in the *Godfather Part III*: "Just when I thought I was out, they pull me back in."

Tonight is the biggest call of all—my monthly conversation with Andrea, which she scheduled for 8:00 p.m. EST. Truthfully I'm a little bit nervous about it. It has to go perfectly. If Andrea figures out I'm in Africa or that I'm not the one doing the actual job, she'll fire me on the spot.

Truthfully, I wouldn't mind. I'm only doing this for Naomi. Had it been anyone else, I would have told them there's no way in hell I'd put myself through this. But this is currently the only source of income Naomi and I have, and Naomi really needs the money, especially if she's going to be able to join me on this trip.

"Hi, Eric," Andrea answers in her southern drawl. "So how's the weather in Miami Beach tonight? Did y'all get the thunderstorms we had up here in the panhandle today?"

It takes a second for me to remember where Miami Beach is. I feel a world away and can't help but stutter, "It's, ah . . . it's, ah," before I think of something safe and say, "Yeah, it was hot and humid today."

"Well, let's get down to brass tacks then. Tell me about Jennifer S.— the system is showing that she's behind in your class?"

Not only do I not know how Jennifer S. is doing, but I don't even know who Jennifer S. is. She joined the class after I turned the job over to Naomi. "I spoke with Jennifer today and she's been sick," I lie, deciding to cover for her. "But she promised me she would complete four assignments by the weekend and be back up to speed by then."

Thankfully, Andrea buys it. She's about as invested in her job as principal as I am at mine as teacher, and we quickly work our way through a few more students. I can tell that the only reason she's on the call tonight is the same reason I call the students each week. She's just doing the bare minimum so she can log it into the system and then move on to the next teacher on her list. She couldn't care less about me or the students.

Everything seems to be running smoothly, but when Andrea gets to the last student on her list, a student named Kassandra, the Wi-Fi drops.

The silence is excruciating. I hold my phone up to Moltenos's bay window, trying to get just a few inches closer to the router, then wave it overhead like a rescue plane is passing by.

The Wi-Fi cuts back in, but now we're on about a five-second delay.

Andrea blames it on the thunderstorms Florida's been having, and I go along with it. "Yeah, it's really coming down out there now." I anticipate when Andrea's about to finish her sentences, and I start speaking about five seconds before I think she'll be done. It only makes things worse, and I decide to stick to yes or no answers. I let Andrea steamroll through the rest of her notes.

I'm about to say good-bye and hang up, feeling like Naomi and I have dodged not just a few bullets, but a major missile, when Andrea says, "Oh, and one more thing."

"What's that?"

"We hired a new head of the Economics Department, and I've scheduled a conference call for you two tomorrow night at this same time. I think it will be good for both of you to get to know one another and go over all your students together."

My shoulders slump, and my head dips in disgust.

I'll never be able to escape this life.

CHAPTER 2
MOZAMBIQUE – MALAWI – TANZANIA
AFRICA

"If you have someone you think is the one . . .
buy a ticket for the two of you to travel
all over the world, to places that are
hard to reach and hard to get out of.
And when you land at JFK and you're still in
love with that person, get married."

— Bill Murray

I'VE BEEN TRAVELING ALONG SOUTH Africa's Garden Route for fifty-four days now, and almost unbelievably, I've exchanged my photography for room and board fifty-three straight nights, sharing my short stories with anyone that will read them and trading my filmmaking for once-in-a-lifetime experiences. I've walked alongside a cream-colored cheetah at a wildlife sanctuary in Knysna, slept in a charming log cabin on the sandy banks of the Mzimvubu River, and watched elephants bathe in red mud under the sun. Things have actually exceeded my wildest expectations; I feel like I'm starting to slowly shed my skin. I've been able to go where I want, do what I want, and scratch every intuitive itch. So why shake things up? Why mess with this bliss-filled balance?

The answer comes as I lift my head out of my Kindle to scan Johannesburg's bustling OR Tambo Airport: *because she's worth it.*

This shakes me. Until now, nobody has ever been *worth it*, not like this. It's new territory. And I'm scared.

In the past when I've made decisions about women, it's always been too quick. When I fall, I fall fast and for the wrong reasons. But with Naomi it's been the opposite. We started out as friends, and it's been a slow burn that escalated quickly in recent months. We've only known each other for a short time, not even a full year yet, and the second she arrives, we'll suddenly be living together.

I fidget nervously in the International Arrivals area, checking Naomi's flight status for the hundredth time, then realize what I'm feeling isn't fear but excitement. She's become my confidante, my best friend, and she can't clear customs soon enough.

I wanted to do something special for her, so I went to the grocery store and picked up some of her favorite foods, including carrots, potatoes, a bag of white cheddar popcorn, and a few dark chocolate bars with the highest concentration of cacao I could find. Then I arranged everything into the shape of a heart on our bed. I can't wait until she sees it. It might be the first ever carrot-and-potato heart anyone's ever made as a romantic gesture, but she wouldn't want flowers or jewelry. She's not that kind of woman. The happiest I'd ever seen her was when I surprised her with a yoga mat she can travel with. She's a gypsy, a yogi, a centered spiritual being, and already I know she's going to be great to travel with. When I told her I bartered us a room at the Ritz in Johannesburg for this week, she got so excited. I felt bad when I had to explain it was actually a hostel called the Backpackers Ritz. But if anything, that only excited her more.

"I always meet so many interesting people at hostels. That sounds better anyway!"

As another mob of travelers spills out of customs, I can't help but think of the one thing we didn't do: we didn't plan. We didn't draft a blueprint for how this is all going to work, nor did we install a system of checks and balances for how two people who are so accustomed to moving through life alone are going to travel as one. Naomi, much like myself, isn't the relationship type. We're both outdoor cats, coming inside only occasionally for companionship.

While I'd undoubtedly consider us a couple, she'd never call me her boyfriend. Her theory is that we don't need to cloud our connection with words just so other people can make sense of it. In a very Buddha way, she wisely says, "Let's just be." She doesn't want us to get into the habit of trying to twist each other into a role we want the other one to play. Instead, she wants us to have the freedom to be our authentic selves. This is just one more reason why I've fallen for her.

Though as I watch a grandmother bend down and wrap her arms and a Bafana Bafana football scarf around her grandson, showering him with kisses, I can't help but wonder what it will be like when Naomi finally appears. Fifty-four days is a long time. Will we pick up where we left off, or will we reintroduce ourselves like it's an awkward first date?

And then she emerges from customs as if she timed her arrival to the second that exact thought crossed my mind.

I smile wide and can't stop from running toward her. All of her belongings are packed sparingly inside her backpack. All of her dreams are spread across a smile that reminds me why I'd rather struggle together than succeed alone. She makes her way into my arms, embracing me in a way that secretly lets me know that this might actually work. It's an embrace that's founded on choice, not necessity—she doesn't complete me, and I don't complete her, but together, we're *better*.

Two souls, greater than the sum of their parts.

#

The first order of business once Naomi has slept off her jet lag and settled in is figuring out where we want to go. And how we'll get there. While standing in front of a floor-to-ceiling map of Africa in the lobby of the Ritz, I run my finger along the first of our three options.

"We could go northwest to Botswana," I say, "or north to Zimbabwe or northeast to Mozambique."

We decide on Mozambique since we're both partial to the long stretch of coastline it provides. The former Portuguese colony's entire eastern edge runs along the Indian Ocean.

"The thought of us sharing a bungalow on the beach is too hard to pass up," says Naomi. I couldn't agree more.

Naomi goes up to the front desk to get information about how we can obtain the travel visas we'll need to enter Mozambique and how much two bus tickets on the cheapest border crossing bus is going to run us.

I begin emailing all the hotels I can find in Nelspruit, South Africa's biggest city en route to the border, and Mozambique's capital, Maputo. Instead of asking them to provide room and board for one person in exchange for my photography and video, I ask if they'd be willing to take on two people. I decide it sounds more professional to refer to Naomi as my assistant. Hopefully this subtle change will do the trick. If not, I'll have to start dipping into the little life savings I've amassed.

Naomi comes back with good news. "We're just a few blocks down the street from the Mozambique Consulate General, and we can go get our travel visas there tomorrow."

I shoot to my feet and give her a high five.

"Oh, and one more thing." She smiles. "The cheapest bus company is called Intercape, and it's only about twenty US dollars to get to Nelspruit from here. It's just a little more if we decide to go straight to Maputo."

My high five quickly turns into a hug and a kiss, and I jokingly say, "Teamwork makes the dream work!"

#

We spend the week wandering the purple petal-filled streets of Johannesburg, where jacarandas are in full bloom, perusing museums and attractions dedicated to Nelson Mandela, and enjoying quiet nights playing gin rummy. By the time we make our way to the coast by bus, I come to realize that sharing such close quarters with Naomi has made it harder to tap into the kind of creativity I've been calling upon. I've taken time away from my film and photography pursuits and I'm starting to feel a little uneasy because of it. The solitude I started with is more special than I realized and while we're enjoying one another's company and growing closer, we aren't quite coming together like I envisioned we would.

That feeling starts to show about two weeks after Naomi's arrival. We've had a grueling day of travel that starts on an unairconditioned bus in Maputo at 4:00 a.m., and ends with us bouncing in a four-wheel drive through the coconut and cashew plantations of Mozambique near Inhambane. The road ended twenty miles back and is now strictly sand. When we clear the final patch of palm trees, my heart skips a beat. I look over at Naomi and giggle like a schoolgirl. The beach that arcs around the bay of Praia de Jangamo is as wide as any this world has to offer, and our cabana sits atop a cliff overlooking it all.

"This is exactly what we've been dreaming about," I proclaim to Ana, the sixty-year-old, sandy-blonde Dutch general manager of the Jeff's Palm Resort as she pulls alongside our cabana. Naomi and I are both rejuvenated from the arduous travel day like we just took shots of vitamin B12. We hop out and grab our things from the cargo bed of Ana's truck. The coastline's cobalt water stretches all the way up to the edge of the atmosphere, and I can't quite believe that we've been able to barter our way here.

"Did you bring your bathing suits?" Ana says playfully before starting in on a rundown of the resort. "We run fishing charters and scuba trips. The reef close by is one of the best spots in the world for snorkeling, and it's a photographer's paradise." Ana's empty hands mimic snapping an imaginary shot. "It's a little slow this time of year, and besides a family of four from South Africa you're our only guests. You're more likely to see a whale than a human here this week."

"Ana, this place is heaven!" Naomi says.

"I'm glad you like it. There's a little general store about a kilometer back where you can buy boxed milk and groceries for the week. Once we get inside your cabana, I'll show you how to turn the propane stove on."

Our cabana mimics the indigenous huts we passed on the way here. It has a thatched roof, and the walls are made of brick and bamboo. But instead of having just one room, our cabana has two bedrooms, a kitchen, and a spacious living room. White mosquito nets hang from fishhooks above each bed, and the kitchen cabinets are filled with worn pots and pans.

"Oh, and the electricity is only supplied from 5:00 p.m. to 10:00 p.m. each day," Ana adds.

As she finishes her sentence, panic starts to spread across Naomi's face. I know what she's thinking. She needs Wi-Fi in order to log into the school's online system each day, and we're about as far away from Wi-Fi as one could be.

"Ana, how can I get internet access out here?" Naomi asks.

"Well, sweetie, there isn't much Wi-Fi out here, but I can let you use my iPad to check your email when you need to. I have a small data plan that lets me return emails and surf the internet for a few minutes each day."

Before Ana even finishes her sentence, there's tension between Naomi and me.

Once Ana heads back up to her office, the next words out of Naomi's mouth are, "I'm sorry to have to say this, but you know we can't stay here."

I play dumb. "What, why not?"

Her whole body tenses as she says, "You know why."

I shrug. "We have food, water, an incredible beach bungalow, and each other. This is the shared solitude we've been dreaming about."

"I know, it's perfect, and I hate to say this, but I need Wi-Fi to check my emails, text the students, and grade all their assignments. There's no way I can spend a week here without doing that. I'd be fired within the first forty-eight hours."

My heart hardens, and I storm out to the porch without saying anything. She's packed and brought my old job to one of the most remote parts of the world; even worse, she's brought the old me. I watch a trail of ants climb up one of the bamboo posts that supports the thatched awning overhead. I sigh. "I don't want to leave, especially for the online school. This is one of the most incredible places I've ever been."

"I don't want to leave either, but I can't lose this job. I need the money. We need the money."

Although Naomi's only making around nine hundred dollars a month, it's more than enough to keep her afloat—and nine hundred more than I'm making. While I've been able to barter my room and board, I haven't actually found a way to make any real money just yet.

My frustrations get the better of me. I raise my arms in disgust and shout, "Where would we even go?"

"What about Tofo Beach? Didn't you say that two hotels there also accepted our offer? Maybe you can email them from Ana's iPad and see if they'd have us a week earlier."

"But that's not the point. I don't want to leave." I point to the ocean's blue top shimmering against the sun. "Why are you asking me to give all this up?" The palm trees that line the sandy beach sway like Bob Marley's serenading the sand they've sprung from.

"But you have to do the live lesson just three days from now, and it's literally impossible to do from here."

Andrea emailed everyone last week, announcing that each part-time teacher would now be required to teach one live lesson a month instead of one every six months. It's a one-hour class taught through an interactive virtual classroom and requires several hours of preparation.

"I don't want to do the live lesson. It's the worst part of the job, and I hate every single thing about teaching economics."

"I can help you. We can study the material together, and I'll even put the PowerPoint together for you." Naomi, always the optimist, adds, "It will be fun!"

My dissatisfaction peaks, and I can't help but direct all my frustrations at her. "You of all people should understand what I'm trying to do, what I'm trying to become. Transforming my life is hard enough, and then with you adding all this extra work, it's becoming damn near impossible." My selfishness settles in the space between us. "I just want to write, film, and do my photography. I don't want to spend my time on a butterscotch beach in Mozambique studying high school economics! All this online school stuff is killing my creativity. Why can't you see that?"

Naomi puts her arm around me, but I pull away. She steps back, and her voice grows quiet. "I know and I'm so, so sorry, but please, just help me out this one last time. I'll figure something out by next month so you don't ever have to do this again. I promise."

"Fine," I snap like a petulant child.

I storm off the porch and then stomp down a dirt path that winds between the prettiest palm trees I've ever seen. I can barely hear Naomi's voice as she shouts to thank me.

#

I end up finding a Wi-Fi-yielding tiki bar on Tofu Beach to do the live lesson, pulling myself out of bed at two in the morning, and saving Naomi's job for at least another month. I don't know if it will be enough to save things between us.

We set off on a forty-eight-hour journey a few hours later that will take us from southern to northern Mozambique, traveling on buses that aren't even buses. They're beat-up, broken-down, old-ass minivans that don't start moving until every single inch is packed tight as a sardine can. Yesterday, a Mozambican couple boarded the bus with a stainless-steel kitchen sink. They sat with it on their laps for eight straight hours. Today, an elderly woman is traveling with a sack of chickens under her seat. During a bumpy stretch of road that sets the chickens clucking wildly, she reaches down and snaps their necks with her bare hands.

I look over to Naomi and, with sweat dripping off my brow, say, "At least we're getting to see the real Africa."

My long legs are pretzeled like the chicken's necks, and the temperatures are in the triple digits. Dust and dirt billow through the open windows, and we were caked like coal miners before we even reached the first rest stop yesterday. This is what I willingly signed up for, yes, but nonetheless the hours spent inside these cramped minivans are taking a toll on each of us.

With one last pit stop to make before we finally reach Tete, Naomi leans over and asks if she can borrow some cash to buy some banana chips and a big bottle of water. I don't think twice about it and pass over all the metical I have left. As we reboard the bus and begin to bounce and bumble over another stretch of terribly tarred roads, I ask, "Why did you need my metical when you have your own?"

Naomi shyly replies, "I ran out of cash. I spent all the money I originally brought with me."

"Okay, no problem, hopefully we can find an ATM in Tete so you can make a withdrawal."

Naomi cringes as she says, "Well, I'm not sure how to tell you this."

"What is it?"

"I didn't bring a debit card with me."

"Huh? What do you mean?"

Naomi doesn't say anything back, so I say, "You mean you left your debit card at our last hotel? I'm sure we can have them mail it to one of the hotels we'll be at next week in Malawi."

Naomi sighs. "The debit card I ordered from my bank back in Miami Beach never arrived in the mail."

Now is not the time for this kind of news.

My face flushes, and I start to raise my voice. "Tell me this is just a bad joke because I cannot believe you came all the way to Africa with no way to access your bank account and no way to help pay for things."

When I first met Naomi, her lack of concern for money was one of the most attractive things about her, but suddenly it's become the opposite. It infuriates me. While we never sat down and hashed out our financial responsibilities, it's an unwritten rule that I would be the one in charge of bartering for our accommodations and she would pay all her own out-of-pocket expenses. That said, I do want to be a gentleman and pick up her tab as often as I can. Her debit card was the only thing I'd specifically asked her to bring. I must have reminded her a hundred times to order it before she'd left for Africa.

Naomi looks timidly over at me. "I'm sorry, but it's true."

My blood begins to boil. If we don't have enough money to keep traveling, then we'll fail—I'll have to tuck my tail between my legs and go back to the old me. "Now I'll have to pay all the foreign transaction fees and cover all the currency conversion costs just to withdraw your paycheck and give it to you. Damn it, Naomi, every dollar counts!"

As the battered van continues to creep toward Tete, I'm running on my fumes' fumes. My nerves are shot, and all my fears and frustrations begin to coagulate in the middle of my mind. Everywhere I look is suddenly red. I turn toward Naomi until our eyes lock.

"Maybe you being here is a mistake." My words are as heavy as the heat, and even before I finished my sentence I wanted to take it back, but it's too late. The damage is done. Naomi explodes with anger.

"You son of a bitch, how dare you! You're such an asshole!" I've never heard Naomi curse before, and I'm taken aback by it.

Everyone is watching us with wide eyes. I feel terrible for what I've just said because here is this incredible woman doing all this for me. Traveling overland wasn't her idea; it was mine. She's sweating through the forty-eighth straight hour of unbearable bus rides that few other women would even consider. Not only that, but she hasn't complained one bit, not a single negative word, heavy sigh, or angry eye-roll about the wretched conditions.

When Naomi's anger eventually fades, it morphs into a deep sadness. As I watch tears stream down her cheeks, my heart breaks twice. First for her and then for *us*. I realize that one of my biggest fears is destined to come true—I'll have to choose between the two things I care most about in this world. It's either Naomi or my dreams.

* * *

The Park Inn in Tete is nice enough to give Naomi and I two separate rooms when we checked in. It's kind of a cool-down period for us. It's generous of them, but since the general manager was only willing to exchange two nights in return for my photography work, we have no choice but to get right back on the road.

We pack up in the dark, and when dawn breaks, we board yet another bus that looks like it's come directly from the demolition derby. It's supposed to drop us off at the Zobue border post. From there, the plan is to cross into Malawi and find another bus that will get us to the hotel we've bartered with in Blantyre by the end of the day.

Once the bus driver has all his passengers penned in like livestock, he puts his foot down on the gas, and we begin to lurch forward toward the border. He drives like a toddler does with his toy trucks, and dirt from the unpaved roads we're traveling down flies through the open windows and cakes our clothes again today. The ride under the baking sun quickly becomes exhausting, and there isn't much to look at other than the occasional thatched hut on the sun-drenched horizon. It isn't until lunch that we reach the border.

I couldn't be happier to finally be leaving Mozambique behind. Although we only spent twenty-nine days here, it's felt more like twenty-nine years. We've traveled over one thousand miles on what have got to be the worst buses known to man, and I'm hoping that maybe once we get to Malawi, not only will the travel conditions improve but Naomi and I will see it as a chance to start anew.

The immigration office is a brick building no bigger than my old studio apartment on the outskirts of the tiny town of Zobue. I slide our passports over a sun-beaten wooden counter to a man in a light blue button-down shirt that's three sizes too big for his pencil-thin frame. I give him my best attempt at a smile, but I'm already spent. It's only getting hotter by the minute today.

The officer flips through my passport, then Naomi's, and then both of them a second time. He looks up at us and says in broken English, "No stamp. You here illegally."

I shoot Naomi a look of confusion. Her look matches mine.

"I'm sorry, sir, what do you mean?" I say.

He holds up our passports. "No entry stamp. You enter Mozambique illegally."

"That's impossible, we have visas." I snatch our passports from him and flip to the pages showing the visas we got in Johannesburg.

"Yes, Mozambique visa, but no Mozambique entry stamp."

"We crossed into Mozambique at the Lebombo border station." I flip through my passport and find the exit stamp I got when we left South Africa and then proudly hold it up. "It's dated November 1. See?"

"Only exit stamp." He tries to find the words. "It's only for South Africa. You need entry stamp to my country."

At the Lebombo border station that day, once we officially left South Africa, we reboarded the same Intercape bus we'd been on, and it drove us about a mile down the road to the Mozambique side of the Lebombo crossing, which is where we got off the bus again and went through the same immigration process a second time, getting our passports stamped by the Mozambique authorities so we could enter legally. However, as both Naomi and I flip through our passports and look for our Mozambique entry stamp, neither of us can find it.

My pulse quickens and fear floods my face. "This doesn't make sense, sir. I'm sure we crossed the border legally."

With a stern and determined look in his eyes, he says, "No stamp, no exit."

"What do you mean?" Naomi asks.

"You go back to Lebombo and get stamp. Then come back."

The thought of backtracking over a thousand miles on all those beat-up, frying-pan buses that got us here and then having to travel all the way back up to this Zobue border post a second time is the most soul-crushing thing I've ever contemplated. So soul crushing, in fact, that it breaks me. My anger escalates quickly. "That's bullshit! What the hell are you talking about?"

Naomi quickly jumps between us and cuts me off, apologizing to the officer on my behalf. Then she pulls me to the side and tries to calm me down. "For some reason, our passports must not have been stamped properly, but you can't take it out on this guy—he's our only chance to keep moving forward and to get to Malawi."

Naomi's right. He's the only one working in this office; no one's come or gone since we've been here. It's just the three of us, and he suddenly has all the power in the world. Worst of all, he knows it. I sheepishly walk back up to the officer and apologize for my outburst, then ask him if there's anything we can do in order to exit Mozambique legally today and move on to Malawi by the afternoon.

"Maybe," he says. "How much money do you have?"

I literally have to bite my tongue so I can hold back all the names I want to call him, but at least now things make sense. The Mozambican immigration officers at the Lebombo post must have only pretended they stamped our passports, knowing that when we'd try to leave the country there'd be no stamp showing that we entered legally, thus opening us up to one of the darkest arts of traveling: bribery.

Even though the thought of having to bribe this man fills me with frustration, I try to play it cool and ask, "How much?"

"Four hundred US dollars."

"What!" I rip our passports out of his hands and walk over and fume in the corner of the room while Naomi takes over and tries to reason with him. He won't budge.

"We don't even have four hundred dollars, jerk!" I yell back over to him. I reach into my wallet and pull out all the Mozambican metical I have. "Here's proof!" It's not enough to pay for lunch, let alone the bribe, and when the officer sees this, he backs away and goes into a small office that's behind the counter. He closes the door without saying anything.

Neither Naomi nor I know what to do, and so all we can do is sit down and wait for him to return. I sit atop Timberland and put my sweaty head in my hands. When I eventually pull my head up and look out the window, I can see the Malawi side of the Zobue border. It's about a half mile down the road—the very definition of *so close but yet so far*. I stand up and walk to the window and look out at Malawi's three-striped flag. Then I squint my eyes and read a sign that's just below the flag.

"That can't be right, can it? Does that say Ebola checkpoint?"

"Oh no, I think it does," Naomi whispers.

Just before I left for South Africa, there was a bad Ebola outbreak in West Africa. It's been affecting countries like Guinea, Liberia, and Sierra Leone and has been getting worse by the day. In September, the deadly disease even made its way to the United States. We've chosen to travel up through East Africa in hopes of skirting around it, but suddenly even heading this way seems like it's going to put us in the crosshairs of this fatal virus.

"Like worrying about malaria wasn't enough, now this," I complain. "How on earth are we ever going to make it around the world without flying. This is impossible! It's just one obstacle after another!"

Naomi's look tells me she doesn't have any answers. "Hang in there. Let's eat our lunch and just try to forget about all this."

She uses the can opener I bought in Nelspruit last month to open a can of baked beans, and I peel the shells off a few hard-boiled eggs for us. It's a sorry-looking lunch, and as we eat I can't help but think how lucky I am to have Naomi here, calming down not just me but the officer as well.

When the officer finally emerges from his office an hour later, he comes out with a bloated belly and a glass bottle of Coca-Cola, condensation running down its hourglass shape. I've never been so desperate for a sip of soda in all my life. What little saliva is left in my throat dries up, and I only get that much more parched.

There is some good news, though. After we finished eating, I remembered I'd hidden four hundred US dollars inside Timberland for emergencies. I never imagined I'd have to bribe an immigrations officer in Mozambique, but I was relieved when I dug through the hidden interior pocket for the money and found that it was still there. Instead of pulling all of it out, I decided to only take out half in hopes that would be enough to keep us moving. To fork over four hundred dollars today would be disastrous, and it's not something I'm mentally prepared to do.

Once I slide the two crisp hundred dollar bills over the worn wooden counter, the officer quickly scoops them up and slides them in his back pocket like he's Cool Hand Luke. Without a word, he marks our passports with the official Mozambique entry stamp we were missing and then the exit stamp that will allow us to keep moving forward. Both Naomi and I double-check the stamps this time, and once he waves us past, we grab all of our things and begin walking to the Ebola checkpoint in Malawi.

* * *

Malawi turns out to be even more challenging to travel across than Mozambique; quite honestly, I didn't think such a thing was even possible. The buses are smaller and hotter, and they seem to break down twice as often. The drivers are constantly pulling over so they can buy soda bottles full of gasoline, which they then empty into the gas tank so we can keep going. As we're plodding around the southern end of Lake Malawi, our bus driver falls asleep at the wheel. Thankfully I'm sitting in the seat behind him and am able to hop up and rattle his shoulders just before he veers off the road.

It's not just the treacherous travel; other issues keep coming up. Embarrassing as it is to admit, our intimacy or lack thereof is one of them. Since the beds are so much smaller here than at home, I'm having a hard time getting a good night's sleep in the same bed with Naomi, so we start asking for two twin beds instead of one queen-sized bed. Sleeping separately only makes matters worse between us. At the end of a long day, she doesn't curl up next to me and rest her head on my chest anymore. Instead, we retire to our own sides of the room, and our gap continues to grow.

When we wake up Christmas morning in Lilongwe, Malawi's capital city, we find ourselves missing our friends and families. We decided to create our own version of Christmas here in Africa. We find a roll of candy cane–striped wrapping paper in the Woodlands Hotel lobby just after breakfast and use it to decorate the lamp in our room. Naomi cuts out several shapes that mimic the ornaments we both grew up hanging in our homes, and I tape them to the lampshade. Once we step back and looked at our "tree," we quickly realized what's missing.

"Presents!" Naomi shouts.

Ten minutes later, we pile into a taxi and head to Shoprite. We spend thirty minutes inside the store, each with a spending limit of twenty thousand Malawi kwacha, roughly twenty-five US dollars.

Back in our hotel room, Naomi peels the wrapping paper off her first gift, a bottle of Pantene Pro-V conditioner. A bright smile spreads across her face. She made a comment the other day about how much damage all these long bus rides had done to her hair, nearly turning it into straw, and about how hard it's been to find the kind of conditioner her type of hair requires here in Africa. She's overjoyed to see it, and I have to stop her from running right to the shower with it.

"Okay, I'll shower later. Your turn," she says.

I reach under the "tree" and pull a rectangular box toward me. I tear into the wrapping paper like I'm five years old and am beyond excited to find a Swiss Army utensil set.

"Yes, this is perfect! Thank you!"

We eat so many meals while in transit, and I always forget to pack a fork and knife, so I end up having to use my dirty fingers to pick at things. This utensil set fits into my pocket and is exactly the kind of thing I never knew I needed. I unfold the fork, then the knife, and finally the spoon and pretend to practice by eating the air.

After a few more small gifts are exchanged, we both reach for our last presents at the same time. The tiny boxes are eerily similar in size and shape. We hold them up to each other and instantly begin to laugh hysterically.

With hopes of working on our intimacy issues, we both bought each other a pack of African condoms.

* * *

Unfortunately, things do not get better between us as we move on to Tanzania. After traveling together for over two months, it's clear I'm not good at balancing my attempt at a creative transformation, the travel itself, and my connection with Naomi. They're all suffering. Maybe I'm just overwhelmed. Overwhelmed by the number of changes my life has gone through lately. Psychologically, I'm still adjusting to a life outside my creative comfort zone, and I'm not sure if I'll ever be able to get used to not having basic things like a home and health care.

The biggest problem is I had no way of knowing that tapping into my creativity would require such large amounts of isolation and silence. But Naomi and I are together nearly twenty-four hours a day, seven days a week. It's not as if I could just walk down the street and sit in a Starbucks to write or get some air; it often isn't safe for her to walk alone, so I feel like I always have to be with her and vice versa.

But writing is a very singular sport, as are photography and filmmaking. The ideas and inspiration I'm trying to invoke come from this very still place inside. In order to get to that still place, I can't just brush the surface, I've got to dive down deep. I know that if I'm able to tap into this creative well enough times, one day it's going to spring a leak. And that leak is going to be the thing that changes life for me. The thing that leads me to a better life.

Indian sage and author Patanjali said, "When you are inspired by some great purpose, some extraordinary project, all your thoughts break their bonds: Your mind transcends limitations, your consciousness expands in every direction, and you find yourself in a new, great and wonderful world. Dormant forces, faculties and talents become alive, and you discover yourself to be a greater person by far than you ever dreamed yourself to be." That is what I was striving for.

But ideas also need time to percolate and work their way up and out of me. I can't just reach down and rip them out. Still, with so little time to focus on my creativity, I keep putting pressure on myself to do just that, and when I can't find that creative sweet spot is when problems arise. I go from light and love to fear and failure. Impending thoughts of doom start rolling in like late afternoon storm clouds. I'm afraid I'm going to revert to the old me once my money runs out again. It's just one stressor after another.

The effect this has on my relationship with Naomi is what you'd expect. I've been growing more distant by the day. Even when we're lying in bed together, my mind is a million miles away. I keep telling her that I'm only acting this way in order to find the internal ideas I'm looking for and that I have no choice in the matter. "It's the only way to keep my dreams alive," I'll say.

This turns Naomi, the normally independent and self-sufficient, world-traveling, lone wolf of a woman I fell in love with, into a shell of herself. That beautiful balance we had back in Miami Beach is now a lopsided landslide of love. The more I withdraw, the more desperately she clings; the more she clings, the more I withdraw. It's as though what I need out of her or anyone is beyond the realm of relationships. We've been spending big chunks of time sitting inside our hotel room each day and analyzing every facet of our relationship—so much time that it's like we don't have an actual relationship anymore. All that's left is a tangled web of overthinking—analysis paralysis in relationship form.

Naomi finally snaps. She's had enough of the distance between us, and comes to me and desperately pulls me in close. Her voice wavers as she pleads with me, "Please tell me that everything is going to be okay."

I can't reply and say that it is. This is the moment we both know that our fate had been sealed. Tears stream down her face.

Instead of feeling sad, like I want to, I just feel more hollow. Somehow I've become the Tin Man.

#

When Naomi's debit card finally arrives the first week of February, she uses it for the first time to book a flight away from me. With tears building in her eyes, she murmurs, "Europe is too expensive, and there is no way I'm going back to Miami Beach." She grabs a tissue to catch her tears. "I need to find a cheap flight to a safe place where my heart can heal."

Crystal-clear waves are lapping so close to our bungalow I can hear the moon slurping them back out to sea. The setting sun is shooting shards of pink across the sky, and we should be the happiest people on the planet. Naomi and I bartered our way into Michamvi Sunset Bay Resort, an all-inclusive, five-star honeymoon resort on the east side of the island of Zanzibar. It's the mecca of my mind's eye, but instead of enjoying its sugary sand beach and the largest lobster tails I've ever seen, we're stuck inside staring at a computer screen.

I know she wants me to reach over and shut off the computer. She wants me to pull her in close and tell her that "we" are going to be okay. I want nothing more than to be able to do that, but I still can't. So instead of reassuring Naomi, I sink behind the walls I've built up around myself and ache with responsibility for everything that's gone wrong.

She believes my writing, filming, and photography needs my complete attention and a deep solitude in order to flourish. The real irony is she stayed behind in Miami Beach for seven weeks to give me a creative cushion for that reason, so I could find myself and establish my new routines. She thinks she's getting in the way, and that's why I'm often so detached even when we're side by side. I think maybe she's right, but that doesn't mean I want her to go. She's still my best friend.

I hesitate to lock eyes with her because I know what I'll see. I'll see everything I've ever wanted in someone else right there in front of me. Maybe there's just something inherently wrong with me; maybe I will never be able to care for someone as much as I do for myself.

I watch in agony as she narrows down her choices to Thailand or Nepal. When it hits me that we won't play another round of gin rummy before bed, I have to get up and walk to the window to try and compose myself. As I look out over the flawless Indian Ocean, it becomes obvious that I can't.

My head dips and then a wrecking ball smashes against my chest.

Naomi looks over at me with exhausted eyes and tells me that she's settled on Bangkok because she's been there before and because the combination of the flight and the cost of living is the cheapest. I can no longer hold back my tears. My heart is breaking. I have no idea how she's going to survive. She only has a couple hundred bucks saved.

"Okay, it's booked," she whimpers. "I leave from Dar es Salaam in two days."

What's left of my heart folds in on itself.

#

As our taxi arrives at the Julius Nyerere International Airport, there's a pile of tissues on my lap and a medicine ball in my throat. Naomi's somehow back to her strong-willed, independent, lone-wolf traveling self. She told me last night that after two months of tears, she's cried out and tired of being tired. She said she was going to put on a brave face today even though she's broken.

I, on the other hand, can't stop the kind of grief-stricken sobs that make snot bubble up and slime out my nose. The enormity of Naomi's departure hit me all at once this morning, and today has quickly become the hardest day of my life. I almost wish she'd given me a reason for things to end this way—that she'd cheated on me or treated me poorly or complained just once about Africa. But she hasn't. She's been a model partner this entire time, and so I know the fault is fully mine.

The taxi skids to a squeaky stop, and our driver pops the car into park. I stagger out into the sweltering heat and help Naomi with her backpack. Then I wait just a few inches behind her, afraid to let her out of my sight even for a second as she checks in for her flight. I've already used the entire box of tissues I brought, so I wipe my eyes with my shirt sleeve, not caring that everyone is staring at me, a giant white man sobbing like a child. We're coming to the end of the line for our love and yet, sadly, I've still not said those three words to Naomi.

I'm pathetic.

We've traveled together for 102 days, and just two or three hours together in Mozambique, Malawi, or Tanzania would have been enough to bring a couple exponentially closer. Naomi has multiplied and enlarged the good in me along the way, and even though I know letting her go is the biggest mistake I'll ever make, I still can't stop myself from making it.

When we reach the security checkpoint entrance, I want Naomi to pull me in close and tell me that "we" are going to be okay. All I want is one more day with her. Almost out of nowhere, there is no limit to my love. Where was this emotion a month ago?

Just before we reach the front of the line, I pull Naomi to the side for a second. There isn't much left to say except those three words I've been holding back for nearly a year. After a long, soul-crushingly sad hug,

Naomi peels herself away from me. I choke back my tears and then look deep into her eyes and softly say, "I love you."

She wipes the tears that follow away from both our eyes.

"I love you too," she says.

It's almost unfathomable to believe that the last thing I'll ever say to Naomi will be to tell her that I love her for the first time. The guard checks her boarding pass and waves her on. She looks back one last time. I try to lift my arm up to wave good-bye, but I can't. She blows me a quick kiss and then she's gone.

I fall to my knees. I drop my head in my hands.

I have no idea how I'm going to make it one more mile.

CHAPTER 3
KENYA – UGANDA
AFRICA

*"I learned that courage was not the absence of fear, but
the triumph over it. The brave man is not he who does
not feel afraid, but he who conquers that fear."*

— *Nelson Mandela*

S OMETIMES ALL YOU CAN DO is put one foot in front of the other.
Traveling north to Nairobi in Kenya a few days later helps me
begin to pick up the pieces of my broken life. It isn't the open road
or the change of scenery that helps—it's the danger.

Rhys, a Brit I'd met back in South Africa, sent me a message asking if
I'd seen on the news what happened at Amapondo Backpackers, the hostel
where I stayed in Port St. Johns, South Africa, the week prior to meeting
up with Naomi in Johannesburg. I'd done a film for them, and Rhys and
his girlfriend were extras in that film. When I emailed him back asking
him to fill me in, he shared a horrifying story with me. A group of masked
men armed with shotguns and knives barged into the hostel and rounded
up all the guests. They raped a twenty-year-old Rhodes University student
in the communal showers and robbed Rhys and all the other guests. This
happened just a few days after I checked out. Rhys ended his email by
saying he felt lucky to be alive.

I'm not normally one to live in fear or be influenced by the news, but

I've been hypersensitive to violence lately because of his email and all the travel warnings that seem to keep popping up. It's not that I've never thought of Africa as being dangerous. Africa is as dangerous as walking down the wrong street at the wrong time of night in America. But when I envisioned traveling across Africa, I never anticipated I'd actually face that kind of danger. It was one of those out of sight, out of mind things. Until last night.

I was sitting in the lobby of the Eden Gardens Hotel in Nairobi just minding my own business and using the Wi-Fi to see if Naomi had emailed me from Bangkok, when a South African woman working on her laptop next to me struck up a conversation. She told me about a hotel guest she'd met here just the day before I'd arrived.

"He was a German man around your age," she said. "He went outside to hail a taxi in the middle of the afternoon, but he returned just a few minutes later completely naked."

I started laughing, thinking there was some sort of punch line coming, but when she told me the details, I suddenly felt fragile. She said a car pulled up pretending to be a taxi and that a group of men with guns jumped out and surrounded him just in front of the hotel. They forced him onto the ground and robbed him of everything he had, including all his clothes.

She ended her story by saying, "You better be careful. I could tell you're an American from a mile away. You're exactly the kind of guy they're looking for."

After I thanked her for the bone-chilling warning, I got up and began to walk back to my room. She called after me as I left: "Don't forget what I said—you've got a big bull's-eye on your back, buddy!"

I'd also been warned by a couple Kenyans I met at my hotel in Dar es Salaam that Nairobi's fallen on hard times. Business is down and crime is up. The travel statement just issued by the US Department of State confirms this, warning, "US citizens considering travel to Kenya should evaluate their personal security situation in light of continuing and recently heightened threats from terrorism and the high rate of violent crime."

Carjackings and armed robberies are currently the most common crimes in Nairobi. But all that pales in comparison to Kenya's biggest threat, which is coming from their next-door neighbor, Somalia. The problem isn't with Somalia; it's with Al Shabaab, a Somali-based extremist group allied with Al Qaeda.

The Somali and Kenyan militaries joined forces to successfully fight off a group of Al Shabaab insurgents in southern Somalia about three years ago, which put a huge target on Kenya's back. After Al Shabaab regrouped, they retaliated by attacking civilians in Nairobi's Westgate shopping mall just last year. I'd been to that mall a few years ago during a previous trip to Nairobi. When I saw on CNN that Al Shabaab had stormed the same restaurant I'd eaten lunch in several times, I froze in fear. They tortured and then killed 67 people while injuring another 175. The attack, although an ocean away from me at the time, hit close to home.

I grew up in a tiny, two-stoplight town in Pennsylvania, in a neighborhood bookended by cornfields. It was the kind of place where nothing bad ever happened. I never had to think about safety while I was growing up, but even when I've traveled abroad I've always felt safe, mostly because of my size. People often tell me that I'm the tallest person they have ever seen. I'm six-feet-ten-inches tall, with broad shoulders that send an intimidating message whether I want them to or not. I might be as big as Goliath, but I feel like David at the moment. My size is now suddenly a disadvantage because I stand out like a sore thumb everywhere I go in Africa. Add in the language barrier, that I'm constantly getting lost, and that Al Shabaab's motto is to shoot first and ask questions later, and I suddenly feel desperately unsafe.

It made me think twice about crossing into Kenya this week, but unfortunately this is really the only reliable route to Cairo. Kenya is still much safer than crossing the Democratic Republic of the Congo to the west. Tanzania's northern neighbor, Uganda, is relatively safe but would only funnel me directly to the doorstep of South Sudan, which is the third most dangerous country in the world behind only Afghanistan and Syria, according to the global peace index.

However, just the sight of the Ethiopian Embassy this morning here in Nairobi adds to my concerns. It looks more like a prison than a place that grants permission for onward travel. Huge rolls of barbwire top intimidatingly tall cinder block walls. I'm buzzed through a very medieval-looking, two-ton metal door that is as unwelcoming as any I've ever stepped through.

By the time I find the consulate office inside the barren building,

I'm hardly surprised to see that there's only one other person here today. As I watch the man shuffle papers together and then present them to the woman on the other side of the plexiglass window, based on the inflection in his accent, I'm all but sure he's Ethiopian. As my eyes scan the rest of the room, I'm startled by the Arabic that's everywhere. It's on the tourism posters that hang on the walls, the brochures on the tabletops, and the forms I have to fill out. It's my first encounter with the language, and the squiggly lines look more like hieroglyphics than written words. In all the countries I've traveled through so far, I often haven't known the language, but at least the alphabet was familiar.

If I can get my Ethiopian visa today, then I can board a series of buses to cross Kenya and be in Ethiopia by the end of the week. From Ethiopia, I'll be able to avoid South Sudan and cross plain old Sudan, which, while still dangerous, would be the lesser of two evils.

When I pass my paperwork and passport to the consular officer, she takes one look at it, shakes her head from side to side, and quickly slides everything back to me. My Ethiopian visa application is denied before I can even submit it. While waiting in line just now, I'd read on the back of the application that only Kenyan residents are able to get the Ethiopian visa at the embassy, but I was hoping that was an outdated policy or that they'd bend the rules for me and my overland dream.

The officer goes on to tell me that the only way I can apply for my travel visa to Ethiopia is within my home country, which sends my arms flailing toward the sky.

"How do you expect me to do that?"

I tell her that it's actually impossible for me to apply in America, but she's unconcerned.

Suddenly there's no way for me to keep traveling north toward Cairo. And while this news is a death blow to my overland travel dream, it only amplifies how isolated I've been feeling without Naomi by my side.

#

Back at my hotel, when the Wi-Fi works long enough for me to finally reach Naomi, I press my ear against the phone so hard it hurts, hoping that will bring her closer to me, but all I get is static.

A long moment passes, and then her soft voice cuts through again.

"Hello."

This is the first time we've spoken since the day she left, and it's as hard now as it was then.

I gulp for oxygen as I ask, "Hello. Can you hear me?"

"I want to thank you for everything—I will never forget the time we spent together in Africa," she says.

My throat tightens, and I can barely get a response out. "Me either."

The Wi-Fi cuts in and out and while we wait, listening, the howling silence widens and deepens like a sandstorm between us.

My mind flips through all the things that went wrong and then stops on the last moment our eyes locked in the airport a little over a week ago.

That image will forever be burned into my brain.

But I can't dwell on that because now we're both fighting for our lives, both living off my modest life savings. The other night I woke up in a sweaty panic from a nightmare that I was getting hauled away to jail because the police had found out that Naomi was really the one doing the online economics work under my name. Unable to shake how real it felt, I immediately emailed Naomi and begged her to resign. Thankfully, she was understanding and agreed with my decision, which only made me miss her that much more. She's sacrificed herself so many times over the past year, and when her email came through letting me know she'd resigned, it felt like she'd fallen on her sword for me one last time.

I can't help but feel financially responsible for Naomi. I'm the one that asked her to come to Africa and ultimately the one who's left her without a penny to her name. And it's not like she can just fly back to the United States; unlike most, she doesn't have a family she can go back to. Her father's never been in her life, and her mother has struggled with unemployment and homelessness. I wired her five hundred dollars this morning, and she's going to try and stretch that out for as long as she can by staying at a flea-infested, five-dollars-a-night Bangkok hostel.

A whooping cough breaks the silence.

"Oh my God, that sounds terrible! Are you okay?" I ask.

"I've come down with something. I'm down to eating only one meal a day so I can save money, but I'll be okay."

"I wish I could take care of you." I can sense her smile, but I can't find mine. "I'm sorry, I'm so sorry for all this."

The line grows silent again for a time. The silence stretches on until it's almost unbearable, and then she finally speaks.

"How is your writing going?" she asks. I can hear the ache in the words.

"It's no easier and I'm no more creative now that you're gone."

Creativity didn't dive into my arms the moment she left them. Instead, like a thief in the night, it took everything I had. It whisked Naomi away under the promise of Hemingway-like pages, but they didn't miraculously appear like I'd assumed they would.

"The blank page is still blank," I say.

What I've come to realize is that the conditions for creativity might never be optimal. The cafes may never be quiet enough, computers quick enough, and myself still enough. I'm scared that it's me. Maybe I'm just not good enough at this artistic stuff.

I change the subject and ask Naomi if she still cares about me.

"I care very much for you—I care in a way that will prove itself over and over again throughout the course of our knowing each other in this lifetime, and perhaps the next."

Naomi whispers into the phone one last time. She tells me she thinks it's best if we don't speak for a while because it's too hard on her heart. She needs time to heal. Then she says the saddest, softest teary good-bye I've ever heard.

My eyes well up. This isn't . . . no, don't . . . I can't.

Click.

* * *

Denied my Ethiopian visa, the only option to keep my overland travel dreams alive is to head west to Uganda. Kenya's neighbor grants me a travel visa and it feels like a safer spot to wait for my other travel visa paperwork to get processed. Once I get to Kampala, the capital of Uganda, I mail my passport back to my parents in the United States with all the paperwork needed in order to get the visas required to enter Ethiopia, Sudan, and Egypt. I've learned the hard way that you can't just show up at the doorstep of a country with a passport and a smile and expect to be let in.

It's incredibly stressful being separated from my passport and, quite frankly, this is the part of traveling that I can't stand. This bureaucratic bullshit. It's not enough to travel with my American passport; I need to get a travel visa as well. Almost every country I've traveled across so far, as well as those I need to travel onward to, insists on additional permissions.

And, yes, I know that the hoops I have to jump through are the fault of my own country. The United States makes it so difficult for foreigners to enter America legally that these countries practice the policy of reciprocity. An eye for an eye, a tooth for a tooth, and a stack of never-ending forms for a stack of never-ending forms.

The result is that I can't leave Uganda until I get my passport back and I end up stuck here for forty days.

I'm staying at the Entebbe Eco Lodge when I learn the care package my parents sent, which contains my passport, has finally arrived at the FedEx office in Kampala. Elias, the short and stout Swiss-born owner of the lodge, agrees to drive me into Kampala this morning (only because he needed to pick up something at an electronics store) and drop me off at the FedEx office.

I've never come across someone who loves to discuss bad news as much as Elias, which is why he's built this hidden oasis in Kitende. It sits just on the outskirts of Kampala. And while its thatched cottages and lush gardens are beautiful, he has hidden behind the huge stone walls of its perimeter for the past fifteen years. Rarely does he venture outside. Although that may also be due to a secret he let slip the other day—that he needed to put some distance between himself and Switzerland due to some unspecified legal troubles.

We're about to leave the breakfast table and head off when a waitress says, "Did you hear the news?"

"What news? No more news!" I say in a panic.

Wide-eyed, the waitress, who's just run in late for her shift, stares at us and then gasps. "The top prosecutor in the Al Shabaab trial was shot dead in Kampala last night."

"We are not going," Elias tells me. "The city is going to riot today— it's not safe for us. I'm sorry, but your passport will have to wait."

The waitress continues, "The prosecutor that was murdered is the one who was trying the thirteen men accused of killing seventy-six people in 2010. "

"Ah yes, I remember—the ones who were watching the World Cup final," says Elias.

I know the story only because I walked in on it playing in the lobby last week. Gruesome images flashed across the screen next to the reception desk. Al Shabaab, the same Islamic militant group that I feared while in Nairobi just last month, carried out the attack. I had no idea their tentacles stretched all the way to Uganda.

At the end of that same news broadcast, a big, barrel-chested Ugandan man dressed in green fatigues came on the screen and said, "Americans may be targeted for terrorist attacks in Kampala. The military has received information of possible threats at city locations where Westerners are known to gather. It's possible that an attack may take place soon." He cleared his throat and then said, with determination, "Now is the time for Ugandans everywhere to be vigilant!"

Having to deal with a bloodthirsty terrorist group that's looking for Americans in the city I'm in is undoubtedly the worst thing I've come across in all my travels. I can't help but replay the words of the woman in Nairobi—"You've got a big bull's-eye on you, buddy"—over and over.

American travelers have always faced scrutiny—the term "anti-American" first showed up in Webster's dictionary in 1828, just a few decades after the country itself was born. Military interventions such as the Gulf War, the occupation of Iraq, and the ongoing war in Afghanistan have increased tensions for travelers. But for the vast majority of Americans like me, who have no connections with the military or American political foreign policy, what's our role in all of this? For the fanatics, like those in Al Shabaab, this is an irrelevant question—we're Americans, so we're guilty.

The awful details keep coming. "The prosecutor was shot twice by two men on a motorbike as she drove home with her three children. They shot her through the window of her car after she stopped to buy fruit on the side of the road."

Something in me snaps. Too much. I'm done. I want out. I *need* my passport!

Without saying another word, I turn and sprint past the wrought-iron front gate and off the property of the Eco Lodge.

It's pouring down buckets of rain, and I can't get any traction on the muddy road, but I keep going. I don't weigh the danger, I don't think about the horrific news. Somehow (I don't know how) I just push it all out of my brain and lock myself into my mission for the day.

The heartbreak, the terrorist threats, the oppressive negativity Elias has been projecting on me—it's all becoming too much to handle.

I splash my way through the tiny village, passing the school I visited to take photos of the students yesterday, then a fruit stall I've been frequenting for fresh mangos, and the water well that everyone within walking distance shares. Eventually I'm back to the main road in Kitende. I stick my arm out to hail a minibus. By the time one stops, I'm soaked. I cram into the middle seat in the second row and wring out the tail of my shirt. Then we wait alongside the road for a few minutes, until every inch of the bus is filled with either a person or a chicken, before sputtering away.

My mind begins to map out how I'm going to get through Kampala's streets quickly. I know the seven hills the city is built on pretty well. Luckily, I called the FedEx office this morning and learned they just moved to a new location, otherwise I'd have shown up at their old storefront when I don't have a minute to spare. I need to retrieve my passport and get to the Kenyan High Commission before it closes at noon. I can apply for my second Kenyan travel visa there. But first I'll need to stop at the mall for cash and to have extra passport photos taken. If all goes according to plan I'll be on a bus heading back to Kenya and then on to Ethiopia within the next few days.

I jump off while the bus is still rolling to a stop at the Jinja Road junction, then wave down a boda-boda. These bikes are the most popular way to get around the city (there are hundreds on offer), but they come with a cost—and it's not just their incessant honking. They are poorly maintained and dangerous. Plus, I know that if I get on the back of one, I will be out in the open, like a big American flag flapping in the wind. That's just asking for trouble.

But this is about speed. They can maneuver quickly through the insane gridlock that fills the downtown streets, and time is clearly of the essence. I have less than an hour to get everything I need. If I take a taxi, I will never make it to the Kenyan High Commission on time.

We shoot off through the rain toward the Oasis Mall, which has an ATM I know will work (I've already found out the hard way that not all ATMs in Africa work or return your card). Within minutes, we pass the Ugandan High Court and take Nile Avenue toward the Uganda Golf Course, then pull up to the entrance of the mall.

The breath whooshes out of me.

Uganda's riot control unit is out in full force. There are armored trucks and fifty soldiers in light blue fatigues positioned around the mall's perimeter. Each soldier has a steely look in his eyes and an assault rifle in his hands.

I think back to the warning: "Al Shabaab is planning an attack where Westerners are known to congregate."

It all falls into place. This isn't a figment of the media's imagination—Al Shabaab really *are* coursing through Kampala and out for blood. Although the prosecutor they murdered last night wasn't an American, it's close enough for my panicked brain. Maybe Elias wasn't being so paranoid after all.

From where we are parked, I can see Café Java. Usually I have a hard time finding a seat inside, but today it's completely empty. I hop off the bike, run up to the café's ATM, punch in my information, grab the shillings I need, and leap back onto the boda-boda.

"Old Port Bell Road!"

The driver is good. He races through the rain toward the FedEx office like he was born on this bike. Every time our bald tires slip against the wet pavement, he gives the bike its head and then nudges it back on track. It's quite a performance.

But no matter how good a driver he is, we can't find the FedEx office. It's already 11:30, and time is running out.

I point down an abandoned street, and just as we are about to fly past the store, I see a tiny FedEx logo out of the corner of my eye.

Roman, the manager, is expecting me and has my package ready. I thank him and pay the fee. (It "randomly" got stopped by customs, so I had to pay duties, taxes, and a clearing charge.) Dumping the contents of the care package into my backpack, I hop back on the boda-boda, and we fishtail through the mist toward the Kenyan High Commission on Nakasero Road.

But of course, the High Commission isn't where I thought it was. It's not where my driver thought it was either. It's simply *not there.*

The driver has to ask for directions five different times. Each time we stop, I can't help but feel like Al Shabaab has a homing device on the bike and is closing in on me. I'm looking over each shoulder like my head is on a swivel. This is *crazy.*

Eventually, a security guard outside Independence Park points us in the right direction. I see the red, green, and black colors of the Kenyan flag waving from a few blocks away, and we pull underneath it at 11:57.

Kenyan security guards at the front gate ask me to leave my backpack with them, but before I do, I reach inside and grab my passport and the letter my parents wrote me.

By the time I clear the metal detector and the body search area and make it to the consulate office, it is exactly 12:00.

As I frantically fill out the paperwork that's required for the travel visa, I realize I forgot to exchange my shillings for US dollars and to get an extra passport photo at the mall. I must have blanked those details out when I saw the riot police outside.

I stop writing and slam the pen down. "You have got to be kidding me!"

Exhaustion. Exasperation. Fear. My clothes are soaking wet, and they feel like they weigh a thousand pounds. Silence. No, not silence—*drip, drip, drip.* I cut my arm while darting around today and so what's rolling off my body onto the ground is a literal combination of my blood, my sweat, and my tears of frustration.

It's just too damn impossible.

I announce my resignation to everyone within earshot of the waiting room.

"I quit!"

I have my passport again. I can just fly home to the US. Maybe I can even call the company I used to work for and see if they'll hire me back. I'll tell my old manager that seven months in Africa gave me a new appreciation for my old job, and that I'm recharged and ready to go. Things will be so much easier. It's almost a relief.

Almost.

Feeling bitter and angry, I lean forward and rest my elbows on my knees as I flip through my passport, looking at the stamps and travel visas I've accrued so far. As I do, I can't help but think of my favorite book, *The Alchemist.* I think of the main character, Santiago, and all the obstacles he overcame in search of his treasure. *How did he do it? How did he keep going when times got tough? Right. He followed his omens to find his treasure. Where are my omens?* I curse myself for comparing myself to Santiago. Then my temper spikes.

That's fiction, you idiot!

When I get to the last page of my passport, a tiny slip of paper falls out and flutters onto the white tile floor, followed by my parents' letter and three twenty-dollar bills, which my dad had stuffed inside as a surprise. I collect the bills, then I reach for the tiny slip of paper.

It's an extra passport photo.

* * *

Now that I've got my travel visa, I can leave for Kenya tomorrow, make a quick pit stop in Kisumu for the night, and then go on to Nairobi the next day. From there, I'll travel north to the Ethiopian border town of Moyale.

Looking forward to finally being able to make progress, I open my laptop to catch up on the news. That's when I see the headline.

No. Please, God, no.

I lean closer to the screen.

Gunmen stormed Garissa University College in Kenya early this morning and killed 148 people.

I click on the article. Al Shabaab rounded up seven hundred students from the university's dormitories and then executed all the Christians.

I'm numb. I take a deep breath to brace myself before I can keep reading.

Collins Wetangula, the vice chairman of the student union, said that when the gunmen arrived at his dormitory, he could hear them opening doors and asking the people who had hidden inside whether they were Muslims or Christians. "If you were Christian, you were shot on the spot. With each blast of the gun, I thought I was going to die."

He said that when he heard the gunshots, he locked himself and three roommates in their room.

"All I could hear were footsteps and gunshots—nobody was screaming because they thought this would lead the gunmen to know where they are," he said. "The next thing, we saw people in military uniform through the window of the back of our rooms who identified themselves as the Kenyan military," Wetangula said. The soldiers took him and around twenty others to safety.

"We started running and bullets were whizzing past our heads and the soldiers told us to dive," Wetangula said. He said the soldiers told the students later that Al Shabaab snipers were perched on a dormitory roof and were trying to shoot them.

I lean back on my chair, unable to process this. The bloody images on my screen are incomprehensible, and the whole thing feels surreal.

Garissa University College is located just a few hours northeast of Nairobi, and it sits close enough to the route I'm supposed to take that I will have to rethink my plans. But there is nothing to rethink. I've already discussed this exhaustively with everyone I've met in Uganda. If I want to get out of Africa overland, and quickly, this is the only way to go. There is no alternate route.

As I read over more of the awful details of the attack, my phone buzzes. It's a text from Roman, the manager of the FedEx store where I received my passport two days ago.

"I don't know how true it is but just beware, Eric. A massive bombing or hostage-taking mission is expected in Uganda in the next forty-eight hours. It's advised to stay indoors. Army deployment is heavy in Kampala. Al Shabaab wants to enter a place and shoot as many people as possible. So avoid crowded places. Please inform your loved ones."

My hands start trembling. I'm not equipped to deal with this. I don't feel safe in Kampala, I don't feel safe going back to Nairobi, and the route from Nairobi to Ethiopia is quite possibly the most dangerous part of all. Everything north of Nairobi is barren wilderness, which leaves the rare bus that runs that route open to attacks by Kenyan, Ethiopian, or Somalian bandits, a common occurrence in the lightly policed region where the borders of the three countries converge.

I'm well aware that I'm here by choice. And while I didn't choose to be in the crosshairs of a conflict that I have no stake in, I know that I am a tall, white, American man with one of the world's most reliable passports in my pocket. I am grateful for all the things I inherited because of where I was born. Plus, I have the power of choice, which is something most people living here don't have. If I want to guarantee my safety, now is the time to exercise the advantages I have in this world. I must book the next flight out.

I run my hands through my hair and begin to search for the cheapest flight to a major European city. The internet spits back fares that are all reasonably priced, but each time I stop and think about boarding a plane, a chisel chips at my chest.

I settle on a flight that leaves for Rome just four hours from now and then sigh as I tell my dreams, "I'm sorry to let you down, but I just can't risk my life for you."

As I hover the cursor over *confirm purchase*, I hesitate. I feel a hurricane in my heart, and all the joy my dreams have brought me over the past two years drains from me. Each time I envision a boarding pass in my hand, it's overpoweringly depressing.

It took everything I had to tap into and truly listen to my heart to find my dreams in the first place and then all the courage I could muster to follow them, but still that's not enough. It feels like a piece of me is dying—and it's not just any piece, it's the biggest and best piece of me. I'll never be able get this part back.

I take my hand off my trackpad to weigh the options one final time. If I fly to Rome, I'll be physically safe, but I'll die inside. If I decide to keep going, I will be risking my life.

I look around the rooftop of the ICU Guesthouse I moved to last night. I wanted to be closer to Kampala since the bus I'm supposed to board to Kisumu leaves at 6:00 a.m. tomorrow morning. There is a worn-out tiki bar in the corner, a refrigerator with a few bottles of water and soda piled inside it, and a couple of lounge chairs facing Kampala's skyline.

I have no idea what to do. I can't quit, but I can't keep going either. I thought finding my passport picture and that spare cash at the Kenyan High Commission was a sign I should keep going. But it's not enough. I need a more definitive sign.

I can hear children playing in the park across the street and birds chirping from the telephone wires. The only book in sight is a Bible sitting on the rickety coffee table right in front of me. I didn't see it when I first sat down, but suddenly I have an urge to pick it up. Something deep inside me tells me that this book has my answer. It's not like I hear a voice or a get a fuzzy feeling or anything like that. In fact, I can't even really put it into words—it's just something I *know*.

To be honest, the Bible has never been an important presence in my life. I was christened in a Presbyterian church, so by definition I am a Christian, although I probably wouldn't call myself that. I hated regular school, so you can imagine how much more I hated Sunday school. On Sundays, all I wanted to do was sleep in and then watch football.

It wasn't until the ninety-day leave of absence I took that my perspective started to shift. During that time, I visited Buddhist and Hindu temples, Muslim mosques, Jewish synagogues, and Christian churches, and my views on religion and spirituality began to broaden. I've cherry-picked and pulled parts I like from each religion to form my own belief system.

My Holy Book is Paulo Coelho's *The Alchemist,* the story of Santiago, a shepherd boy, who has a recurring dream which tells him that he will find a hidden treasure if he travels to the Egyptian pyramids. He sells all of his sheep and decides to take the risks required to pursue his Personal Legend. Many of the characters Santiago meets along his journey use the word *Maktub,* which in Arabic means, "It is written." The word *Maktub* typically appears to Santiago when he is about to take a big risk. As Santiago learns, fate always cooperates with those who pursue their Personal Legends, so as long as he remains true to his heart, he can be at ease.

I decide I'm going to close my eyes and blindly open this Bible to a random page, and then I'm going to spin my index finger in circles and plop it down. Whatever that line tells me to do is what I'm going to do.

I close my eyes and tilt my head up toward the sky. I think about how desperately I want to stay true to my heart and make it to those same Egyptian pyramids Santiago saw. They've never felt farther away than they do now.

I flip open the Bible to a random page.

There are 783,137 words in the King James Bible. My finger is so fat that it lands underneath five of them. I whisper them to myself as tears flood my eyes.

Jesus answered, "It is written."

CHAPTER 4
ETHIOPIA
AFRICA

"What matters most is how well you walk through fire."

— *Charles Bukowski*

Nairobi's streets at 2:30 in the morning are grim. Huge piles of garbage line the broken sidewalks, and the smell of raw sewage obliterates every other scent. Small piles of trash burn in the middle of each intersection and give the city's eerie darkness a lawless, postapocalyptic feel.

Most of the dangling streetlamps don't work; the dim headlights of the taxi I'm in barely illuminate the pitch blackness. I feel anything but safe. But much worse than the darkness is the statement that Al Shabaab released two days ago: *Kenyan cities will run red with blood.*

I'm in one of those cities—a poor suburb of Nairobi called Eastleigh. Its nickname is "Little Mogadishu" as it's inhabited mostly by Somali immigrants. Since 2012, this neighborhood has experienced several attacks linked to Al Shabaab. Most of the buildings we pass are crumbling; some look bomb blasted. One actually is—a blast killed six people here last year. There are only a handful of people walking the streets at this hour. They look as tough as you'd expect.

The taxi driver I've hired, who assured me he knew where the bus station was, can't find any of the streets he's looking for.

He slows the car without looking at me and then pulls over and rolls the window down. A stranger emerges from the shadows. This is exactly how Western tourists end up on the news.

The driver asks him a question in Swahili—directions, I surmise. They both look confused.

This is the most dangerous thing I could be doing here. To my relief, the driver finally pushes the pedal down, and off we go again. A few minutes later, still no bus station, so my driver pulls over, and we repeat the same hair-raising process. It feels like just a matter of time before we're carjacked.

A homeless man helps us out, pointing down the street and counting up from zero. He's telling us it's the tenth street on the left. Pulling away, the driver regains his confidence and tries his best to reassure me. "It's very safe, nothing to worry about."

We both know he is lying.

We count the streets out loud together as we pass. There are no street signs.

Tenth street. Left turn.

At the end of the block, I see a long white bus with "Moyale Liner" painted on the side. This isn't so much of a bus station as it is a bus stop. My blood pressure spikes, and I fidget in my seat. This is it—we've arrived. I was almost hoping we wouldn't. Our car creeps around crater-like potholes.

When I told the manager of Khweza Bed and Breakfast I would take this bus to Moyale last night, she stopped clicking through the photos I'd taken on my computer screen and started pleading with me not to go. I told her it was the only way.

After an eerie silence, she said, "The bus will most likely have two armed guards on it."

"I'm not sure if that makes me feel better or worse," I replied nervously.

The bus will pass through the part of northern Kenya that has recently become a hotbed for Al Shabaab activity. Their attacks are often aimed at buses just like this one.

As we pull closer, I notice that the bus appears to be riddled with bullet holes. My taxi driver pulls alongside it. I wish we were good friends. I wish he could tell me a funny story or reassure me that all this is routine, no sweat. The only thing he says is how much I owe him.

"I'll be right back, wait here," I say.

I leave my bags in the taxi so he won't pull away while I inspect the bus. When I get up to the driver's side, I find that the "bullet holes" are metallic stickers of oddly shaped stars. It's an appalling choice of decal, considering where this bus is headed.

I circle the dilapidated vehicle, looking for someone in charge. There's a group of Ethiopians wrapped in blankets drinking camel-milk tea. By their side, a homeless teenage boy sleeps on the sidewalk. He is using newspapers as blankets and his lone shoe as his pillow.

"Does anyone work here?"

No one blinks. No one responds. No one seems to care.

I run back to the taxi and ask the driver if he can wait for me or if I can wait inside the taxi with him. He points to his watch and says, "I have to be at the airport to pick someone up in a few minutes. I must leave right now." I offer him more money to stay, but he has to go. He gets out and dumps Timberland and my camera bag onto the pavement.

As he pulls away, I watch his taillights disappear into the wasteland-like night.

Behind me, someone appears in the doorway of the bus. He's a dark man with a long black beard. His once-white T-shirt and tan cargo pants are filthy. He waves over the group of Ethiopians and begins collecting their tickets. I walk over and ask in a panic, "Is this bus safe—do you think it will make it to Moyale without being attacked? I heard that the bus has two armed guards on it, is that true?"

He shrugs. He can't understand a word I say, and neither can anyone else. Everyone here speaks Arabic. I see no armed guards anywhere.

Kenyan cities will run red with blood.

People push past me to board the bus. No one is smiling, no one is cheerful, and no one looks like they are going to enjoy the long road ahead—a nerve-jangling, fifteen-hour ride, a good portion of it likely on unpaved roads.

The man collecting tickets motions for mine. I pull it out of my pocket and look at it. It says boarding time, 3:00 a.m.—the same time that's showing on my phone. This is literally the point of no return. If I step onto this bus, there's no turning back.

Just how much am I willing to risk for my dreams?

I can just go back to the hotel, go back to bed, and then fly to Addis Ababa, Ethiopia's capital, in the morning. No one will ever know!

The man collecting tickets officially loses his patience with me and angrily waves his hands for mine. There isn't going to be some miraculous sign this time; I'm going to have to make my own feet move.

I have to finally find out what I'm made of, to stick with what I initially set out to do, just this once. I've quit too many times in my life. Who knows what kind of man I might become if I can summon the courage to push forward. This might be my only chance to ever truly test myself. With the flames at my feet, I take one last deep breath and tell myself, *don't quit, keep going.*

I reach into my pocket and fish around for my ticket. After I pass it over, I rest my hand on the windshield and say a quiet prayer.

Dear God, please protect everyone on this bus. Please let us arrive in Moyale safely. Help get us there in one piece. And please don't let my journey end like this.

And then I step on board.

* * *

It's pitch black, and I can't see my hand in front of my face, but I can feel something. As I start to regain consciousness, the pain intensifies. It feels like tiny pieces of my skin are slowly being gnawed out of my body.

I jump out of bed and flick the lights on. It's a disturbing scene. Hundreds of beady-eyed mosquitos are hovering just above my bed sheets.

I was so tired from not sleeping last night that when I finally found a room in Moyale, I threw myself into bed. Now I see there is a hole the size of Alaska in my mosquito net. I frantically try to shoo the pests away, but they're not going anywhere. They love me. If anything, I'm only getting them riled up.

Now I understand why this room at the Koket Borena Hotel was only ten dollars. By the time I got to the Ethiopian immigration office last night, it was closed, and since there were no guards at the border, I simply walked across it and onto Ethiopian soil. I guess technically I'm here illegally, but this side of Moyale is slightly more built up than its Kenyan counterpart, and I was told that this is the nicest hotel in town. If this is actually true, then I can't imagine the conditions at the other ones.

My left arm is throbbing, and when I look down at it, I can see that a pimply rash has broken out. I know this rash. This isn't from mosquitoes. It's from bedbugs. They're occupying the filthy sheets I've been sleeping in.

Not bedbugs again.

I'm so drained from the roller coaster of the last seventy-two hours that it almost doesn't matter. I tie a knot in the mosquito net, dust down my sheets as best I can, put on my jeans and the only long sleeve top I have with me and then tentatively lay back down. When I close my eyes, I can't help but wish I were anywhere but here.

#

I can't stop clawing at my skin the next morning when I enter the Ethiopian immigration office.

"Hey, white man!" someone yells as I walk in. This immediately hits a nerve. I'm a deeply unreceptive audience for sarcasm this morning. But as I remind myself to stop taking things so seriously, I realize the tone's friendly, playful. It's ironic banter from another traveler.

It's a funny thing: the more seasoned a traveler you are, the less you seem to need names. Today is no different. Instead, we exchange info about where we've come from and where we're headed. His strawberry-blond hair and blue eyes were minted in Denmark, and he too is trying to travel across Africa overland, doing the reverse of my route, Cairo to Cape Town. He has covered all the ground that I am about to embark upon. I've stuck to my guns and refused to use guidebooks or Google searches for travel tips so far. What good is a map if you can't find yourself? But bumping into another traveler like this, in such an isolated part of the globe, is serendipity at its finest!

He answers all my questions about what I can expect in Ethiopia and the safety situation in Sudan. He also tells me about a ferry that will take me across Lake Nasser, right up to the Egyptian border. In return, I answer his questions about the route he will need to take through Kenya, Tanzania, and Malawi. I tell him to double-check his passport when he enters Mozambique so he doesn't fall victim to the same scam I did, and lastly I tell him to make sure not to miss Tofo Beach.

And just like that, with a five-minute chance encounter, I have all the information—and maybe more importantly, the confidence—that I need to keep pushing forward.

But there's still one snag in my plan. I had to wait for the Ethiopian immigration office to open this morning so I could legally enter the country, which means I've missed the only bus going to Addis Ababa today. There is absolutely no way I'm going back to that bug-infested motel I was at last night, so once I get my official Ethiopian entry stamp, I decide to head to the empty field in the center of town that serves as Moyale's bus station. There's only one bus left in the dusty lot, its destination unknown to me, but it can only be going one direction, which is north. I clamber on.

This bus is half the size of the Moyale Liner that I was on yesterday and more reminiscent of all those tin can minivans Naomi and I used to get across Mozambique and Malawi. One of the seats isn't even a seat: it's a bucket turned upside down. The driver waits until twenty people are uncomfortably penned into fifteen seats before he makes any sign of preparing to leave.

Just after ten, the engine starts jerkily—and even though I'm squished into my seat and my knees are in my throat (again), I'm feeling rejuvenated.

It's exciting not knowing where this bus is going. It's the ultimate freedom in the midst of a life that's turning into one gigantic leap of faith after another. So far, all along my route, I have arranged my accommodation by bartering with hotels in advance, but this is different. There's something magical about being on this bus. It's just me and everything I own, bumbling down an unknown road in Ethiopia.

I'm surrounded by people who only speak Arabic, except for one other passenger. He's around twenty-five years old, and in awkward English he tells me that he works at the bank in Moyale, and that we're heading to Yabelo, where I can transfer to another bus to Hagere Maryam. Apparently there's a cheap hotel there where I can spend the night and then get a bus early the next morning that will take me the rest of the way to Addis Ababa.

I reply and show my gratitude with a very Fonzie-like double thumbs-up.

Even though this bus puts me a day behind the room I've arranged ahead of time with the Juniper International Hotel in Addis Ababa, I'm not too concerned because I'm on the move again, which feels infinitely better than hanging around a bedbug-infested motel room in the sketchy city that is Moyale.

As the engine drums and we track across a sand-swept highway, it slowly starts to dawn on me that Sudan and the Sahara Desert are the next obstacles on my overland list. Even though the Danish guy I met this morning seemed to think Sudan was safe enough to venture across, it has always been the one country I've been most concerned about. I've tried to push it out of my mind, but as the bus inches forward, Sudan inches closer.

As the bus rattles down yet another Swiss-cheese stretch of road, the two guys in the seat in front of me stand up, scream at one another in Arabic, and start swinging their fists at each other.

After a few wild haymakers, the bus sways off the road and the fight lands on my lap. I try to stand up, but the bus swerves again, and we all fall forward. I'm now smack-dab in the middle of the fight, and fists are flying underneath my chin. (This is one of those moments that I'm really glad I'm tall.) I reach down and push the combatants away from each other, stretching my arms out as wide as they'll go. The bus erupts into chaos.

As I keep the two apart, another passenger jumps up and grabs the aggressor until everyone cools down.

The tension lingers throughout the morning. It doesn't help that we are being stopped at every police checkpoint along the way. Every thirty minutes, we have to file off the bus so an officer can inspect our luggage for weapons and contraband. I'm always singled out and separated from the group and asked to unpack my belongings under the watchful policeman's eye. The tripod I carry causes the most problems. At first glance, most of them assume it's a weapon, so I have to unfold it and show them how my camera fits on top.

Under the midafternoon sun, the bus stops in the middle, and I mean the *middle,* of nowhere. It's definitely not a police checkpoint, and I'm praying that we don't have a flat tire because all I can see is miles and miles of sand. If the sand were the sea, we'd be considered castaways.

Suddenly, rising from the horizon like a beautiful mirage, come six women swaddled in bright red and yellow clothes. They run up to the bus with giant smiles, carrying enormous jugs of creamy-white camel milk. Understandably, every Ethiopian is enthusiastic about this kind of interruption, and I watch closely as the jugs are carefully passed through the open bus windows in exchange for a few Ethiopian birr.

The man who's been sitting next to me all morning looks rather intimidating, and even though our shoulders and legs are touching, we haven't said a word to one another since we left Moyale. He has a piercing stare and is dressed like a devoted Muslim, with a long, flowing white kurta and crochet taqiyah or skullcap atop his head.

I watch him buy the biggest milk jug of all. The container it comes in looks like it's designed to hold antifreeze. This should be interesting.

After everyone completes their purchases and the bus huffs and puffs away, I watch him lift the jug to his lips. Just as he takes a giant swig of milk, the bus hits a monstrous pothole. Everyone is launched out of their seats, and my neighbor spews a throatful of milk all over me.

I'm drenched with it. My face, my arms, my legs. And it's *warm*. Because it used to be inside a person. (Exactly as gross as it sounds.)

When we bounce back into our seats, the joke's on me, and I have a very important life decision to make. I must decide if I am going get really pissed off or if I'm going to find the humor in it. The tension quickly rises, and everyone's eyes widen as they wait for my reaction.

And suddenly, a weight lifts from me. The unbearable tension of the last week, the heartbreak, the fear, the stress—they leave me completely, for the first time in . . . I can't remember how long. I laugh so uncontrollably that the staunch (and probably worried) man next to me laughs too. And then, like a row of dominoes, the rest of the bus falls into crazy fits of laughter.

At the next police check, everyone files off the bus again—but this time it feels different.

As I'm waiting outside in the hundred-degree heat, I'm cool and relaxed.

I see a potbellied little boy with pencil-thin legs digging through the trash along the side of the road. He is barefoot, and his tattered clothes are covered in soot. All I have with me is a single cookie, but I walk over and place it in his hand. He smiles and holds it like it's gold. As I walk back toward the bus, I turn around so I can wave good-bye.

The boy isn't looking back at me. He has broken the cookie in half and is sharing it with his little buddy.

* * *

My days on the bus usually fall into a natural rhythm. I try my best to open my body language up for a chat with my neighbor, but almost always the language barrier between us keeps those conversations to just a few short sentences.

I make it a point to not count down the time left or the miles remaining but instead get lost looking out the window, like I did as a child. Today, it's been impossible to focus on anything other than the elevation. Much to my surprise, Ethiopia isn't as flat as its East African neighbors. The Ethiopian highlands haven't been much fun, though. I've been holding my breath for most of the morning. At one point, the bus teetered like a tired top when we hit the tightest hairpin turn I've ever seen. With a thousand-foot drop just inches beyond our tires, I had to look away from the windows and then again as we glided down the backside of a mountain pass like the bus was born without brakes. When a family of monkeys blocked the road in front of us, everyone was finally able to relax, rushing to the windows to witness the scene. A collective laugh came when the driver threw a handful of fruit onto the shoulder of the road in order to get them to step aside.

We finally stop late in the afternoon for lunch. Since I've already eaten the omelet I brought with me in my trusty Tupperware, I'm nearly starving. The ramshackle restaurant doesn't exactly look appetizing, but I follow everyone inside because there's absolutely nothing else around. If I can't find something to eat, I can always order a soda or a fragrant, full-bodied Ethiopian coffee. Ethiopia is the birthplace of coffee, after all. But as soon as I walk through the front door, the idea of coffee goes out the window.

A bloodstained butcher welcomes our group in with a smile and open arms like a hostess at TGI Fridays. Carcasses hang on hooks behind him and cuts of meat are arranged in the dimly lit, nonrefrigerated case in front of him. Everyone oohs and aahs when they walk by the case. Some meat slabs are pink, and others are a deep shade of red, almost brown. Each piece of meat, regardless of its hue, has a moatlike pool of blood surrounding it. There are so many flies buzzing about that it's of no use to swat them away. When I see a handful of them land on a piece of pink meat, I'm reminded why I've stuck to eggs these past three days.

Just as I'm about to turn around and walk back outside, the man who has been sitting three rows behind me on the bus points to a hunk of fatty pink meat and then excitedly says something in Arabic. The butcher shoos away the flies and uses his machete-like knife to cut off a golf ball–sized chunk. His bare hands pass it to my bus mate's filthy fingers, which in turn pop the meat into his mouth like it's a piece of gum. As he chews, a bright smile spreads across his face. Shock spreads across mine. It takes a second for me to process what just happened. Did this man just eat a chunk of raw meat? My stomach clenches, and I have to look away to keep from vomiting.

Once I pull my insides together, I look around at the people seated at the wooden tables. Every single table has a huge platter of raw meat sitting on it. There's also injera, the spongy traditional Ethiopian bread, and a few glass bottles of soda, but all I'm able to focus on is the massive amounts of raw meat.

That everyone is eating.

I've never seen anything like this.

A group of men who aren't traveling on the same bus see my reaction and wave me over to their table. Their faces are welcoming. As I walk toward them, one of the men jumps up.

"My name is Etefu, please join us." He offers his own chair. He speaks surprisingly good English.

In an effort to be as polite as possible I insist on pulling up an empty chair from another table. Then, not so politely, I proceed to stare at the mountain of raw meat sitting atop their silver serving tray. Etefu cuts off a tiny piece of raw red meat, stabs the tip of his knife through it, and holds it just inches away from my face. I know how rude it is in some countries to turn down food, but this is one invitation that I cannot accept.

"Thank you, but I'll get sick," I say as I rub my belly.

Etefu dips the meat into a small bowl of senafich, a spicy mustard sauce, and then pops it into his own mouth with a devilish grin.

After Etefu finishes chewing, he speaks. "It started during wartime. Fighters didn't want to expose themselves in the mountains by starting fires to cook their meat, so they ate it raw."

"But doesn't this make you sick?"

"No, no, our bodies are used to it. Plus, what makes the meat so delicious is the blood. That's what gives it the flavor."

"Anytime I've ever ordered a burger or a steak in my life, I always insist upon getting it well done, almost burnt. So the idea of blood adding to its flavor gives me the chills." I'm not sure if everyone at the table understands my English, but the group politely plays along and laughs with me.

After a few minutes, I excuse myself so I can wander up the road and look for something a bit more edible. I don't even trust injera bread here because of all the flies I saw swarming around it. However, the only other food I'm able to find are two sleeves of chocolate-chip cookies at a makeshift newsstand. I buy both sleeves, which will have to serve as lunch and dinner.

#

By the time the bus finally limps into Addis Ababa, it's well past midnight. I'm completely exhausted and as hungry as I've ever been. After seventy-five hours crammed into African buses, my legs ache, and it feels as though my back might actually be broken. I've had the same filthy clothes on for four days and I've not seen a shower since Nairobi. But I made it. Arriving in Addis Ababa feels like the prayer I said back in Nairobi has been answered.

When the bus pulls up against the curb and stops for the last time, I let out an exhausted but excited sigh of relief. Finally, a decent meal and clean bed.

I've arranged my stay here with the Jupiter International Hotel on the north side of the city. They accepted my barter agreement for the week, and their website's promise of clean sheets, a big Western bed, and an all-you-can-eat breakfast buffet has me salivating.

As I wait alongside the bus for Timberland to be untied from the roof, I tell Alif where my hotel is. He tells me that it's too far away and too dangerous to take a taxi all the way across Addis Ababa at this time of night. Alif is an English-speaking Ethiopian who boarded the bus with his teenage son and daughter after lunch. They took the row of seats in front of me, and we talked intermittently along the way. They've been kind and caring, and I have no reason not to trust what he's saying. He grew up just outside the city and knows it well.

Once Timberland is passed down to me, Alif gestures at a group of sketchy-looking men who are waiting by the taxi stand and then warns me about them.

I don't want to believe him. I want clean sheets, running water, and room service in the worst way, but I've taken enough risks the past few days just to get here. Alif tells me that he and his children are headed to a hotel that's right next to the bus station and says that I'm welcome to join them. I decide that it's not worth trekking across the city at this hour and begrudgingly take Alif up on his kindness. I can always just take a taxi to the Jupiter International Hotel first thing tomorrow morning.

I follow Alif and his children around the bus and down the adjacent street. Clumps of exposed electrical wires hang from telephone poles like split ends, and trash blows across the street like tumbleweeds. Alif promised a respectable and cheap hotel, but when I see the state of the place he's taken me to, I realize right away that I've made a huge mistake.

The hotel isn't actually a hotel but a three-story concrete housing complex that occasionally rents out its rooms for the night. After just a minute inside, I realize that the place is overrun by rats the size of cats, and when I see the state of the bed in my room, I get even more annoyed with myself for listening to Alif. It's so dirty that not only do I have to sleep in my clothes, but I have to use the rest of my clothes as makeshift bedsheets. I take all my T-shirts out of Timberland and tie them together at the arms to form a blanket and then slide a pair of mesh shorts over the stained pillow that was lying on the cement floor when I walked into the room. I attempt to rest my head on the pillow, but the mattress is crawling with so many bedbugs that it feels like there are snakes in its springs. Even worse are the sounds I hear. As rats scurry back and forth across the tin roof doing who-knows-what, their tiny claws sound like fingernails on a chalkboard. It's impossible to sleep knowing that if I close my eyes, even for a second, I'll undoubtedly wake up to a soccer ball–sized rat sitting on my chest.

In the middle of the night, I get up to kill time by taking a shower. God knows I need one, but when I discover that the shower is actually just a communal bucket of stagnant brown water at the end of the hallway, that too is out of the question.

The second the sun comes up, I bolt out of the crumbling building and onto the streets of Addis Ababa. Before I know it, I'm humming through the middle of Meskel Square in a taxi that's the equivalent of an oxcart with an engine. The brakes scream for help when they're asked to do their job in the dead center of the square. It's as lawless as India in this intersection, and I grab my neck to make sure it is still there after a hard stop.

Cars are buzzing by like worker bees around their queen, and once I get my bearings, I quickly figure out why. Twelve lanes from four different directions all funnel to this very spot, and almost unbelievably there isn't a single stoplight in sight.

When my taxi pulls up to the Jupiter International Hotel some thirty minutes later, it's a sight for sore eyes. It would normally be considered a *nice* hotel, but suddenly everything about it looks like a plush five-star resort. It feels strange to hear the woman working at the front desk speak near-perfect English, and I'm awestruck by the beauty of the chandelier hanging above us. I've grown so used to dirt, dust, and cinderblock walls that I'd forgotten just how lovely nice things can be.

After the woman at the front desk hands me my keycard, the bellman in a slightly wrinkled maroon suit calls the elevator for me, and I take it up to the fifth floor. As I slide my keycard into the lock and open the door to my room, the magnitude of the past week lands on me like a two-ton weight. Maybe it's seeing the big Western-style bed with crisp white sheets or the two bottles of purified water on the nightstand or the sleek flat-screen television mounted on the wall, but something about walking into my room sends my body into shock.

As I make my way toward the king-size bed, a tiredness that I've never experienced in my entire life washes over me. When I collapse into the middle of the bed, everything I've just put myself through finally sinks in. I felt close to death for the first time in my life, and I can feel the fatigue from the chances I've taken deep down in the marrow of my bones. I've looked over my shoulder so often, I've nearly forgotten how to face forward.

I know that I need to get up and eat something, but I have nothing left to give. Not even a single blink of my eyes. For the life of me, I can't keep them open any longer, and when they finally close, I fall into the deepest sleep of my life.

CHAPTER 5
SUDAN – EGYPT
AFRICA

"Africa changes you forever, like nowhere on earth. Once you have been there, you will never be the same. . . . Could it be because Africa is the place of all our beginnings, the cradle of mankind, where our species first stood upright on the savannahs of long ago?"

— Brian Jackman

"GET YOUR HANDS OFF ME!"
I rip my right arm free and beads of sweat fly from my face.

"Where are you taking me?"

No one answers.

"I'm not going any further until you tell me what I did wrong."

Still no one responds.

I stop in the middle of the street. A donkey saunters by, too slowly, like it's eavesdropping. I don't want to make a scene, but hell, I need answers and I need them now.

"Who are you?"

The men around me lash out in Arabic. Their tone is relentlessly hostile. I've clearly done something to upset them, *but what?*

Everyone in the street stops what they're doing and stares at me—actually, strike that, it's like they're looking through me.

The three men who are forcing me forward tighten their circle around me, and I'm left with no choice but to keep moving. Their body language is abrasive, and they keep bumping into me in order to make me move. I'm about to totally lose my cool—but I can't because this is Sudan, and even though I've been here for a few days, it's still very much a mystery to me. I have to play along.

They lead me across the street and into the courtyard of Khartoum's chaotic bus station. A high chain-link fence surrounds the property, and I'm guided into a brick building and up a flight of steps and then down a long, empty hallway. The rules of the real world are starting to feel further and further away with every step I take, and my stomach starts to churn. I have no idea who these men are or where they are taking me.

All three wear worn-out khaki pants and ratty, button-down dress shirts—not police uniforms or anything that looks remotely official. And they just came up to me out of the blue while I was waiting to buy my bus ticket to Wadi Halfa and forced me up and out of my seat. One of the men is heavyset and looks like a nightclub bouncer; another is older and balding, with a bad comb-over; and the youngest one possesses a militant attitude that's really starting to rub me the wrong way.

At the end of the hallway, we turn into a nearly empty room with yellow paint peeling off the walls. The room feels swollen and ready to burst. It is 108 degrees outside but feels about 140 degrees in here. I'm instructed to sit in the single chair that's in the middle of the room. They've seen way too many bootlegged episodes of *NYPD Blue*.

As I take a seat, nervousness spikes within me. I want to lash out and scream but know I need to remain calm and play dumb, and if all else fails, mention Manchester United. The Red Devils are most Africans' favorite soccer team, and I've found that discussing them usually gets me out of trouble quicker than anything else. I also know no one wants to deal with a smart-ass American.

The three men motion for my passport, which thankfully I happen to be carrying with me so I could purchase my bus ticket. I slide it across the warped and splintered desk and watch them flip to the page where my Sudanese visa is printed.

Desperation creeps into my voice. "Can someone please tell me what I'm doing here?"

The youngest flips through the rest of my passport and demands,

"Registration." It's not enough to have a visa to enter Sudan; you are required to register your passport with the Aliens Department within three days of arrival. Luckily, I knew this from my chance encounter with the Danish traveler. I politely flip to the page where my registration is.

I'm starting to sense that I could be in some serious trouble, so I ask again as sweat slithers down my face and arms, "What am I doing here?"

English has been hard to come by in Sudan, but after a long pause, the answer I've been looking for this whole time finally comes.

"Kam-er-A."

Ahhhhh! I should have known. Makarus, the manager at the 5M Hotel I've bartered with this week, told me yesterday that taking photos or filming inside Sudan required a photography permit from the government of Sudan. I didn't go through the lengthy registration process because I didn't think I'd be here long enough to actually need one. This is why he escorted me around the city yesterday when I was filming tourist attractions like the Presidential Palace and Nile Street. Anytime a police officer came up to me, he'd quickly pull the officer aside and assure him in Arabic that he had the proper permits for me to be filming there. But Makarus isn't here. And without him, each time I pulled my camera out this afternoon I've been taking risks. Big ones.

While I was waiting for the bus companies to reopen after their afternoon lunch break, I killed some time by filming a few shots of me walking through the alleyway behind the bus station for the next episode I'm planning to put on my travel blog. I didn't think what I was doing was any cause for concern. I just assumed that what I was filming was so harmless and insignificant that it didn't matter, but I blame that on my own American ignorance. The rules are different here, and I should have realized that I was doing something wrong by the anxious look on everyone's faces when they saw me set up my camera. I mean, people in Africa *usually* stare at me when I'm walking through the streets for any number of reasons (my size, color, tattoo, beard, long hair, baggy shorts—take your pick) but it went to a whole new level today when I set my camera down, then ran back twenty-five yards so I could record myself slowly walking past it.

Even with the right permissions, photographing military areas, bridges, train stations, broadcasting infrastructure, slum areas, or other defaming objects is strictly forbidden. People have been arrested for taking pictures where the Blue and White Nile Rivers meet in Khartoum, which is actually one of the places I was filming last night.

The worst-case scenario is that these guys think I'm a journalist who has secretly been sent here by one of the big media outlets. Sudan is known to harass and arrest journalists and sometimes detain them without charge. It's an intimidation technique, but news media independence has long been under assault here, and government censorship was clear from the first moment I tried to surf the internet from my hotel room.

As I pass over my camera, I remember a headline I read not too long ago. It was about a journalist who was arrested a few months ago for "fabricating" news on a Facebook page called Sudan News. My nerves ratchet up a level when I remember that all the footage from yesterday is still on my memory card. I never got a chance to transfer the footage onto my computer and then wipe the memory card clean like I normally do. And I'm skilled enough now that it will come across to them as professional and polished, not tourist snaps.

Shit. This could bad.

As the men begin to inspect my camera, my right leg begins to fidget. I envision myself in a Sudanese jail. Dirt floors, metal bars, and one scoop of dirty rice a day. A worse experience I cannot conjure up, so I think about making a break for it. I'm much bigger than these men, and I'm sure I could outrun them, but then I remember the chain-link fence that surrounded the bus station. The only way in and out is through a turnstile controlled by a police officer.

I decide to stick with my initial plan to stay calm and confused. I carefully watch the men as they turn my camera over and over like a child with a Rubik's Cube, like it's the first time they've ever seen one. Thankfully, it's just my point-and-shoot camera, small enough to fit into my pocket. Most of the footage from yesterday is on my big DSLR, which I've left back in my hotel room today, but I still used this one enough that it could cause a problem.

The men make a motion like they want me to turn my camera on. Then they point at the LCD screen, which I take to mean that they want me to show them all the photos and video I have taken while in Sudan. After I flip through the entire catalogue of images from yesterday and today, they leave my camera in the center of the desk while they turn their backs to me and huddle in the corner to talk things over. Best-case scenario is that they're going to confiscate my camera and then insist on a bribe just so I can be released, so while the camera is sitting on the desk, I hatch a new plan.

If my camera is confiscated, I'll lose the extraordinary images I've captured here. And it's not just the photos that I want to keep, it's the memories. Since I don't collect souvenirs, this footage is all I have. The traveler in me really wants to be able to look back and remember moments like the sight of three hundred Muslim men in long white robes standing in the sandy courtyard of the Al Kabir Mosque. They were gathered around a solitary man who was slowly beating a calfskin drum as the sun set behind the mosque's Mecca-facing minaret. One of the elder men with a wispy long white beard saw me filming at the edge of the mosque, and I suddenly realized that I was making an egregious error in cultural etiquette. However, instead of chasing me away from the circle, he invited me inside it. And then he insisted not only that I continue to take more photos of them but that I join them in the photos as well.

After I passed my camera over to one of the men so he could snap a photo of us, five other men crowded suspiciously close to my side. But then, just as the photo was about to be taken, all the men raised their arms up and rested them on one another's shoulders, including mine, and I followed suit. The photo quickly became my favorite picture to date because of how wide and genuine the smile across my face is. It felt like the Universe had paused to say, "Hey, I know that it's been pretty hard lately, but keep doing what you're doing, and don't ever forget that you're always surrounded by love."

But this isn't just about retaining my photos; it's about keeping me out of serious trouble.

So while the men are still huddled together, I casually slip the camera into my cargo pocket and open the compartment door where the memory card is located; I slip the memory card out and into my pocket, then close the door like nothing ever happened. Just as I quietly set the camera back on the desk, the heavyset bouncer guy turns his head, giving me a funny look and motioning at the camera again. As he reaches for it, he waves his hands in a chopping motion, which I take to mean that I must delete all the footage that's on the memory card. He passes the camera over to me, and I pretend to push a few buttons and—presto, empty camera. I proudly hand it over and show him the blank LCD screen. Just as he looks down at it, the words *no memory card* start flashing across it.

My heart stops for a second, and I pray that he can't read English.

He seems satisfied that I have in fact deleted everything.

I've gotten away with it!

However, the men don't let me leave. It isn't until the four of us sit in a sweaty, tense silence for thirty more minutes that they finally mutter something to each other in Arabic and then look over at me. The man with the bad comb-over walks over toward me and motions to the door. I am free to go. Just like that. I'm shocked. I can't believe it.

Before they have a chance to reconsider, I turn and walk out, as fast as my trembling legs will carry me.

* * *

When I reach the pyramids in Cairo, Egypt, I proclaim that I've officially completed the first part of my mission. The Great Sphinx and all six Pyramids of Giza are just about the most beautiful things I've ever seen.

Thousands of seats have been set up for a concert, but there are two in particular I can't take my eyes off of.

It's nearly a hundred degrees outside, but a shiver rushes up my spine and goose bumps prick the skin on my forearms.

What are the odds of me running into these numbers here, yet again, at the very spot I've been trying to get to all this time? Seats 44 and 43 are facing the pyramids, and the numbers run together: 4443.

The numbers 444 have appeared frequently in my life, sometimes as often as five or six times a day—on a license plate in front of me, as part of a telephone number I needed to call, embedded in an address I'd have to travel to, or as the amount of change I was due back after purchasing something. They've been by my side from the first moment of this Impossible Idea. The morning I created my gigantic vision board and put pen to paper they were there. At the time I had $444.08 to my name.

It isn't just that I see these numbers a lot. It's the feeling I get when I see them. It's always when my negative, self-sabotaging thoughts are trying to strip away all the positive gains I've been making. Each time I see these numbers, I get this comforting feeling, as if something greater is watching over me and trying to nudge me in the direction of self-belief instead of self-doubt. They seem to reinforce the same message: I am on the right path.

My friend Alba told me that the numbers 444 are my angel numbers; seeing them indicates when angels are near me, and seeing them frequently means I am on the path of spiritual awakening. She said their purpose is to remind me to pay attention to my intuition because it will lead to the success and fulfillment I'm looking for.

I've never downplayed their importance, even when a close friend told me that it was just a stupid coincidence and that I only see them so much because I purposely look for them. It doesn't work like that, but since he was the kind of person I could never convince otherwise, I let it go. It's best to let the skeptics go on thinking they're right. Deep down, I kept smiling at the power the sequence possesses.

Even though I've seen these three numbers a million times before, today is perhaps the most special, most mystical of all because it was here, at the Egyptian pyramids, that Santiago's journey ended.

The plot twist in Santiago's story is that once he arrived and began digging into the dunes where he thought his treasure was buried, all he found was more and more sand. He didn't give up, however. That night, as he continued to dig, a group of men surrounded him. They assumed he was digging for gold and forced him to continue while they waited nearby to rob him of it. When Santiago was unable to find his treasure, the men grew frustrated. They beat him until he was bruised and bleeding and nearly unconscious. Just as they were about to walk away, the leader walked up to Santiago and told him about a recurring dream he had about a treasure buried under a sycamore tree near a ruined church in a Spanish field. The man added, "I'm not so stupid as to cross an entire desert just because of a recurrent dream."

Upon hearing this, Santiago immediately realized two things. The first was that his treasure was actually buried back in Spain under the sycamore tree where his journey began. The second was that his entire journey across Africa and to these very pyramids was just a means to reveal to him that the real treasure was not a chest full of gold coins but what he'd become in pursuit of those gold coins. This is exactly what I've learned today too. It's what I've become while in pursuit of these pyramids that matters most.

With this sense of self rushing through my body, I walk toward the

Great Sphinx of Giza. It feels as big as Africa, and even though I'm seeing it in person for the first time, it still looks mythical. Just as I bring my camera up to my eye, a camel slinks by. When it turns its head in my direction and sticks its tongue out at me, I snap an unforgettable shot.

Seconds later, I put my camera away because I want to take a few minutes to enjoy just how far I've come. I find a spot in the sand and just sit. Oily incense washes by in waves from the street stalls just beyond the entrance. I look up and lock eyes on Khafre, the tallest pyramid. Time has taken its toll on this colossal achievement and it's only at the very top of the triangle that the original limestone casings survive. Still, the way it pierces the vaulted blue sky is the most magical thing about being here. It's hard to imagine that at such a historic spot, we still don't know exactly how all this beauty was built, but now that I'm here, it's also hard to fathom that the same sun I used to get up early to watch rise in the east way back in Miami Beach is the same sun that's dipping toward the silver sands behind the Sphinx this afternoon.

I shake my head in astonished disbelief at the amazing world we get to live in and my astonishing journey through it.

* * *

By the next morning, I'm ready to move on. While Africa has taught me more about myself than anyone or anything ever has, it has beaten me to a pulp. I had to throw out all my T-shirts because no matter how many times I washed them, I just couldn't get the sweat stains out of them.

I've managed to book seven free nights at the Marriott in Cairo by using most of the points I racked up while traveling across Florida and covering for coworkers at my old corporate job. One of the additional perks of my platinum status is full access to the beautiful Executive Lounge, which includes the most knowledgeable concierge service I've ever come across. Though Kamilah's got to be tired of me by now. We've spent the past hour together, poring over ways for me to get out of Africa and into Europe without flying, but it actually seems impossible.

Ever since the Egyptian revolution in 2010, the tourism industry here has suffered. Cruise lines have either scaled back service or just stopped coming altogether. So taking a ship across the Mediterranean Sea, like I had assumed I would do, isn't an option. Libya, Egypt's neighbor to the west, is in the midst of a civil war. Although Israel, Egypt's neighbor to the east, does have a border crossing at Taba, to get to there I would have to cross through the northern part of the Sinai Peninsula, which is ungoverned and one of the most dangerous strips of land in the world. It's been the launch site for several terrorist attacks against tourists, which is one of the major reasons why cruise ships no longer sail to Egypt.

Once again, I find myself at a dead end. While I've suffered setbacks before, none have felt as impenetrable as this.

I lift my head up out of my hands and glance over Kamilah's shoulder out the window at the Nile. We're twenty-two stories up, and I can see the shimmering blue snake nose its way through Cairo's Zamalek district. It's a magnificent sight.

I simply cannot bear the idea of my dreams dying after having come so far, and it takes only my next breath to remind myself that I won't be defeated. If I've learned one thing during this Impossible Idea, it's that impossible situations are not here to stop me. They're here to test my resilience and determination.

And I can assure you I want this more than I want my next breath.

Like a match has been scraped against my insides, I feel a spark in my belly, and I'm reminded that I can't just mope around and hope that diplomatic relations in North Africa and the Middle East magically clear up overnight. I can't expect the world to roll out a red carpet for my overland dream. The old me might have done that, but not the new me.

Knowing full well that this is my final African exam, I jump up and insist that we take one last look at the map Kamilah has pulled up on her computer screen.

"Can you think of any other way for me to go?"

As Kamilah hunts for a route, I try to manifest an idea into her mind. I'm concentrating so hard on her that if I redirected my thoughts toward the pencil on her desk, I know I could make it move.

A few seconds later, she interrupts the silence with a wonderful sound. "Ah!"

"What is it? Please tell me!" I say.

"No, never mind. That's probably not a good idea."

"What is it?"

"It's probably too dangerous as well, and I don't want to be responsible for sending you that way."

I beg and beg until she finally relents. She zooms in on the map and moves her finger around the southern rim of the Sinai Peninsula, and then up and across to the middle of its eastern edge.

I squint and read the word just above her finger: "Nuweiba."

"It's a tiny Egyptian port, and I think that there might be a bus that goes from Cairo to Nuweiba. It's still a risk, but the bus doesn't travel through Northern Sinai, which is the most dangerous part of Egypt. Instead, this one travels across Central and Southern Sinai."

"Okay, what happens once I get to Nuweiba?"

"A few months ago, two guys who were staying here travelled along this very route. The bus gets loaded onto a ferry, crosses the Gulf of Aqaba, and docks in Aqaba."

Kamilah zooms in even further on the map and points to a small sliver of land no bigger than a matchstick between Israel and Saudi Arabia.

"Aqaba is on the southwestern coast of Jordan, and from Aqaba the bus continues on to Amman. That's where those two guys came from. They did the reverse route you'd be doing and traveled from Amman to Cairo this way. But again, you would still have to cross through the Sinai Peninsula, and I wouldn't recommend anyone try that, let alone a very large American like yourself. Plus, I believe that the bus ride itself takes about thirty hours."

I dry my palms against my shorts. They've begun to sweat at the prospect of finding a way to continue.

"If you make it to Jordan, then you could cross into Israel. The Israeli-Jordanian border is much safer than the Israeli-Egyptian border, and I remember seeing on the news that one ship still sails from somewhere in Israel to . . . Turkey? Or was it Greece? Either way, I believe that's the only ship in this part of the world that still sails to Europe."

I stand up and begin pacing back and forth in front of her desk. Kamilah watches me with concern.

"I don't want to get your hopes up, however, because I'm not sure if either the bus or ship are still running. Both might have been cancelled by now. Plus, you will need to get a travel visa to enter Jordan, and since you're American, I'm not sure how quickly you can obtain one."

But I do get my hopes up. My heart is about to beat out of my chest. I feel like a cat that's found out he has a ninth life. "This is great! At least there is an option."

"I will check on all of the things we've just discussed and call your room as soon as I find out more information."

I thank Kamilah about five hundred times and head back to my room, where I try, and fail, to process all that's just happened. Maybe one day I'll be able to look back and see the shape of all of this, but not now.

I flip my computer screen open and study what the US Department of State has written about travel through Egypt, because I know that's the first thing my parents will read if this new plan actually comes together. The advisory emphatically warns against any kind of overland travel outside of Cairo and specifically notes the dangers of the Sinai region and of Egypt's borders zones—exactly where I might be heading. One of the lines even reads, "US Embassy personnel in Egypt are currently prohibited from traveling to the Sinai Peninsula."

The room phone rings.

Before I can even get a hello out, Kamilah starts talking. "So I have some interesting news for you. The bus to Jordan is available, but it only runs once a week, and it takes thirty hours to get there, like I remembered."

"Okay, that's great news!"

"There is a Jordanian Embassy in Cairo, and you can get a travel visa in one day for eighty-five dollars."

"Yes!" I scream into the receiver.

"Also, I was able to track down the ship I mentioned. It's a cargo ship, not a cruise ship, and it sails from Israel to Greece, but it only has room for six passengers. It leaves from Haifa, Israel, and docks in Lavrio, Greece. That ship leaves once a week, and it takes four days to cross the Mediterranean Sea, but you'll have to arrange your ticket directly with the shipping company."

I listen to Kamilah take a sip of something before she continues. "Would you like me to book the bus to Jordan for you?"

The route will be as dangerous as any I've traveled so far. ISIS and Al Qaeda are both said to be in and around the Sinai Peninsula. It's entirely possible that I might not make it out alive.

Before I reply, I take a second to think about who I've become thus far and who I might yet become at the end of this journey. As I stare out the window at the Nile, I can see my reflection in it. Having not cut my hair since I left America, it dangles just above my shoulders, and my beard is equally long. I look exactly as you'd expect someone to look after they have spent eight months crossing Africa overland, but beyond that I can almost see the outline of my future face in the reflection. Of the person I'm becoming. I know that if I fly once, I'm done. The core of my dream crumbles to dust, and so too does the man in me that I'm starting to see.

Kamilah interrupts my reverie. "Sir, the next bus for Jordan leaves on Thursday—would you like me to book a ticket for you?"

I take a deep breath and call upon all the struggles, setbacks, and obstacles I've gone through to get here. I think about all the times I've been knocked down and then about all the times I've gotten back up. At crossroads like this, I've always called upon Santiago's story for strength, but now I'm ready to call upon my own.

"Hell, yes, book it!"

* * *

Even though the Sinai Peninsula is just about as dangerous as it gets, that hasn't taken away from its beauty. The jutting rock formations and deep canyons we're winding through are awe inspiring. The soft light from a slowly rising sun is hitting them at just the right angles, and it looks like we're driving through one colorful kaleidoscope after another. It's too bad that there aren't more people here to see this, but since this is such a risky strip of land to cross, the bus is nearly empty. There are only five other passengers on it besides me.

We're still fifteen hours from Amman, and the sun is just over my right shoulder, deep orange, big, and comforting. There must be something about the desert that draws it close. It feels like it's within arm's reach. Seeing it like this has pushed away my need for sleep and, as crazy as it may sound, I'm glad I'm here. I'm glad I had to take this dangerous detour.

I turn and smile at the Palestinian family I first met when the bus departed Cairo last night. Elham and her teenage daughter, Aram, are so sweet, always smiling and waving at me. They can tell that I'm nervous and out of place, and they've been looking out for me. They're traveling home to Palestine after visiting Elham's sister in Cairo, and they check on me every hour or so. They offer me crackers, and Aram translates for Elham so they can give updates on what to expect in terms of bathroom breaks and possible dangers. They are the very definition of "the kindness of strangers."

Many hours later, as we near the edge of the African continent, tears begin to slide across my eyes.

I'm not exactly sure what's making me so emotional. Maybe it's because this is my final day in Africa, or maybe it's because I didn't quit all the times when I probably should have. I can't help but feel a deep gratitude for each and every setback I've encountered thus far. The moment quickly becomes overwhelming. Tears stream down my cheeks, and as they fall onto my lap, Elham turns around and asks me if I'm okay. I blink, sniff, rub my eyes.

"It's just allergies," I say.

An hour later, after watching our bus get loaded onto the ferry at Nuweiba, I walk over to the edge of Africa. I look down past my sneakers; there's a hole in the toe, the soles are peeling off, and the laces are frayed. I look past the rickety plywood pier I'm standing on and deep down into the Gulf of Aqaba. I'm instantly awed by its complexion. It's the deepest shade of blue my eyes have ever seen, and yet at the same time it's as transparent as the air around me. Fish with neon zebra stripes and lime leopard spots are swimming in synchronistic schools. It's quite possibly the most mesmerizing thing I've ever seen, and as I let myself get lost in it, I can't help but think of the old adage: Give a man a fish, and you feed him for a day. Teach a man to fish, and you feed him for a lifetime. Africa has been my rod and reel.

As I crossed the continent, I stumbled upon a side of myself I never knew existed. An inner strength that I never knew I had. I was willing to die for my dreams and now, with the roles reversed and Africa finally being the one that's up against it, I'm able to feel the cumulative effects of tapping into that kind of courage.

Getting here has been the toughest, riskiest journey of my life, and as I bound into the boat to Jordan and take my last step on African soil, I can feel my soul strengthen.

CHAPTER 6
GREECE
EUROPE

"My parents are my backbone. Still are.
They're the only group that will support you
if you score zero or you score 40."

— *Kobe Bryant*

"HOW MUCH IS YOUR CHEAPEST private room?"

"It's thirty euros per night."

Sweat trickles down my temples. I shake my head. "Really?"

"Well, since you don't fit in any of our bunk beds, the only option is a private room, which has a queen-size bed."

Dimitris is right. My height is my Achilles' heel today. Before I booked a dorm room, I ran upstairs to see if my long legs would fit on the bunk beds. They didn't, and I couldn't even hang my feet off the end of the bed because the frames have an impenetrable metal footboard built into them.

"You'll be in room 6B. It's up the stairs and to the right. There's a shared bathroom at the end of the hallway."

I hesitate as I reach for my wallet. I'd rather slice open my side and pass over a kidney than this much money. I've been playing with house money so far, having gone 303 days without having to pay for a place to sleep, the only exceptions being the odd nights when I was just passing through somewhere in transit. But right now, it feels like a hollow achievement. All I feel is frustration. I thought that once I finally made it to Europe, everything would magically become easier, but—of course—day one of this continent is proving just as tough as everywhere else. Promised land? Not so much.

The burst of exultation I'd felt at finally finding my way to Europe was erased just an hour after I'd arrived. This morning, I was unceremoniously kicked off the bus I was taking from Lavrio to Athens. No one was selling tickets as we boarded the bus, but thirty minutes into the ride, a woman finally popped up from the front seat and came around offering them. When I told her I didn't have any euros, she simply said, "No euros, no ticket." I should have known that the Greek bus company wasn't going to accept my leftover Israeli shekels, but I boarded anyway because there was nowhere to exchange money in or around Lavrio's port, which is where the cargo ship had docked. I figured they'd have some way to run my credit card once we got to the station in Athens. I begged and begged the bus driver to let me stay, but he pulled over anyway and yelled at me in Greek until I got off. It was embarrassing, which made the two-mile walk to the nearest town feel that much farther.

Welcome to Europe, Eric. It took an hour to find an ATM machine and then two more hours to track down a bus that would get me to Athens.

The old wooden stairs creak like a coffin door closing as I spiral up them and toward my room. Awful electronic dance music rattles each room I pass. 6B is sparse—just a bed, cracked ceiling, and paint-chipped walls. As I set Timberland down in the doorway, I wonder what I'm doing here. I'm too old to be sharing a bathroom with teenage party animals who will be going to bed when I'm waking up.

I start to panic.

What if my idea to barter with hotels only works in Africa? What if I can't find a way to make money doing this job I love? Then what?

I can't go back to my "old life," the one that Ellen Goodman sums up so perfectly: "'Normal' is getting dressed in clothes that you buy for work and driving through traffic in a car that you are still paying for—in order to get the job you need to pay for the clothes and the car, and the house you leave vacant all day so you can afford to live in it."

The further I've gotten away from that cycle, the more insane it's looking. If I've learned only one thing from these past nine months on the road, it's that most human beings are not spending the time they're given here on earth in the way that best suits them—sometimes by necessity but sometimes by choice. That's maddening.

But, madness or not, I can't solve the world's problems because I haven't fixed mine yet. I need to find a cheaper accommodation. It's not like I haven't already tried my damnedest. I emailed my standard offer to exchange my film and photography work for a room to over two hundred hotels here last week, and then today, under the sweltering summer sun, I traipsed across the city with all my things and tried to barter in person with about twenty more hotels. They all turned me down—and I discover why after I settle into my room and read the local news headlines.

Greece is in the midst of one of the most catastrophic economic crises the world has ever seen, sparked by the revelation in 2009 that the country had not been reporting accurate deficit figures. As a result, Greece was shut out from international financial markets and has been relying on bailouts to stave off bankruptcy. I arrived here the day before it all started coming to a head.

Tomorrow, Greek citizens will vote on whether or not Greece should accept the bailout conditions proposed by the International Monetary Fund, the European Central Bank, and the European Commission. Do they accept the proposals of Greece's creditors, which the government has already rejected? Voting "yes" means Greece will remain a part of the Eurozone and suffer even further budget cuts. Voting "no" means they will reject the demands of Greece's international creditors and risk exit from the Eurozone.

All the banks are closed, and tensions are high all across the city today because the cash machines are running out of money. Long, angry lines stretch down most blocks, and Greeks are only permitted to withdraw sixty euros per day. I could not have picked a worse time to hustle my work.

My money problems pale in comparison, but they're all I can think about. I sit down on filthy bed sheets that haven't been changed all week. Some hostels I've stayed at have a policy that they only change the bed linens on Sundays, and I can already tell that this hostel is one of them. I feel gross just thinking about it. But it's nothing next to the financial hole I too could soon find myself in.

If a private room is going run me thirty euros a night times seven nights, that's 210 euros a week and 840 euros a month—and that's just for the cheapest room. There's food and transportation, both of which are *way* more expensive than in Africa. I am looking at a minimum of a thousand euros a month ($1,050 in US dollars) and that's on the low end. On top of those challenges, I need new parts for my camera and new clothes, probably including a jacket because it will be winter soon enough and I don't own anything other than T-shirts and tank tops. While I still have a decent chunk of the life savings I started with, that isn't going to be nearly enough if I want to make it the rest of the way around the world.

I need to start making money.

But I don't want to make money for money's sake. I don't want to be what Julie Cameron calls a "shadow artist" and settle for a "shadow career," which is when an artist compromises their craft and chooses a path that's close to their desired art, even parallel to it, but isn't the art itself. I don't want to go on press trips to really nice resorts or write articles for online travel magazines. That defeats the whole purpose of my travels and negates my attempt to go from corporate to creative. I'm painfully aware there isn't much of a career path for what I want to do, but I just want to write, film, and photograph for myself and my own travel blog and somehow earn income from that.

Money doesn't motivate me like it does others, and I've always believed in two simple theories about my finances. The first is the idea of abundance, which is a mindset that I will always have enough of what I need when I need it. Thankfully, up until this point, that's been true. The second is something my father has instilled in me: "Do what you love, and the money will find you." Here, on my first day in Europe, I'm putting both of these theories to the test.

Some of my income is the result of small donations from family and friends. And though I'm grateful for every penny, I can't live on that. And while I haven't had to cover the cost of hotel rooms, I've had plenty of other expenses—all those bus rides, and the cargo ship this week, which set me back $1,200, the meals; the absurdly expensive travel visa fees; and the writing coach I hired to help me develop my skills as a writer and look over my short stories.

On top of all of that, even though we haven't spoken in months, I'm still financially supporting Naomi. It's a way to alleviate my guilt. I asked her to come to Africa with next to no money and I asked her to resign from the online teaching job that was her only source of income. While those were her choices too, it feels like I'm the one that's left her with no home and no income. Though I worry all the time that my modest life savings isn't going to last through my journey, I still have so much more than Naomi's got in her bank account at the moment. Sure, she could go back to the United States and get a job like almost everyone else, but deep down some part of me doesn't want her to do that. She's trying to find and follow her own dreams, and it feels like she's on the brink of a breakthrough of her own. I know how demanding that process can be, and maybe I'm overly sympathetic to the cause. I guess what it boils down to is that I'm willing to keep sending her money while she tries to find her place in this world. But is it the right thing to do? I wish I knew.

I stand up and walk over to the window. I run my finger across a long, lightning-bolt crack, and my breath becomes short and shallow.

What happens if I can't find where I fit in this world? Then what?

* * *

My parents arrive in Athens just a few days after I do, much to my relief. They'd been planning to come and see me as soon as I made it out of Africa, and initially it's great having them here. Their presence lifts my spirits and eases my money woes. We take a ferry from Athens to Mikonos and then a second ferry to Santorini a few days later. They let me stay in their hotel room with them, and I jump at that offer, relieved not to have to spend any money on lodging.

I end up sleeping at the foot of their bed on a tiny rollaway cot too small for someone half my size. Between that, my father's snoring, and nearly seeing my mother naked on more than one occasion, the whole thing has me feeling like a failure. I'm thirty-four years old, not four.

My dad is . . . well, let's call him "conservative" with his money. He'll be the first one to tell you that he loves to buy his clothes at a discount store and while he's happy to pay full price for things, he'll hem and haw about it for a few minutes afterwards. So instead of booking a second room for me, he'd rather sacrifice all of our sanity to save a few bucks, which he has every right to do since it is his money. My parents have always been kind, caring, and supportive of each other and everything I've ever tried to do, including this Impossible Idea. However, if I had to pick one thing that's caused just the slightest ripple in our relationship, it's been money.

They have it, and I don't.

My father was very successful in business, and he sold his company and retired at the early age of fifty-five. I have no idea how much he got for the business, but I'm sure it's more than enough to live on comfortably for a few lifetimes. And while I don't want a single dollar from his success, people often assume that's how I'm financing all this long-term travel. A few days ago, a college friend commented on a photo I'd posted of my parents and I smiling in front of the Acropolis: "It must be nice that your parents are paying for you to travel around the world." While my parents have let me stay in their room and have picked up the check for meals while they've been in Athens, I'm on my own for the rest of the trip, and the comment rubbed my perceived privilege raw.

Most people think I have some golden ticket through life, but I've never asked for a handout from my parents, not even when I got laid off and was collecting unemployment four years ago. Even if I did want their money, they wouldn't just give it to me. My family lineage includes a long line of Pennsylvania coal miners who were tough as nails and earned every dollar they had. They're the guys in the old black-and-white photos you'd see coming out of the dark mine shaft covered in soot and never smiling. Things aren't just given in my family; they're earned, and that's the way it's always been.

So I'm mostly mad at myself for my inability, or reluctance rather, to pay for my own room. After a full week of this arrangement, something inside me short-circuits. But rather than take responsibility, in the moment I irrationally channel the anger at my father, who doesn't deserve it. He has been the best father on the planet. Even when he was working sixty hours a week, he never missed a family dinner or a Little League game. He never missed a Little League *practice*. He coached every team I ever played on. I've often told myself I would be happy if I could be half the man he is one day, but I've never told him that.

I find him out by the pool, sipping his morning coffee. He has no idea of the hurricane that is heading for him. My voice cracks when I say, "I'm sick of this shit—you're so goddamn cheap! You've flown all this way to see me, but you've got us living like refugees in this tiny hotel room!

Why couldn't you just have paid a little extra for a second room? I'm sure you've got the money for it!"

As the words fly out, I know I sound like a spoiled brat. I just kept thinking of the comment my college friend made. As my mom comes running up between us, I turn my back and begin to walk away. They both plead for me to stay, but I just race through the lobby and out of the hotel with all my things like a man on fire.

#

With Santorini's scorching summer sun beating down on me, my hair has worked its way loose and flops like a fish trying to escape a net while I try to retie it. I look like a disheveled mess when Chara looks up from behind the front desk of her villa-style hotel to greet me. She quickly asks me if I have a reservation. I tell her, "Unfortunately not," and then go right into my sales presentation, the same one that got shot down twenty times in Athens just a week ago. I pull out my laptop and ask if I can show Chara my photography portfolio, but before I can even load up the first photo, she stops me.

"I'm sorry." She shakes her head. "We need dollars." My head dips, and large spears of sweat splash onto the ground. I'd sell my soul for a room right now. As I inch toward the brink of my second breakdown of the morning, Chara adds, "But maybe the manager at Milos Villas . . ." Chara motions me around the front desk and cranks open a tiny oval window, stretching her slender arm to point at an iconic Greek windmill at the edge of the horizon.

I hadn't noticed Milos Villas while walking around the past few days with my parents. It's toward the sea, where Fira and its cube-shaped cafes, shops, and restaurants are spread atop the western edge of the island's cliffs. The way everything here clings to the cliffs is the very thing that draws people to the whitewashed island, and rarely does anyone ever look the other direction. Chara promises that she'll call Kostas, the manager, on my behalf, but before she can even pick up the phone, I'm out the door and beelining toward the place.

Milos Villas is a sprawling complex. Underneath the ancient windmill is a sparkling sapphire pool, surrounded on three sides by white, modern buildings trimmed with bright blue. It's a beautiful boutique hotel and most likely has a four-star rating, which makes me cringe. I can't imagine they would want to take a vagabonding, stressed-out amateur photographer in off the street on the spot.

Before I make my way into the lobby, I stop by the restroom and splash some water on my face, change my shirt, brush my teeth, and wipe the redness out of my eyes. I compartmentalize the outburst I just directed at my father and tell myself that I can't take *no* for an answer. The only other option would be to tuck my tail between my legs and head back to the same parents I just stormed away from. At this moment, I don't think I could take that kind of failure.

After I introduce myself as professionally as possible, the front desk receptionist escorts me into Kostas's office. His olive skin matches his shirt; he gestures to a seat while offering me an espresso. I don't know much about sales—in fact, I've never made one—but I do know that the more likeable you are, the more likely you are to seal the deal, which is exactly what made my father so successful. So even though I don't want the espresso, I sip slowly and listen to Kostas talk about the hotel. He tells me that the windmill is 250 years old and notes the distance from Fira as an advantage: "People can relax here—not so much noise."

I nod in agreement.

Kostas then explains the renovations he's in the midst of overseeing, which have been completed in fifteen of the twenty rooms the hotel offers. As he takes a sip of his espresso, silence fills the air. I see my window and pounce. "I could photograph the new rooms and make a film of the entire hotel for you. You could update your website with the images, and you wouldn't have to pay me for anything!"

Then, with my laptop already in hand, I start up a slideshow of the very best hotel photos I took while in Africa and then a short film of a hotel I shot in Mozambique, which catches me off guard because it reminds me of Naomi. She was by my side when I filmed it and even jumped in the pool for a shot. As that exact shot flashes across the screen, my thoughts drift toward her. Today is her birthday, but we haven't spoken for almost five months now. Last year for her birthday, we went to her favorite vegetarian restaurant in Miami Beach. We laughed all night and then walked along the ocean on the way home. The whole world was still out in front of us then, but now I'm not even sure what country she's in. I've given her the space she's asked for and was hoping she'd reply to the birthday email I sent her. But she hasn't.

How can every wall be caving in all at once?

Kostas shakes me out of my slump. "Impressed with your work," he says with an industrious smile. "But we are not ready to have photographs yet. Still renovating. Five rooms to go. Come back next summer, and we have deal."

As Kostas escorts me out of his office and back to the lobby, I dip into one of the other traits that's made my father so successful: his dogged determination. I've got to be relentless if I want this to work. I ask Kostas to reconsider. "If you could give me just three nights, I'll be able to photograph all fifteen of the renovated rooms as well as film around the five rooms that are not complete. And I'll shoot the pool, the restaurant, the lobby, and even the windmill at sunrise and sunset!"

Kostas takes his last sip of espresso while he lets my offer sink in, and then he asks me to wait in the lobby so he can think it over for a second time.

There's still a sliver of hope.

A steady stream of people comes in and out of Kostas's office over the next hour, and the wait is agonizing.

Eventually, Kostas emerges from his office. When he walks in my direction, my blood pressure spikes and my palms begin to sweat. His hands are in his pockets, and he surprises me when he pulls a key out from one of them.

"It's for room 204," he says. "We have a deal—let's begin filming after lunch."

I crack my first faint smile of the day, and then I thank him as though I've been struggling against the sea and he's pulled me back into the boat. Once Kostas returns to his office, a primal urge unlike anything I've ever felt pushes me outside, and I find a quiet spot behind the windmill where nobody can see or hear me. I pace in small circles and then I pound my chest with pride and let out a lion-like roar.

However, this exalted feeling has come at a cost. My relationships with the three most important people in my life—Naomi, my mother, and my father—are in shambles.

\#

The next afternoon, I receive two visitors, my mother and then my father. I have long talks with each of them out by the pool, and now that the dust has settled, I think we're all better off for it. Sometimes an explosion is for the best—it gives you a chance to start anew. And thankfully this turned out to be one of those times.

After I explain the origins of my outburst and apologize, my father does the same even though he didn't need to. He makes a point of apologizing for all the times he's ever pinched his pennies, not just for the recent cramped quarters. He even offers to book me my very own king-sized bedroom back at their hotel, but I respectfully decline. It's not because I don't want to go back but because of how much I have learned about myself since I stormed out of that hotel. I feel a new hunger driving me and even though I felt up against it in the moment, I wouldn't trade the awareness it brought me for all the money in the world.

You can learn a lot about yourself at the end of the rope.

My new responsibilities at Milos Villa mean I don't have much time left to spend with my parents. I am, however, able to sneak away and meet them for dinner on our last night on the island.

We sit in a bright white restaurant high atop one of the jagged cliffs that overlook an Aegean Sea so breathtakingly blue I have to periodically shield my eyes, careful not to overdose on the view. And as my parents and I share an order of fried zucchini chips with tzatziki, we ease back into our familiar roles. When our entrees arrive, I offer up a toast and then share some good news with them.

"A hotel in Belgrade just emailed me back and has accepted my film and photography offer. That's where I'll head next," I say. I see the pride they have for my pursuit in their eyes as they congratulate me, and although it will be a two-day train ride to get there, the relief of having a week's worth of room and board out in front of me is exactly what my journey needs most at the moment.

We meet up again the following morning in Fira to take the ferry back to Athens. While my parents load their luggage into the trunk of a taxi outside the Port of Piraeus, I find a spot for mine against the curb. Then we say our final good-byes. I'll have to make my way halfway around the world—across Europe, Asia, the Pacific Ocean, and most of North America—before I'll see them again. As we embrace, I have a hard time letting them go.

All this traveling is amplifying my emotions.

Or maybe it's as simple as having two people who care more about me than they do themselves within arm's reach and not wanting them to go.

* * *

The ride away from Athens is filled with remarkable scenery: I pass through the vast mountains south of Larissa, along the sparkling Aegean Sea, and past Mount Olympus, all while sipping on a cappuccino. However, after just a short walk across the platform and a quick change of trains in Thessaloniki, everything changes. It's like I've stepped back in time. I'm now in a dreary and graffiti-filled cabin that groans each time the train swerves. And I'm no longer alone. I'm sharing my compartment with five baby-faced student travelers. We've had to stack our luggage awkwardly in the tiny aisle that separates the two thinly cushioned benches we're sitting on.

As we introduce ourselves and shake hands across the aisle, our knees knock against one another's. I seem to be the only one who's a little unnerved by our accommodations because no one else mentions it. Instead, the canoodling French couple that's on my side of the compartment strikes up a conversation with the three British students from Oxford University who are across from us. They start discussing the social changes the Italian aristocracy faced during the Renaissance (or something sophisticated like that). As they repeatedly try to outdo one another and assert their intelligence, it becomes clear that I need to move to another car if I want to maintain my sanity. After politely excusing myself, I'm surprised to find a row of empty compartments just two cars down. I settle into one and spread myself across three red leather seats just as the sun starts to fade.

Right as the train begins to hit its stride and chugs powerfully toward Macedonia, a skinny, bare-footed traveler joins me. His long hair is as greasy as the bottom of a fast food bag, and he asks in a very polite and self-aware French accent if he can join me. It turns out to be the start of a conversation much more to my liking. He tells me he's been traveling through Europe for seven years and that he's poor on the outside but enriched on the inside. His appearance confirms his story: the bottoms of his feet are as dark as charcoal, but he has a bright presence about him like he knows it all but doesn't feel the need to *prove* it.

Just as my French companion starts in on a fascinating story about a time that he lived in an enchanted German forest, the train lurches to an unexpected halt.

"I thought we were going straight to Belgrade without any stops," I say.

"Oui, oui," says the Frenchman.

I stand up and walk over to the open window in our compartment and pop my head outside. We've pulled alongside a tiny green platform, but it's barely visible. It's been swallowed up by a mob of people. The platform is so crowded that people are spilling off it and out onto the tracks just in front of the train. I sense an odd energy in the air. Everyone looks listless and in serious discomfort. The other thing that catches my eye is that the skin color of the people surrounding the train is much darker than the people of the Balkans. Something strange is happening.

I briefly lock eyes with a tiny Greek woman in a white polo shirt, and as she spins around in a panic, I read out loud the words that are written across her back: "Aid Worker." I realize these people must be part of the wave of Syrian refugees that have been flooding into the country. She's having a hard time trying to keep everyone on the platform organized. Everyone is trying to board the train. The crowd creeps past her outstretched arms and toward the open doors without her permission. I scan the faces of the people closest to the train. Exhausted eyes meet mine. I have never seen such a beleaguered group of people in all my life. Confused, I call out the window to one of the conductors. "What's going on?"

He's angry, and in broken English he yells back at me, "Compartment for refugees! You move. Go to first car." When I freeze for a second to take in the weight of his words, he loses what's left of his already thin patience and shouts, "Now!"

I grab my camera bag and Timberland and start moving toward the front of the train with my new French friend. It's a mad dash to find a new seat as other conductors scream at us to hurry down the corridors. I end up in an empty cabin with a young Greek woman named Zita. She's from the island of Lesbos and tells me she's heading to Belgrade to teach English for the summer. After telling her an abridged version of what I've been doing, I turn my attention back out the window.

I watch in utter amazement as hundreds, if not thousands, of Syrian refugees board the train car I was just in. They are tired and bony, and they have all their belongings with them. I do too, but while my clothes are folded neatly into my travel-specific bags, their stuff is hanging out of potato sacks, boxes, and battered suitcases.

I know from watching the news that Greece is their gateway into Europe, but since Greece currently has enough problems of its own, refugees are having a hard time here. The Arab Spring and the euro crisis have taken a hefty toll on everyone. Most refugees cannot get the Greek government-issued pink card—the temporary resident permit they need to legally stay in the country for three to six months. Without it, many Syrians have been arrested and put into detention centers. As if that wasn't bad enough, trying to leave Greece without papers is *also* illegal. It's a no-win situation for them.

It takes about an hour for two aid workers and a handful of conductors to sort out which Syrians are allowed to board and which will have to wait on the platform for tomorrow's service. The ones given permission are assigned to the second and third cars, carefully separated from all the other passengers like they're carrying the bubonic plague.

About two hours later, I'm still consumed by what I've witnessed, and so I sneak out of my compartment and walk down the corridor while the conductor in my car isn't looking. I peer into the first car the Syrians are in like I'm eavesdropping on a conversation. My eyes widen with shock, and my heart breaks for humanity. They're jammed in like livestock. Some people are even sitting on top of one another. Bedrolls are laid out, suitcases are unpacked, and empty water bottles are strewn about everywhere. They make the crowded African buses I was on seem luxurious. I remember telling my father he had us living like refugees just days ago. Now that I'm face-to-face with actual refugees, I feel such shame for those hasty words.

A small group of Syrian men spill out of the car and into the vestibule in front of me. I take a few steps toward them. I don't know what to say, apart from a sheepish, "Hello."

The men return the greeting in near-perfect English. Their clothes are torn and as dirty as a mechanic's at the end of the day. I can't help but stare like a stupefied deer transfixed by headlights. My eyes must ask them how they got here because one of the men tries his best to explain.

"We took a rubber boat from Syria to Turkey, then we walked across Greece. Our homeland . . . is not safe."

His situation is horrific. Syria is currently in the midst of an extremely violent civil war. The unrest began in the early spring of 2011 when pro-democracy protests began to challenge the dictatorship running the country. The nationwide protests demanded President Bashar al-Assad's resignation, and he retaliated with violence. After months of military sieges designed to terrorize the civilians into submission, the conflict escalated as civilians began an armed rebellion.

The Syrian government has been accused of violating human rights, including committing war crimes and massacring civilians, including children. Chemical weapons have been used against the Syrian people. Protesters and activists have been imprisoned and tortured. I'd recently read a horrible headline that said the death toll had risen above 300,000.

As he's talking, I get lost in the look in his eyes. I've never seen anything even close to it. He is tired, he is scared, he is lost, and he is hurting on levels that no human should ever have to know exist. He has nothing left. He looks like he has been living on the verge of tears for years. It is without a doubt the most soul-crushing encounter I've ever had with another human being.

"We have been walking for a month, and we are trying to get to Germany to meet our family. They left six months before we did, but we don't know how far this train will take us. We've heard that Syrians are now banned from public transportation in Macedonia—but we aren't sure if that is true."

I reach into my wallet and offer all I have.

"I would like to help you. Please take this."

I try to pass over fifty euros—it's the only way I can think of to help them. To my surprise, no one in the group will accept it. One of the men tells me that he was a lawyer in Damascus and that they have money, but they have no respect. He tells me the most helpful thing I could do would be to find out where the train tickets they bought are taking them.

"We are hoping these tickets will take us all the way to Serbia, but no one who works on the train will talk to us and tell us."

I take their tickets and hunt down the conductor in charge of my car, who tells me that all the Syrians must get off at the next stop, which will be the Greek-Macedonian border. The Syrians' fears are justified: once they get to Macedonia, they are prohibited from using public transportation. They will have to walk across the entire country in order to reboard the train at the border with Serbia. I take my anger out at the conductor.

"What kind of world are we living in? How could you make these people get off the train and walk? Do you know what they have gone through just to get here?"

He shrugs and unfolds his newspaper. For him, it's just another day on the rails.

As I turn around and walk back down the corridor to deliver the bad news, the train screeches to a halt. The Syrians are ushered off the train and into the Macedonian darkness before I can get back to them. I watch out the window in shock. They don't know where to go or what to do— and it's truly the most awful thing I have ever witnessed.

There is such an extreme divide between those that get to travel for pleasure and those seeking safety that I can't quite wrap my head around it. The Syrian refugees are as intent on reaching their destination as I am. I can continue my journey in a reasonably safe, somewhat predictable way. But the Syrians? Nothing is predictable. Nothing is safe. Even in broad daylight, they're all walking into the dark.

The only conclusion I come to is an ugly one. Life isn't fair; it just can't be. As if fleeing a gruesome civil war in their homeland wasn't enough? Or hearing of their friends or family being tortured or killed? No. Macedonia's government decided to turn the horror up another notch by forcing them to walk hundreds of miles to reach safety. I don't think I'll ever understand that decision.

I hear their feet slap the wooden track ties as the last few refugees jump down to disembark the train, and I imagine that this is what life has been like for them since they left Syria. Just a series of walks into the unknown, triggered by tragedy and the small-minded fears of others.

All across Europe, similar stories are playing out. Tens of thousands of them, right this second. So much pain and misery and fear, aggravated by international bureaucracy, by ignorance, by so many failures in basic human decency toward people who never asked for this.

The train's brake pads hiss as they loosen their grip; my car shimmies and heaves forward. My ride resumes, but darkness engulfs everyone we've left behind.

CHAPTER 7
ENGLAND – BELARUS
EUROPE

*"I am lonely, yet not everybody will do. I don't
know why, some people fill the gaps
and others emphasize my loneliness."*

— *Anaïs Nin*

"WE NEED A GOAL, LADS!" is passionately screamed into my left ear by the North Londoner who's been guzzling pints of beer behind me. Sixty thousand Arsenal supporters leap to their feet in anticipation at this must-win Champions League match.

I lean over the barrier that's meant to separate the spectators from the field. I'm almost in play. I left my seat in the nosebleed section at halftime and snuck down to the only open seat in all of the Emirates stadium, which happened to be in the front row, right behind the lanky goalkeeper for the Olympiacos, the Greek League champions. It's a trick my dad taught me when I was a kid, when he took me to Philadelphia Phillies games. At the start of the game, he would look for two empty seats behind the Phillies dugout and keep his eye on those seats during the first few innings. Then, around the fourth inning or so, we'd sneak down when the ushers weren't looking and claim those seats as our own.

Theo Walcott cuts inside a Greek defender with one lightning-quick touch and lofts a glorious cross into the box. As the ball floats through the air, time seems to slow for everyone in the stadium—except Alexis Sanchez. He ascends like a rocket and attacks the ball with his head. I'm trying my best to will the ball into the goal. In the two months I've been in London, Arsenal and their sleek attacking style have won me over, and I've pledged my allegiance to them.

Initially, Adrien, the manager of Ibis Hotel in Whitechapel, only agreed to give me four nights in exchange for my film and photography work, but when I told him about the length and breadth of my travels and how desperate I was to stay in one spot for longer than a week, he did something truly incredible for me. He cut me a deal, allowing me to stay up to three months for only a couple hundred bucks a month. I'd have been an absolute fool not to take it.

I had spent much of the summer in Croatia. I wound around the Adriatic's sapphire sea from Dubrovnik to Split, and couldn't get enough of the castles and cathedrals on cliffs, but since it was peak season hotels had the upper hand when it came to my offer. They would negotiate me down to one or two nights, which meant I was always on the move. When I ran out of real estate in Split, I boarded an overnight ferry to Ancona, Italy and hopped on a train later that same day. I disembarked when it stopped in Milan to stroll around the Duomo, then overindulged in pasta and pizza that weekend. Before I knew it I was back on a bus, this time headed towards Switzerland. After having to pay $45.00 for a night in a bunkbed and $13.00 for a latte in Geneva, I left at midnight on a bus, then changed to another bus headed to London underneath the Eiffel Tower's shadow as the sun came up. When I arrived in London's Victoria Station I was exhausted and once again worried about my finances. I just couldn't keep up the blistering pace I'd been traveling at any longer.

My apartment at the Ibis—or, as the Brits like to call it, my "flat"—is located just a few steps from a cultural axis of London's population, one of many. The BBC once reported that over three hundred languages are spoken in London each day, and I wouldn't be surprised if I've heard about half of them spoken on my block. I'm right where the skyscraping financial district of Moorgate ends and the Bengali neighborhood of Whitechapel begins. Just a few blocks north is the gentrified hipster haven that is Shoreditch, and a stone's throw south is the London Docklands, which was built on the backs of hardworking immigrants.

On any given day, I could be walking between a multimillionaire in a perfectly tailored three-piece suit and a shaggy-haired, leather-pants-wearing hipster, while smells of sweet ginger, turmeric, chili, and cumin waft around us. This is just one of the many reasons why I love living in east London. Another is the electric energy that Champions League nights like tonight provide.

Sanchez's diving header ricochets toward the left corner of the goal. Olympiacos's goalkeeper dives for it. His fingertips graze the stitching of the ball, but the power behind the header won't be denied, and both Sanchez and the ball end up in the back of the net.

The crowd erupts. Gunner flags go a-flying, and my eardrums ring with excitement.

I'm caught up in the sensational atmosphere around me, and I punch the air and yell, "Arsenalllllllllllllll," like I've lived here all my life.

I turn to my left to celebrate, but the couple next to me are having their own private hug-fest. I turn to my right, but those friends who came together are chest-bumping and high-fiving. Same with the people behind me. Everyone's here with someone.

Everyone except me.

A strange, unfamiliar, all-encapsulating feeling shoots through my system. It's bleakly ironic. I am surrounded by sixty thousand people, yet I've never truly gotten lonely or homesick out here on the road until this very moment. It's a double-edged sword some days; I love being alone so much that I'm nearly a recluse now. I sit in coffee shops and work on my writing, which can really only be done alone, and I'll go days without having a conversation with anyone other than my own thoughts. Still, that's the way I like it. Whenever I find myself making plans with someone in London, I secretly hope they'll cancel. When I'm actually in the middle of a face-to-face conversation, my mind drifts, and I think about something Paul Theroux wrote in his book *The Great Railway Bazaar*. He was traveling by himself from London to Beijing; after having a chat with a woman in the dining car, he wrote, "I need to be alone after seeing people, sort of put myself back together." It's taking me longer and longer to put myself back together, though I can't pinpoint the reason.

My alone time in London, up until now, has been all but perfect. I've stepped further and further away from societal norms, and since I have nowhere to be, no bills to pay, and no set schedule, I often lose track of what day it is. If it weren't for the ever-changing weather, I wouldn't know if it was January or June, which honestly is an amazing feeling. I'd have to say that I'm just about where I wanted to be when I originally set out to pursue this Impossible Idea.

I feel rejuvenated and refreshed, and the city has provided me with a series of *firsts*. I did my first live television interview, talking about my journey across Africa, and I published my first stories about my overland journey in publications other than my own. I sold my first short travel film (for a decent payday), and I celebrated my first full year on the road by sinking my teeth into a delicious double cheeseburger at the Five Guys that's just a few blocks from Big Ben.

The other day, a complete stranger came up to me and said, "Oh my God, are you the travel photographer TravelTall?" (That's my social media moniker.) When I said yes, it became the first time I was ever recognized for anything other than just being really tall. And the amazing part is that when this woman recognized me, I was sitting down. At six-feet-ten-inches tall, I'm used to people blurting out something about my size or reciting the world's worst joke, the one I've already heard twice today: "How's the weather up there?"

I love being tall and wouldn't trade an inch for anything in the world, but when this woman asked me if I was the travel photographer instead of a basketball player, it was a wonderfully unexpected out-of-body experience. It made me feel like it's not just my travel plans that are working but also my creative transformation. As the woman who recognized me was walking away, I called out to her, "Wait, what's your name? How can I follow you back on Instagram?"

She ran back and put her business card in my hand, saying, "I run a little boutique clothing store here in London, and I go by The Alchemist on social media sites."

For a moment, I was speechless. I gave her a beguiled smile and told her, "Maybe I am the real-life incarnation of Santiago. After all, the one and only person that's recognized me on my journey is The Alchemist. What are the odds of that?"

But after meeting The Alchemist and all those firsts and the bursts of euphoria that follow, I've been left with a lingering feeling that I couldn't quite put my finger on, until now.

There's no one for me to share all those wonderful moments with, and again tonight as I look for someone in the crowd to high five, there's no one to celebrate Arsenal's game-tying goal with. So with my arms outstretched and raised up toward the heavens, it hits me hard.

I miss *Naomi*. I really, really, really miss Naomi.

I thought that time was supposed to heal all wounds, but the longer we've been apart, the deeper mine have gotten. I'm befuddled about why I pushed her away in the first place. In this moment, it immediately becomes clear what I need to do. I have to track her down in Thailand. I need to right my wrongs. I need to win her back.

I take the London Underground back to my flat after the game, disappointed that Arsenal lost but clearly knowing what needs to be done.

I walk over to the window in my room and look out over the twinkling lights of "The Gherkin," the iconic cone-shaped skyscraper that punctuates London's skyline, and I think about what, if anything, has changed about me since she left. Would things be any different if we tried again? Has she moved on and met someone else? Is she even in Thailand anymore? If I really give myself to her, will that connection run roughshod over my creative process and detour my journey? I wonder if, after everything I put her through in Africa, she would even want to see me again.

My window reflection doesn't have any answers.

I think of the advice Elizabeth Gilbert writes about in *Eat, Pray, Love*. When she was worried about pursuing a man after finally finding her own balance, her Balinese friend said, "To lose balance sometimes for love is part of living a balanced life."

I'm nearly there. I'm close to finally cracking the code on how to make all this work—but I can't seem to move on from Naomi. My mind, body, and soul are yearning to have her here with me once again. As if on cue, the Universe senses my sadness, and raindrops start pattering against the window.

Missing *anything* this much is foreign to me. In an interview I did this week for my hometown newspaper back in Pennsylvania, the reporter who used to cover my high school basketball games ended the interview by asking, "What do you miss the most about the United States?" I couldn't think of anything, and just as the interview was about to end in an awkward silence, I blurted out, "Hot dogs." That's right: after a year of being away from friends and family, the only thing I could think to say that I missed was junk food. This is how locked in on this Impossible Idea I've become. Nothing else seems to matter.

Except Naomi.

But it's nearly October, and we still haven't talked since that excruciating Skype session back in Uganda. We haven't emailed much either. I heard from her for the first time in what felt like forever just over a month ago. She told me she'd been volunteering in a Buddhist temple in Thailand, which is also where she lives in exchange for keeping the temple clean. Since most monks don't require Wi-Fi to find enlightenment, she rarely has access to her email. The only time she even checks it is when she heads to the nearest Thai town, wherever that is, so she can stock up on supplies and chia seeds.

How many temples are there in Thailand?

I sit down on my bed and flip open my laptop.

As I type in her email address, my hands shake and my heart thumps. Then I take a deep breath, and I begin to write the most important message of my life.

* * *

"I've got to get to Asia if I want to see Naomi again. This might be my only chance to fix things with her!" I tell Liu.

Liu begins to flip through my passport for a third time, not knowing who Naomi is or why I need to get to her. He still can't find my United Kingdom entry stamp. Even though the sterile bureaucratic atmosphere of the Chinese Visa Application Service Center on Old Jewry Road in London is about as different as it could be from the Zobue border station in Mozambique, the situation is eerily reminiscent of the time Naomi and I had been bamboozled while trying to cross the Malawi border.

This can't be happening again. Not in England.

"I'm sorry, sir, but the entry stamp is one of the requirements we request in order to apply for a Chinese visa. Because yours is missing, I cannot accept your application," Liu says firmly.

"I'm 100 percent sure the entry stamp is in there somewhere. Please pass it back to me, and I'll find it for you."

Liu slides my passport underneath the plexiglass window. As I slowly flip through it page by page, I think of Naomi. She hasn't yet replied to the email I sent her last week asking her to meet me around Thanksgiving in

Beijing, where I'll enter Asia. I don't want to have to wait until I've made it all the way to Thailand to see her again. We can resume traveling together from there. But first I've got to get across Russia, which is why I've already purchased a non-refundable ticket on the Trans-Siberian Railway.

When I get to the back page of my passport, I look up at Liu, as befuddled as I was at the Mozambique border. I took a bus from Paris to London, crossing under the English Channel via the Chunnel and arrived at Victoria Station in London exactly two months ago to the day. I specifically remember seeing the solid steel stamper smack flush against an empty page inside my passport before I retrieved it and slid it back into my pocket.

Although there was a bit of a mix-up at the border. When the immigrations officer asked me what I did for a living, I felt a strange shame. So I lied and said that I was a high school history teacher, which was my first job out of college over a decade ago. In response, the immigrations officer asked as he flipped through my well-worn passport, "What kind of teacher gets to travel this much? Looks like you've been across Africa this past year. You even have a visa for Sudan in here."

I dug the hole even deeper. "Um, yeah, I'm on a one-year sabbatical," I said.

"Oh, yeah?" the officer said with suspicion. "What's the name of the school you're employed at back in the States?"

When I scratched the bridge of my nose like a bad bluff before replying, he knew right then that I was lying. Just moments later, when I wasn't able to provide proof of onward travel, I got pulled out of the line and asked a long list of questions in a separate cell-like room, which nearly made me miss the bus I'd been traveling on.

Lying for no reason was beyond stupid, and I nearly didn't get into England because of it, but I couldn't get the words *I'm a photographer, filmmaker, and writer* out of my mouth. My creative confidence was particularly low that day, but even so, I've still never been able to call myself any of those things. I take those titles seriously, and while I do take photos, make short travel films, and write short stories, I don't think my work is worthy of such lofty titles. But I couldn't backtrack and tell such a stern-looking immigration officer the origins of my insecurities.

Eventually, I was able to work my way out of the mess by owning up to the fact that I was unemployed and by providing a copy of my reservation at the Ibis Hotel.

"This is crazy, Liu, but I can't find the entry stamp either. What are my options without it?"

"Well, technically you are in the United Kingdom illegally, and you won't be able to leave when you try to exit the country. I'm sorry, but I don't know how you can fix this. We only issue Chinese visas here. Perhaps the United States Embassy can help you."

"It's just got to be in there," I groan.

Liu pulls a small black flashlight from his desk drawer and holds it just a few inches above each page as he flips slowly from front to back one last time. When Liu gets about halfway through my booklet, he mysteriously pauses above an empty page. He squints and moves his flashlight another two inches closer. "I think I found it," he whispers, like we're suddenly in a library.

Liu points to a spot in the center of the page, but I don't see anything. "Where?"

"Right here." He pushes his index finger into the page and then moves it around in small circles.

"The page is blank, Liu."

"The stamp is really faded and barely visible. The only thing I can think of is that the stamper must have been low on ink the day the immigration officer stamped your passport."

I was so mad at myself for lying to the immigrations officer and in such a rush to make it back onto the bus before it left me behind at the border that I never stopped to make sure the entry stamp was actually there.

"What a relief," I say, still not seeing the stamp.

"Well, the good news is that the entry stamp is here, but the bad news is that when I send your passport and paperwork to our visa approval team, they won't be able to find it either, and so they won't be able to issue you a Chinese visa."

"What happens if I submit my visa application today and it doesn't get approved?"

"Once someone's visa application is denied here, they can only reapply at the Chinese Embassy or Chinese Consulates General in their home country, and they must do so in person."

"In person!" My thick eyebrows scrunch together, and my head tilts sideways like a dog waiting for its dinner. "So you're telling me that if the person who's reviewing my application can't see my faded United Kingdom entry stamp and I get denied the Chinese visa here in London, I have to go all the way back to the United States to reapply for the visa in person?"

Liu nods as I continue, "This is crazy. I can't go all the way back to the United States just because the United Kingdom's stamper was out of ink. There's got to be something you can do to help me out here. Please, I'm begging you."

Without access to the gigantic landmass that is China, I'm all but stuck. China is the third-largest country in the world, and there really is no other way to get to Naomi overland than to cut across China. The only other option would include crossings of Iran and Pakistan, which would bring me close to the borders of Iraq and Afghanistan—two nations my country has been at war with for the past fifteen years. I'm sure it would be all but impossible to get travel visas to enter Iran and Pakistan on the fly like this. The only other option would be to reverse my route and head west once I leave London, but that would mean I'd have to find a way across the Atlantic Ocean, which would take me farther away from the rendezvous I've been envisioning. It would also mean I would lose the $1,100 I've already spent on my Trans-Siberian train ticket. I can't cope with that kind of financial failure right now.

Liu writes something in Chinese on a Post-It note and then draws an arrow in the direction of my faint entry stamp. "What would you like to do, sir?"

"What are my chances, Liu?"

"I would say about 25 percent, sir."

"If I apply for the visa now, how long will it take until I hear if I've been approved or not?"

"It takes five days, sir."

As the line begins to grow behind me, Liu repeats, "What would you like to do, sir?"

I rock back in my chair and stare up at the ceiling while I think over my options.

Who am I kidding? I don't need to think things over. I already know what I'm going to do.

"Here's the rest of my paperwork. See you next week!"

* * *

I find out about the status of my Chinese visa application when I open my credit card statement on my computer to pay my bill and see the $140.00 charge. But my elation about getting the chance to keep trekking on toward China and Naomi has waned. It's been over a month since I emailed her, and I still haven't heard back.

Each day I run myself through the exact same excruciating gamut of emotions. I start out hopeful and optimistic that today, yes, *today* will finally be the day she responds, which quickly leads to missing her like mad. Then an awful feeling of anger and betrayal sets in. I can't *believe* that she has the audacity to ignore me after all the things I've done for her. The next day, the cycle starts all over again.

I still have no idea how she feels about reuniting with me, but I've bullishly gone ahead with my initial plan.

I'm sitting in a comfortably modern four-berth cabin on a train that's rumbling through a chilly Eastern European October night. I'll pass through Belarus tonight and then arrive in Moscow in the morning, which is where my long journey on the Trans-Siberian Railroad will officially begin. Even though it's only 5:00 p.m., it's already pitch black outside.

My life could take so many trajectories right now. It's entirely possible that I could get to Beijing and still not have heard from Naomi. Then what? It's also entirely possible that she could email me tomorrow and our reunion in Beijing would be the beginning of a forever relationship. Or we could meet in Beijing and things could unravel. I shudder at that last possibility.

I picture her in a Thai temple. I imagine her meeting someone else who's more her speed, the yin to her yang—and then I wonder if *that's* the reason I haven't heard back from her yet.

Maybe she's met someone else.

You would think I would have learned my lesson by now about how wasteful it is to worry, that I would have learned to trust the process. But I can't. I remain as fallibly human as I ever was.

After a few hours of mental warfare, I unhinge my tiny berth from the wall and crawl up a small metal ladder and into it. I let the train rock me to sleep, and as I drift away, I hope that I'll get to see Naomi again soon . . .

Even if it's only in my dreams.

CHAPTER 8
RUSSIA
EUROPE

"Everybody has a plan until they get punched in the mouth."

— *Mike Tyson*

ALL THE COOKIE-CUTTER HOTEL ROOMS I've been sleeping lately in are starting to blend together, and it takes a second to remember what city I'm in. Then it hits me. "Novosibirsk. How could I have forgotten I'm in the middle of Siberia?"

I'm hung over from all the exhausting train travel, but that doesn't stop me from doing what I've done every morning for the past six weeks. I swipe my phone off the nightstand and pull up my email. Maybe this is the day Naomi finally responds and accepts my offer. I'm getting worryingly close to Beijing, and I still haven't heard back from her.

I flick some junk mail aside. Ugh.

Suddenly, there it is. For the first time in months, I see Naomi's familiar email address at the bottom of my inbox. My heart leaps out of my chest, and my fingers get clumsy with excitement.

I'm picturing us meeting in Tiananmen Square later this week, she on one side of it and me on the other; when our eyes meet, we race across, and she leaps into my arms like a scene from *Gone with the Wind*. It all looks absurd against a backdrop of modern China, but neither of us will care—we'll just be ecstatic to be in each other's arms again.

After letting me know that all is well on her end, she cracks a couple of inside jokes like we haven't spent a day apart. I skim through all the small talk—I can go back and read that later—and desperately look for her answer.

I find it in the middle of the email.

I read it out loud to the pillows and bedsheets around me, hanging on every letter. "Maybe I can meet you again someday down the road, but it is evident that we are a bit too off-sides to make much movement down the field of life together."

My heart hardens, and I'm momentarily confused. Not by her foggy football analogy but by the rejection. While I knew it was a possibility, it never truly dawned on me that she would turn me down. I always thought—or maybe I should say my *ego* always thought—that she was just waiting around for me until I invited her back into my life. I figured it was just a matter of time until she read my email and responded with a "Yes, I can't wait to see you too, of course I'll meet you in Beijing!"

I let out a stunned breath, and then my mind goes blank.

Eyes glazed with sorrow, I look out the window at the snow that's piled high atop the rooftops across the street. I watch the outline of a burly Russian man lean out of his bedroom window. He puffs on a cigarette and then exhales the smoke up toward the stark sky. I watch everything and think nothing.

I figured Siberia would be a good place to stop for a few days so that I wouldn't have to spend seven straight days crammed inside a tiny train car. Besides wanting to break up the journey from Moscow to Beijing, I was also curious to see what Siberia was like. But now that I'm here, I'm wishing I weren't.

I'm wishing I weren't anywhere.

Novosibirsk isn't anything special. It's just like any other midsized industrial European city, except colder. Depressed-looking skies and far-below-freezing temperatures make this one of the harshest places on the planet to spend the winter, and the choice to stop here at this time of the year would be, in hindsight, extremely stupid. The motherboard inside my camera shorted out because of the extreme cold, and karma's backlash has been hard at work ever since I arrived. Yesterday I realized I'd left my external hard drive on the train that brought me here, and thus I've lost all the photos and films I created as I traveled across Africa that didn't already make it onto my blog. It's been a bitter pill to swallow, and my anger at that mistake is only amplified after today's rejection.

I drop my head into the pillow by my side, wondering if there is anything I can say that would get her to change her mind.

But I already know there isn't.

#

While hopelessly staring up at the popcorn ceiling of my Siberian hotel room, a sinking suspicion sneaks up on me. I race over to my backpack and unfold my train ticket. It's printed in a mix of Russian and Chinese characters, but I can read the numbers: 14/11/15. I still haven't become accustomed to the European style of listing the day before the month. Worse, I realize that after two nights of poor sleep on the train from Moscow, I'm hazy about what day it is. I flip on the TV and turn to an international news channel; the date is stamped in the bottom right-hand corner.

Today is in fact November 14. I scan the ticket for the departure time, which I remembered being noon.

"Shit!"

Twelve a.m. It's not in military time, and I missed the a.m. notation the first time I'd read it. I throw it up into the air in frustration, and as it flutters to the ground, I punch a nearby pillow in absolute anger. "You have got to be kidding me. How could I have missed my train to China by twelve fucking hours?"

Dollar signs fill my brain. Not only was this ticket the second-most expensive thing I've purchased along the way, it also required me to navigate a maze of bureaucracy. I booked and paid for the ticket while in London, but I had to pick up the ticket in person at a very out-of-the-way Moscow office. I have no idea how to rebook it—or if rebooking it in Siberia is even possible. And on top of all that, I don't know when the next train leaves. Novosibirsk to Beijing in the middle of November, when it's negative ten degrees outside, isn't exactly a popular route for locals or tourists.

"This is a disaster!" I scream into the empty air.

My attention is momentarily pulled back toward the TV by breaking news. There's been a massive terrorist attack in Paris. Men armed with assault rifles and explosives killed over a hundred innocent people in and around the city last night.

I don't know who's responsible for the attack—nobody does yet—but my mind goes right to the Syrian refugees I met on the train in Greece. I imagine that they are going to catch the backlash for this. Some people are going to find a way to blame *them* for this atrocity. The right-wing press will drum up some sort of story about how the borders were weaker around Europe because of these Syrian refugees seeking freedom, which made it easier for the terrorists to make their way to France and carry out today's attack.

I shake my head in disgust.

My phone warbles on the nightstand, and I walk over and see that a text has come through from my dad. My grandmother collapsed at my cousin's wedding in Florida last night and was rushed to the hospital.

How can all this be happening at once?

I decide that enough is enough—someone owes me some answers. That someone is God. I get up, put on my jacket, and take the elevator to the ground floor. It's bitterly cold outside, but I push through the revolving door. Snow tumbles out of a featureless sky. The temperatures plummeted last night, and the cold nips at my exposed flesh, gnawing at me through my clothing.

By the time I walk across the street to Lenin Square, I am already frozen. The temperature at the southern end of the square feels, if possible, even colder, as if its gigantic stone sculptures of Soviet-era soldiers are pulling all the remaining heat out of the world. We stand there, five statues and one man, feeling nothing.

There's no time to properly introduce myself. I figure that God knows me well enough by now, at least from my side of things. We've gotten close these last few years, so I cut right to the chase. "I need to know what the hell you want from me because this—this is bullshit!"

I look up through the snowflakes and without sugarcoating my feelings, I demand answers from the Creator of the Universe.

"I thought this is what you wanted me to do with my life. So why are you making this so damn difficult?"

I pace back and forth between two snow-covered park benches.

I am so depressed, so utterly at the end of my rope, so delusional that I fully expect an answer. Not one of those symbolic answers that comes in the form of a cosmic sign, like that time in Uganda when I randomly flipped open the Bible and my finger landed on the words "It is written."

And not something that I need to decipher either, like a series of 4s, but an answer given audibly, spoken in words, clear cut and in English. I need to hear from God with literal clarity so I can know exactly why every single part of my life has just fallen apart in the span of a few short minutes. I'm waiting for the snow to stop, the heavens to open up, and a bellowing James Earl Jones voice to shake the earth with a thundering response.

I wait, and then I wait some more, but all I hear is the silence of snow falling on the lifeless ground.

I have begun to shiver uncontrollably. I yell up at the statues, "It wasn't supposed to be like this!"

I sense people staring at me as they bustle across the square on their way to work, and I'm tempted to yell at the pack of Russians, "What are you looking at?"

I shake my head in disgust at myself. *What am I doing here?* Deep down, I thought that what I'm doing, or trying to do, would actually make a difference in the world, but it's not even making a dent on my closest friends. My buddy Shaun asked me how my flight to Moscow was last week, not even remembering that the most basic principle of my journey was to not take any flights. Maybe I'm delusional, like the tone-deaf contestants that go on *American Idol*. Maybe I'm the William Hung of travel blogging, and it's just that no one has told me this yet.

I know what my friends and family will say if I give up and fly home, and how they'll try to comfort me. They will look at how far I made it and say something like, "Even though you didn't end up making it all the way around the world, you got to see some pretty cool places, and you had some awesome experiences."

And while they would be factually correct, it's of little comfort.

I look back up at the muted sky and watch black smoke billow into it from the industrial side of the city. I want to place the blame for misreading my train ticket and Naomi not wanting to see me on anyone other than myself, and who better to find fault with than God?

"What did I do to deserve this?" I yell. I stretch my arms out wide. "I've done all the things you've asked of me: I've tapped into my deepest dreams, I've trusted my intuition, I've taken the leap, I've risked my life, and I've had just about as much faith as any one person could have, so what more could you possibly want from me?"

I lose what's left of my fractured patience and begin to throw nothing short of a tantrum. I scream, grunt, and curse like a maniac as I stomp deep holes into a nearby snowbank. "I thought this is what you wanted me to do with my life!"

Snow rushes through the hole that's in the big toe of my right sneaker, but I keep stomping. I stomp and stomp until my socks are soaked and I'm nearly out of breath.

I wipe my wet hair away from my eyes and peer over at the statue of Vladimir Lenin, and then I take a few steps back and run up and kick at a chunk of dangling ice with all my might.

"No matter what I do, it's never enough for you!"

The feeling in my toes and fingertips is long gone. I try to take a deep breath and blow warm air into the knit gloves I picked up in Moscow last week, but they're not nearly thick enough to fight the frigid conditions.

I look up at the sky again and defiantly say, "FINE, YOU DON'T WANNA TALK? THEN I'M DONE WITH YOU!"

I reach a level of hopelessness that makes me think God might not exist after all. And that's when it hits me that my dreams are nothing more than far-fetched fantasies. I picture my friends laughing at me behind my back, and it makes things worse. I yell up to God one last time, "I guess you want me to quit, huh? At least be a man about it and come down here and say it to my face!"

I fall to my knees, the word *quit* echoing in my brain. My mind slows down for a second as I process what it would feel like to quit. I put on my old corporate clothes, the slacks from Banana Republic, the button-down shirt from J. Crew, the shoes from Kenneth Cole. Then I sit in traffic on I-95 north. I go through my old routine. I even flirt with a cute barista at Starbucks while I wait for the latte I always ordered after lunch. When I feel its foam spread softly against my lips, that's when a deeper understanding snakes up my spine.

My old life never had the power to bring me to my knees.

Nothing about that life would have led me to demanding answers from God while stomping through snow and ice while stranded in Siberia, which is precisely the problem I had with that life. This moment is the living embodiment of the Charles Bukowski quote that's written on the first page inside my leather-bound journal, the one I read through every morning: "If you're going to try, go all the way. Otherwise, don't even start. This could mean losing girlfriends, wives, relatives and maybe even your mind. It could mean not eating for three or four days. It could mean freezing on a park bench. It could mean jail. It could mean derision. It could mean mockery—isolation. Isolation is the gift. All the others are a test of your endurance, of how much you really want to do it. And, you'll do it, despite the rejection and the worst odds. And it will be better than anything else you can imagine. You will be alone with the gods, and the nights will flame your fire. You will ride life straight to perfect laughter. It's the only good fight there is."

I never fully understood what Bukowski meant when he wrote that, but now I do. This is the good fight! And even though I'm currently at the wrong end of the emotional totem pole, I finally understand the essence of his words. This, this shit storm, is the gift. Success and failure are one and the same. I've lost everything this morning, including my mind, but when I strip away all forms of judgment about whether this is good or bad, I feel as alive and in tune with myself as I've ever been.

A sliver of gratitude follows; as it settles over me, a deep appreciation for all this mess courses through my core. Instead of losing faith, almost miraculously, I find it.

I realize that while I've always pursued the goal of a creative transformation, I'm in the midst of a much deeper transformation. Somewhere along the way, the lotus has emerged from the murkiness of my mind. As the petals have begun to slowly unfold, I've gotten to know parts of my true, authentic self, which Deepak Chopra described as the purest part of oneself. The roads I've really been traveling are internal roads, which have been leading me to that self, the person I'm meant to become. This isn't an overland journey around the world—it's a journey over, under, and around all the obstacles I've been encountering to my wholeness.

But right now, I'm hanging on to that new self and those dreams by the thinnest of margins. While part of me is afraid that I might not actually make it around the world without flying, a bigger part of me is afraid of losing touch with me, *this* me. The *real* me.

I lift my forehead back up to the sky and whisper through my shaking lips, "Nothing is going to stop me! Nothing is going to stop me! Nothing is *ever* going to stop me!"

I must say it a hundred times, laughing manically while simultaneously on the verge of tears. I too have found that perfect laughter Bukowski mentioned.

It's in this moment that God finally responds.

God's voice doesn't sound like James Earl Jones, nor does it move a mountain or rattle the earth. God's voice is calm and still like my intuition. But it isn't my intuition. It comes from an even deeper place. It comes from the bedrock of my being. God's voice parts the sea of fears and doubts that have flooded my chest and rolls through that open space like molasses. And as it inches its way through, it coats every bone, nerve ending, and muscle fiber in its path.

When I hear God's voice for the first time, I almost laugh because I immediately recognize it. God's voice is deep and baritone, just like my own—because it is my own.

The voice that I've summoned from the strongest part of my soul says, "I know exactly what you need, and believe me, *this* is it."

I freeze for a second, too in awe to take a breath. As the corners of my frozen lips turn up, I feel God begin to retract back into my soul—but before God leaves for good, I hear two more words ever so faintly . . .

"Trust me."

* * *

If there was ever a time for a stiff shot of Russian vodka, this would officially be it. I'll even down the cheap stuff if it keeps me warm.

I yank down on the drawstrings of my hood and tie them together until only my eyes and nose are exposed. Then I reach for my zipper and try to pull it up even higher, but it won't budge; it's already at the end of its track. My teeth begin to rattle against one another in a frigid chatter. I always thought that only cartoon characters with elastic faces could make their jaws move that quickly. Boy, was I wrong.

I look down my nose and then out at train tracks covered in equal parts snow and darkness. After being stuck in Novosibirsk for the past five days, I'm finally ready to resume my journey east and hop back on the world's most iconic train, which if I'm reading my ticket correctly this time, should be here within the next sixty seconds, at 12:43 a.m. It seems like an odd time to board, but it's the only ticket out of town this time of year.

I've made some major strides since my breakdown and breakthrough in Lenin Square a few days ago. Besides figuring out how to rebook my Trans-Siberian train ticket and then using my remaining Marriott points to check into the nicest hotel in town, I've tried my best to truly listen to the two words God whispered to me: "Trust me." I've probably repeated them close to a million times by now, especially in regard to Naomi not wanting to see me. I figure that the more I say them, the more likely they are to sink down into the hardest part of my heart. I've tried my best to see all of the setbacks I've experienced here as tiny gifts from God, put in my path to help loosen my consciousness and catapult it to the next level. What that next level looks like, however, is still a little hazy.

I wrap my arms tightly around myself and squeeze, but I can't stop shivering. The fact that I'm the only human being on the platform makes me feel even colder. Atop the Novosibirsk train station, a digital clock flashes the time and the temperature:

Its 12:42 a.m. and negative 22 degrees Celsius.

Just as the neon clock on the platform ticks forward, a single light cuts through the darkness and begins to steamroll toward me.

"Right on time."

I grab Timberland and shuffle down the platform to where I think car twenty-three will end up. As the first couple train cars pass me by, I see yellow Chinese characters painted on the green sides of the train. I can't help but gasp; the excitement of Asia looming in the distance steals my next ice-cold breath. I assumed that I would be boarding a Russian train tonight, just like the one that took me from Moscow to Novosibirsk.

It took the Russians twenty-five years to lay nearly six thousand miles of track, and the Trans-Siberian railway was built specifically for harsh weather just like this. Back then, it was what connected Moscow to the Far East when all of the rivers and roads were frozen five months out of the year. But for travelers like myself, I think the words "Trans-Siberian" primarily fill us with a romantic sense of wanderlust. As I was crossing Europe a few weeks back, every time I told someone that I was planning to take this route, they would always say, "Aww, man, that's on my bucket list—one day, man, one day!"

There's something about a lengthy journey by train that's magical. I envision myself sitting in the dining car with a few good books and a warm cappuccino, unable to focus on the page in front of me because the landscape on the other side of the window is so interesting that I can't concentrate on anything but the horizon. So, believe it or not, I'm actually looking forward to spending the next five nights on the train. No TV. No

Wi-Fi. Just me and whatever else happens to be out there. The ticket I purchased goes east to Irkutsk and then cuts south, right through the heart of Mongolia, and then east again until it reaches the Beijing Railway Station. Once the train steamrolls to a stop, a sleepy Chinese conductor slinks down the steps. His uniform is filthy, and the arms of his jacket hang five inches past his hands; he looks like an overgrown schoolboy in it. His teeth are terribly misshapen, and he doesn't speak a lick of English. I don't expect him to, but I can't help asking anyway, "Is this the right train?"

His only answer is to punch a hole through the top left corner of my ticket. I lift my luggage up the steps and climb aboard.

Inside the vestibule, a cloud of soot and disgusting black smoke greets me. The first thing I see catches me off guard. Even though I have a second-class ticket (which is the cheapest option available), I am half expecting to see a waiter with a glass of red wine and a pair of slippers waiting for me; this is the charming Trans-Siberian Railroad, after all. But instead, what I get is another Chinese man whose face is caked with soot; he's bent over a furnace and is shoveling coal around the open flame like he's single-handedly responsible for making the entire train move. I glance into the bathroom when I pass by it because its door has swung open. A god-awful odor is cascading out of it. It's filthy and smells worse than the stalls at Wrigley Field on dollar beer night.

A conductor strides toward me. Without saying a word, he grabs my bag and leads me down a corridor that's so narrow I have to turn sideways and shimmy just to make my way.

I call out to him, "This isn't exactly what I had in mind."

The Trans-Siberian Railroad was completed in 1916, and I wouldn't be surprised if this train car was part of that maiden voyage way back then.

The conductor slides open the door to my compartment. It's ice cold and empty. It's a cramped four-berth closet of a room. It has a tabletop bolted into the wall and a beige blanket atop each pancake-thin mattress. I swing my bag and myself into the room, and the conductor follows me in.

"Um, it's freezing in here. Can you turn the heat on?"

He has no idea what I'm saying, so I pretend to shiver, which doesn't take much pretending, and I say, "Cold."

I put my hand to the frost on the window, expecting it to be on the outside, but it's actually on the inside. Then, as I inspect the rubber rim that's around the window, I notice that tissue paper is pushed in between the glass and the rim, which means that this Bible-thin tissue paper is my only insulation against the harsh Siberian winter.

I crouch down in a panic and run my fingers underneath the heating vents that are beneath the tabletop.

I can't feel anything coming out.

The conductor finds two English words: "Heat on."

It's in this moment that I think my unquenchable appetite for travel is forever quenched.

"I am not prepared for this," I say to the conductor, but by the time I turn around, he's gone.

Just a few days ago, it took everything I had inside to pick myself up and dust myself off, and now I'm already finding myself on the wrong end of things again.

The train shudders and starts to move. The lights of the station and then the smokestacks on the industrial side of Novosibirsk quickly disappear.

I sit down on the frigid bottom bunk that's about as wide and soft as an ironing board. I look out the window. My body rocks as the train rocks. I resist the urge to cry.

I grab a blanket from the empty berth across from me and pin it up against the window, and then I work the window's roller curtain down, hoping that will provide some sort of insulation. I dig into Timberland and pull out all the long-sleeved shirts that I own, which is a total of three. I put them all on.

I turn out the lights and crawl into my berth, wrapping myself from head to toe with the three blankets from the other berths.

I pull my wool hat over my eyes and nose, and I begin to mentally prepare myself to sleep in my jeans, sneakers, and jacket for the next five nights. I remind myself that times like these are why I chose to start this journey around the world in Africa, and that if I could make it there, then I can make it anywhere.

With that thought repeating in my brain, I listen to the wind whistle as the train creaks through the darkness.

CHAPTER 9
CHINA – VIETNAM
ASIA

"Traveling is a brutality. It forces you to trust
strangers and to lose sight of all that familiar comfort
of home and friends. You are constantly off balance.
Nothing is yours except the essential things:
air, sleep, dreams, sea, the sky – all things tending
towards the eternal or what we imagine of it."

— *Cesare Pavese*

I WAS JUST ABOUT THE ONLY passenger on the Trans-Siberian the five days it trudged toward Beijing. I ran out of food two days before our arrival because the dining car was disconnected without warning when we stopped in Mongolia. By the time I made it to Beijing, I was so weak I wobbled when I walked. After ten days in Beijing I took a high-speed train to Shanghai. The difference between the two cities was immediate. Beijing, the historical hub of the country with its antique streets and its seven UNESCO World Heritage sites, made it feel five hundred years older than it's sleek sister.

Shanghai stretches to the sky so it's easy to lose track of where you are. It's a vertical city and I'm constantly looking up in awe at its architecture. The view from the Bund, a one-mile long waterfront promenade is one of the best I've ever seen; on the opposite side of the Huangpu River the skyscrapers are showcased each night. The bulbs in each building sparkle under the sky and some rooftops even disappear into the clouds (if they're lying low enough).

I manage to barter rooms for my work at three hotels in Shanghai, but it takes longer to get my Vietnamese visa than I expect, and I have to extend my stay at the last minute. The problem is I quickly run out of places to barter with on such short notice. Worse, I have to leave my passport for three days at the Consulate of Vietnam.

I zigzag up and down Sichuan North Road, go into every hotel I see, but the story is always the same: no passport, no room. I'm not even trying to barter anymore, just pay outright for a room, but none of them will even let me do that, not even when I show them the crinkled color photocopy of my passport. Although, even I have to admit the passport photo doesn't look like me; it's from seven years ago, when I was clean-shaven with short hair. Still, never in my wildest nightmares would I have anticipated so many hotels declining my money.

As dusk turns to darkness, it begins to rain. I decide to duck into a tiny café. I order an Americano, the cheapest thing on the menu, just so I can get access to the Wi-Fi. I decide to try the Yangtze Hotel, which was the first hotel I bartered with when I arrived in Shanghai. It was a beautiful, four-star hotel just a few blocks from the Bund in central Shanghai. I took about seventy photos for them and made a short two-minute film of their property, and they comped me five nights in return. I type out my predicament to Liz, my contact there, and I ask her if I can come back for just one more night, which should give me enough time to figure out my next move. I think this might work because they have my passport on file, so checking in there shouldn't be much of an issue. Plus, Liz was really on board with my overland attempt; she even helped me plan out the route I'll need to take to get across southern China and into Vietnam.

Liz responds just seconds after I click send: "Sorry, Eric, we are all out of complimentary rooms, and since you don't have your passport, unfortunately we cannot let you check in even if you were to pay for your own room."

Strike one.

I think about emailing Sue; she's my contact at a hostel I bartered with here. However, the hostel was like an infirmary, everyone constantly coughing all over everything, hunched over and shivering in the communal areas because the heat wasn't really working and the rooms were infested with mold. When Sue first showed me where I'd be staying, I asked, "Why are the windows open in the middle of winter?" Once I closed the window and caught the ungodly odor of the mold, I understood. I also started coughing so violently it felt like I had cracked my windpipe.

I gutted it out there for four nights, only going to my room to shower and sleep, but by the last night there, it became so excruciating that even if you paid me, I just couldn't go back.

So that's out, strike two.

The other hotel I bartered with in Shanghai was a small bed-and-breakfast called Quintet. It was in the French Concession, a neighborhood popular with expats, where the streets are lined with cool boutiques and coffee shops. I did a few photos for them in exchange for two nights, and it's possible that they might take me back for a night.

It's 6:58 p.m. and I remember that the owner, Po, leaves at 7:00 p.m. every night, and once she leaves, there is no way to get a room. Each houseguest has to check in before then, and if you need something after 7:00 p.m., then you're out of luck. I quickly pull up my Skype account and dial Po's local number.

Of course, the call doesn't go through. I look down at my phone and quickly realize that I forgot to set the country code; it automatically defaulted to the United States. I try it again, but this time I type in +86 in front of the number.

"Please answer!"

The call goes through and starts ringing.

"Damn, I bet she left already."

If she doesn't answer, I honestly don't know what I'll do for the night. I think about what it would be like to spend the night on the street in Shanghai. I look out the window; it reminds me of London, gray and raining. The only difference is there's a neon bowl of noodles glowing across the street.

Ring, ring, ring.

I gnaw at the skin around my fingernails as I wait for someone to pick up. Please pick up.

"Hello, Quintet B and B."

I can't help but ramble, "Po, oh Po, thank God you answered. This is Eric, I am the really tall guy that stayed at your B and B last week. I took photos of the rooms for you. I don't have my passport, long story, but none of the hotels in Shanghai will let me check in without it. I don't have anywhere to go tonight, and I'm hoping you have my passport on file. Do you think you could possibly give me a complimentary room again tonight?'

"Well, we have one room open, but we wouldn't be able to comp you again. We can give you a discount, though—how does 650 yuan sound?"

I quickly do the conversion in my head; that's about a hundred dollars.

"Well, Po, thank you, but I really can't afford that. What if I leave first thing in the morning, could you go even lower?"

"Hmmm, well, 500 yuan is as low as I can go, but I'm just about to leave for the day—can you get here right now?"

Even though eighty dollars is more money than I typically spend in a week, I'm officially out of options. I agree and thank her.

"Are you sure that I can check in without my passport?"

"If you get here in the next fifteen minutes, you can check in without it—we still have your information on file."

I hang up and take a breath to steady myself. Then I grab all of my things and sprint out into the soggy Shanghai night.

* * *

In my old life, before I set out around the world, I was a relatively healthy eater who only allowed for cheat meals after a raucous night of drinking with friends. But ever since Naomi turned me down, I've been doing a lot of emotional eating.

China is a food lover's paradise, and everything I've tried here is an explosion of flavors. I've eaten pork belly atop jade-colored tables and garlic prawns mixed with butter over a mountain of chili and spices that made my taste buds and temples sweat. I've plucked dumplings the size of bear paws out of steaming bamboo baskets on busy street corners. I've eaten all kinds of chicken—braised chicken, stewed chicken, deep-fried chicken, stir-fried chicken, and chicken that drips with molasses like barbeque sauce.

But McDonald's is the one and only place that's been able to provide me with any kind of familiar comfort. Well, that, and it's entirely possible I'm getting addicted to the food. When the combination of sugar, fat, and salt gets into my bloodstream, I'm left regretting the decision I made to come but also already counting down the time until I get to return.

Then there's the price. It's the cheapest food I can find. I can't afford the food at my hotel, a really fancy five-star Hilton in Haikou, an island in the South China Sea. The Hilton is set in a sprawling building with Romanesque pillars at every turn. My room is the definition of modern luxury and has a balcony that's bigger than my old apartment. The view from my room looks out over the hotel's never-ending maze of infinity pools, which run right up to a sugary beach. It's the nicest place I've ever stayed, and I obviously couldn't afford it on my own, not even for a night.

When I emailed the Hilton's marketing team a few weeks back, they didn't have any interest in letting me stay for free in exchange for my photography and film work, but my parents stepped in and helped out. They own a timeshare in the United States that was set to expire if it went unused by the end of the year. Since they weren't going to have time to use it, they exchanged their unused week and gifted it to me as my Christmas present so I could use it in China.

I think they could sense that I've been hanging by a thread lately and that I needed some sort of break. Crossing Russia and China during the middle of winter was far harder than I could have expected. When I arrived at the Hilton after a grueling, two-day train ride in a compartment crowded with people and saturated with cigarette smoke, the marble lobby and champagne spritzer that greeted me were the most welcome sight of my life. I nearly fell to my knees in appreciation.

My goal since arriving has been simple—to do nothing, to switch off. No writing, no filming, and especially no thinking. I've been staying up late watching the kind of mindless shows on Netflix that I normally avoid, lounging by the pool during the long and lazy afternoons, and then sneaking off to McDonald's for dinner almost every night.

"Merry Christmas, Ronald, Merry Christmas," I mutter sarcastically as I give the ceramic statue of Ronald McDonald a high five.

I shake my head in shame as I walk under the Golden Arches and into China's best attempt at Americana for the fifth time this week. I keep my eyes down to make myself as small as possible and quickly make my way to the register. I want to get this over with as soon as possible for two reasons. First, because of my size, everyone in China stares at me every time I step out in public. Second, I'm embarrassed to be eating my Christmas dinner alone at McDonald's.

I begin the process of trying to order. Key word: trying.

"I'll have the number two value meal, hold the onions, and then two double cheeseburgers, also without onions."

The employee, Chung, looks as though he's seen a ghost; he has no idea what I just said. I can't blame him; I'm the one in a foreign land. Imagine the look someone would get trying to order a Big Mac in Chinese in Oklahoma or Atlanta. I should be speaking his language or at least trying to speak his language, but I don't have the energy or desire to learn a single word of Chinese. Based on my time here so far, I can't imagine ever wanting to come back.

As I try to think of another way to place my order, I get that *here we go again feeling*. Every single thing I've done since I stepped foot in this country has been about as fun as a trip to the dentist.

I hate to say this, but it's the Chinese people themselves who have been testing my patience. I expect to be stared at because of my height, but not laughed at, which happens about thirty times a day. I don't know if you've ever had someone walk up to you and laugh in your face for no reason and then turn and run away without saying anything, but after a while, it starts to rub you the wrong way. It's become such an issue that I only go out in public if it's absolutely necessary.

I hate it here.

I point at the blazing red-and-yellow McDonald's menu behind Chung's head and hold up two fingers.

He smiles politely as he punches in my order.

"Hold on, Chung, I'm not done."

I want to order two more double burgers, but here's where I've been running into problems all week. The number two value meal is actually the double burger meal, and I don't know how to explain with body language and hand signs that I want two additional double burgers instead of two additional number two value meals. Essentially, there are too many twos; it's a lot for anyone to handle even if we did speak the same language.

I hold up two fingers and, as expected, Chung thinks I want an additional number two value meal. I point to a picture of fries on the menu and wave *no, no, no* with my arms. Chung gets the message behind my madness and types in just the two extra burgers.

"Okay, good. Now we're getting somewhere."

I think he's got my order right so far, and I admire his patience because mine was left for dead a few weeks back. But before either of us can celebrate, there's still one big hurdle: I loathe onions, from their smell to their texture to their taste. I pull my phone out of my pocket and open an archaic app that translates English words into Chinese phrases. It's the only translator that's free and works offline. I type in the word *onions*, and the only thing that comes up in Chinese is the sentence, "I can eat anything other than onions."

It's not exactly what I'm trying to say, but I show Chung the Chinese characters on my screen, hoping that he will put two and two together.

Chung slides my order over on a green plastic tray, and I duck into a dirty corner booth in the back of the establishment. As expected, everyone is watching me like I'm going to do something crazy like take off all my clothes and eat with my feet. I unwrap my burger with the utmost care, like I want to save the paper so I can use it again next year. Then I lean in for a bite. Since everyone is still staring at me, I close my eyes as I begin to chew. The salty burger is a welcome shock to my system, and it takes me far away from this tiny island in the South China Sea. It takes me home. I'm gathered around the Christmas tree with my family. My dad's blasting the Andy Williams song "It's Beginning to Look a Lot Like Christmas," which in my family means that it's time to open the first present. My mother is rolling her eyes and telling him to calm down and to turn the music down while secretly enjoying his enthusiasm. I'm reaching under the tree, hoping for the latest Sega Genesis game or WWF action figure. Our dog, Niko, caught up in the excitement, is running laps around the tree like all of the presents are for him.

I go in for a second bite still thinking about Christmases gone by, and immediately I'm thrust back to real time.

I swish the bite around my mouth just to be sure. My eyes fly open, and I peel back the bun.

Onions.

* * *

I don't have a bucket list anymore, but if I did, Ha Long Bay in Vietnam would be at the top of it. It was first listed as a UNESCO World Heritage Site because of its "outstanding, universal aesthetic value." It has been a dream destination ever since I saw it in a *Travel and Leisure* magazine ten years ago. I would pay full price to see it even on my shoestring budget.

The bay features thousands of limestone karsts and isles that have formed over five hundred million years. Each limestone island is topped with thick jungle vegetation and rises spectacularly from the ocean. Five hundred years ago, Nguyen Trai praised the beauty of Ha Long Bay in *Lộ nhập Vân Đồn*, calling it "Rock wonder in the sky." There's something about the emerald labyrinth of channels and hidden lagoons that's been calling my name.

I somehow stumble out of the fog and funk I've been in traveling through Russia and China and land smack-dab in the middle of this dream project. After the bitter cold in Siberia killed the motherboard in my camera, I had it repaired in Shanghai and shipped it to Hanoi Central Backpackers Hostel in Vietnam, so that it's waiting for me at the front desk. The hostel also happens to run a tour company out of their lobby, and the marquee tour is a two-day backpackers booze cruise through the same picturesque waters of Ha Long Bay I'd taped onto my gigantic vision board way back in Miami Beach.

On the bus, I literally cannot stop talking. I work my way up and down the aisles like a politician hungry for votes, asking everyone where they're from and what they do for a living. Eight scruffy Argentinean backpackers; three Australian couples; two British women; a few sets of Dutch, Danish, and Norwegian couples; one Japanese traveler; myself; and our guide have a four-hour bus ride to the Quang Nihn Province in Northern Vietnam ahead of us.

I must have said, "Hi, my name is Eric. It's nice to meet you," to every single person, and we haven't even left the parking lot. It's so unlike me. I'm typically quiet and reserved and tend to keep to myself whenever I'm around a big group of rowdy backpackers, but today I want to know everything about everyone.

As I'm talking to a group of Argentinean guys in the back of the bus about the River Plate–Boca Juniors soccer rivalry, which takes place in their hometown of Buenos Aires, our Vietnamese tour guide interrupts us. He stands up at the front of the bus and announces, "My name is Tuan, but you can call me Snake." Then he smiles slyly and swivels his hips like he's auditioning for Chippendales.

Snake's playful gyration and smile is infectious, and even though he's only five foot two, his energy is bigger than the bus. After the laughs and catcalls die down, he pulls out his clipboard and starts going over our itinerary for the next two days.

When Toi, the owner of the hostel, told me about the tour company he runs, I perked up and quickly offered him an idea. "Toi," I said, "besides doing photos of the rooms and restaurant here at your hostel, if you can get me a complimentary seat on the next tour to Ha Long Bay, I will put together an amazing film for you that you can use to promote your booze cruise."

Toi looked me over like I had a hidden agenda, which of course I did, but then he agreed once he realized that sending me along to film the tour wouldn't cost him a dime. He found space for me on the next bus out of Hanoi, and all I have to do in exchange for the trip is to film it.

Toi told me that he wants me to get absolutely plastered. He said, "In order for you to get the full booze cruise experience, you need to act as though you're a backpacker and not a filmmaker." He wants me to kayak and swim, and he insisted that I jump off the roof of the boat with a beer in hand at sunset. He wants me to dance, play drinking games, and party all night long.

I'm not much of a drinker anymore, but who in their right mind could turn all that down?

After Snake finishes going over the itinerary, I work my way back toward the front of the bus with my camera in hand. I sit next to Dan, an Australian electrician, and immediately begin to bond with the guy. As we're getting to know one another, I notice he has brought along a garbage bag filled with party-sized bags of potato chips. For a two-day trip.

Typically this is the kind of thing I'd ignore, but for some reason I just can't stop running my mouth.

Dan chuckles as he starts in on his explanation. "I was buying a few bags of crisps for the bus ride today, and the Vietnamese woman working in the store came over to me and said, 'Buy eight, get one for free.'"

Dan's buddy Rodney affectionately chimes in, "You idiot. That cannot be a real sale, mate. You're the only person dumb enough to believe her."

"Ah, shud up, would ya?" Dan sarcastically snaps back before continuing. "So this little old Vietnamese lady just started stuffing bag after bag into my cart, and I didn't know what to do. I couldn't say no. At one point she had seven bags piled up, and it was like if I just buy one more, then I get the next one for free."

Dan holds up his garbage bag like he's just caught a five-foot trout and says, "So I ended up with nine bags of crisps. I didn't know what to do with them, so I brought them on the trip!"

Everyone in the front of the bus, including me, erupts into laughter. Dan has clearly been hustled. I know the feeling well, so his story has nearly got me in tears. He retells it a second and third time, and the story only gets funnier to us all as he adds details, like how he tried to check his potato chip trash bag into the hostel's luggage lounge just before we left, but they wouldn't allow it. Hearing that pushes me over the edge. I'm hunched over and panting and grabbing my sides to keep them from exploding.

I've been so isolated the past two months that I've kept my mouth all but shut. Not only have I been keeping everyone at arm's length, but I couldn't tell you the last time I laughed, like really laughed a sidesplitting laugh.

Until now.

As Dan tells the potato chip story yet again to another group of passengers, I can feel the enthusiasm that had dried up and deserted me begin to course through my veins again. I feel this silly serum slide down my shoulders and up my arms. Then, as it seeps through my core, my heart begins to flare up and drum to a new beat.

Each time I laugh, it burns away a bad memory of the past few months and reminds me why I'm doing this. For me, travel has always been about the people, not the places, and that's what I've forgotten lately.

And it is why I can't stop talking today.

I am on a bus bouncing toward one of my dream destinations; the sun is shining, I'm surrounded by wonderful people from all over the world, I've got my camera on my lap, and I haven't had to pay a dime for any of it. I've worked so incredibly hard to get here, and if I can't enjoy this, then I can't enjoy anything.

I look out the front window, knowing that I've found my resolve and thinking that perhaps the open road is in fact where I belong after all.

That thought is hammered home ten hours later when I snap a photo of the bay and then pass my camera over to Dan so he can hold it for me. I step to the edge of our traditional Chinese junk boat and let my toes curl off its side. I'm three stories up, and I've got a Heineken in my hands. I chug down the rest of my beer while everyone I've befriended on the boat chants my name from the deck behind me.

I want to make sure I don't miss anything about this moment. I gleefully gaze across the water's edge at the stunning seascape in an effort to freeze all these feelings of fun in my mind. The last droplets of daylight are drying up in the sky, and a purple sun is dipping into an emerald ocean like a cookie into milk. I glance back at the group of people I've spent the day alongside with a smile that stretches from ear to ear. I give a thumbs-up to the guys from Argentina who have offered to take me to a Boca Juniors game if I ever make it to Buenos Aires.

And then I jump.

As I sink under the surface, a deep satisfaction washes over me.

I have fallen back in love with my journey.

CHAPTER 10
THAILAND – INDONESIA
ASIA

"Life will give you whatever experiences are most helpful for the evolution of your consciousness."

— *Eckhart Tolle*

I T FEELS ABOUT A THOUSAND degrees inside this sizzling Cambodian bus, and of course the air-conditioning isn't working. It's a fourteen-hour bus ride from Siem Reap to Bangkok, Thailand. The bathroom at the back of the bus isn't working either, so I've hardly drunk any water the whole day because I have this weird fear that I'll have to ask for an emergency stop and relieve myself on the side of the road in front of everyone. In the midst of my misery, I think about Naomi.

There were so many happy couples cuddling during the booze cruise, by the end of the night, I couldn't help but feel empty without her. She's still my favorite person to be around and the deepest connection I've ever made. When she turned down my offer to meet up in Beijing, it was devastating. However, she also wrote, "Maybe I can meet you again someday down the road."

I'm holding on to that sliver of hope she left me. In the back of my mind I've been thinking that we'll eventually find our way back together. So just before I left Hanoi, I wrote her again and asked her if she'd rejoin me out here on the road.

Naomi hasn't said yes yet to meeting me, but she also wouldn't say no. Over the past few weeks in Cambodia, I've begun to feel strung along, always waiting and wanting to hear something definitive from her.

When I was waiting for her to respond to my first invitation, to meet me in Beijing, she was living in a Buddhist temple in Thailand and didn't have access to the internet. Now she's back in Miami Beach, and yet nothing's changed. I still barely hear from her. During our rare Skype conversations, I end up feeling like a used car salesman trying to sell her on the same clunker she's already test-driven and turned down.

As a result, I'm not out living life like I should be. When I showed up to Angkor Wat, a crimson sunrise silhouetted the crumbling cone-like Khemr temple towers. I should have been in awe at the sight. Instead, I shrugged my shoulders, snapped a few photos, then left so I could check my email. For a few days there in Siem Reap, I slipped into a hapless state where I thought that maybe I wasn't worthy of love. *From anyone.*

The closer we get to Bangkok the quicker the landscape changes, from waterlogged farmland to midsized brick buildings, which eventually give way to a sprawling skyline. The city smells like fried fish as it's smack dab in the middle of the Chao Phraya River delta and the interconnected waterways are ten times busier here than they are in Venice.

Bangkok is vibrant and everything about it is exciting. Food hawkers sell skewered meat underneath red and yellow neon signs, while the buzz and horns of what seems like a hundred speeding three-wheeled tuk tuks fill every street. But I'm too miserable to truly pay attention to any of it as I practically fall into a cab and direct the driver to my hotel.

#

The first thing I do my first morning in Bangkok is lift up the receiver on the phone and press zero. I hear a voice on the other end and make a desperate plea, "Can you please have the housekeeper bring ten bottles of water up to my room immediately? I don't feel so—"

Before I can finish the thought, I drop the phone and make a mad dash for the bathroom. My stomach tumbles like a bag of rocks in a washing machine.

I push the bathroom door open with what little strength is left in my body and fall to my knees.

I rock from side to side, and cold sweat oozes from every pore. As the bathroom begins to spin, I try to fight it. I reach for a bottle of pink Pepto-Bismol that's on the sink and take a shot like I'm at a bar with my buddies. Then I put a damp washcloth around my neck in a futile attempt to calm my body, but the hot and cold flashes keep steamrolling through me.

I crawl over to the toilet and kneel before it like it's the holiest of Thai temples. I stop fighting and give myself permission to let it fly. The bathroom begins to blur.

I fold my arms on the toilet seat and rest my head against my arms while I wait for the next army of parasites to mobilize. I'm dazed but not confused; I know full well what's going on. This is a soul-cleansing experience, but I can't help but wish that I didn't have to turn my insides out in order to move on.

I lie back on the cool tile floor, knowing that although it's not the most romantic of places, it's time. I know that this is much worse than severe dehydration—it's the final scene in the final act of the play that is my love life. This is Naomi's soul disentangling from mine and leaving my body, forever.

Kahlil Gibran envisions the soul not as a presence locked inside your brain or body but as an entity that can be everywhere at once: "The soul walks upon all paths. The soul walks not upon a line, neither does it grow like a reed. The soul unfolds itself, like a lotus of countless petals."

Ever since I left America, it feels as though I've been walking upon my path. And in turn, I've been getting to know not just myself but my soul. Through all the trials and tribulations of trying to find, follow, and then stick with my dreams, it's been inevitable. At my core, I'm not this six-foot-ten-inch American man with long dark hair who likes English soccer, white sandy beaches, and double cheeseburgers (without onions). There is so much more to all of us than our skin and bones and what we've come to know in this lifetime.

Courage, creativity, and cultures have been the conduit, and my soul has blossomed inside me with each shot I've snapped and bus ride I've sat through. And because of it, my faith is filled with firsthand experiences that transcend anything I've ever been taught.

So as I stare up at the ceiling, I ask for Naomi's soul to rise to the surface of my skin.

Within seconds, it does. Her presence is so palpable that I can practically feel her touch on my skin. Then I hear her voice, and the first thing she tells me is that she too knows that it's time to do this.

Next, she says that she is uncharacteristically sick today, stuck in bed with a bad sinus problem, and that my soul is choosing to leave her body through her nose. We have a good laugh about that because the most sensitive part of my body has always been my nose; I broke it badly while playing basketball when I was in high school, and it has given me problems ever since.

"I'm snot, how fitting," I say.

For this final good-bye, we don't need to rehash what happened in Africa; we are just one cloudlike spirit that knows it's time to travel in different directions. Our bones and bodies are of no use to us in this moment, and we've come together in this final congress in a love that knows no opposite. I feel her soul push through my pores and then watch it swirl around the room like steam rising from a teapot. After it mixes and mingles with mine one last time, our particles fully peel apart. It's a thing of beauty.

As her spirit floats toward the ceiling, we're instantly freed from the spell we've both been under. The roller coaster ride we've been on for the past two years has come to an end.

Naomi wishes me well and tells me that I'm going to become all the things I'm trying to become.

I thank her for every moment we shared together and tell her that I'll always be there for her if she ever needs me.

Simultaneously our souls say, "I love you," and then, simply, one final good-bye.

* * *

Five years ago, when I was traveling as part of my three-month leave of absence, I got lost on a chalky road in Malaysia's capital city, Kuala Lumpur. I happened to stop outside a towering Hindu temple while trying to recalibrate the sense of direction that always seems to be eluding me. I had certainly never come across any place even remotely similar to the soaring structure that stood before me.

The outside of the five-tiered entrance rose high into the sky and was decorated with hundreds of colorful figures. Some had eight arms like Dr. Octopus, and they reminded me of comic book characters I watched on

TV when I was a child; others had animal heads and human bodies. I had never seen anything like this in all my life, and I wondered what kind of person could believe in so many gods that all looked so different from one another.

As I walked around the outside of the temple that day, wondering what to do next, I thought of something Ralph Waldo Emerson was quoted as saying: "I like the silent church before the service begins, better than any preaching." I decided that since the temple was empty, and because I was lost, that it was a sign.

I slipped off my shoes and entered the interior prayer hall. Sounds from a percussion instrument immediately put me on edge. The temple wasn't quite empty after all. Two men were stepping slowly in adoration around its perimeter. One held a serunai that made a sound like a high-pitched English horn, and the other circled while beating a calfskin drum. The deeper into the temple I walked, the darker the sounds became.

I forced myself forward.

Once inside the prayer hall, shades of blue and purple exploded around me. Multiple shades of violet eased into lavender, which complemented the lilac that spread across the interior's onion-shaped dome. Just a minute before, I was schlepping through the streets like a lost tourist, and then suddenly everything around me began to dissolve into an elegant orchid.

It is said that purple or violet assists those who seek the meaning of life and spiritual fulfillment; it expands their awareness, connecting them to a higher consciousness. For this reason, the color is associated with transformation of the soul. If someone exudes a purple aura, this is said to be the highest vibration of the human spirit.

The closer I got to the belly of the temple, the louder the serunai played. It rose to near-deafening levels, as though its shrieking was attempting to pierce not only my eardrums but also my soul. I could feel my fears just beneath the surface of my skin, and I couldn't help but start to question if I should even be there. But instead of turning back, I let the experience rush through me.

As I stepped closer to the shrine, the large temple bell rang out. I hesitated before stepping out onto the raised cobalt floor, unsure of local customs. The belly of the sanctum was polished so finely that it looked like a sheet of glass and reflected the ceiling, creating funhouse-like illusions.

After a deep breath to steady myself, I gingerly stepped toward the front of the temple, each tentative touch pulling the shrine closer. Every time I planted my bare foot, chills broke over my body. The drumbeat grew more insistent.

I arrived at the foot of the shrine and was now face-to-face with something I knew nothing about. The man with the calfskin drum closed in on me and then called out in English, "This is Mariamman." The deity was about six feet tall and radiated a pink hue from her cheeks. She wore a maroon dress trimmed with light green that matched the base of the shrine. The man continued, "One of her hands is displaying a mudra, which wards off fear." I looked toward one of her other hands, which held a trident. "That weapon is said to destroy the three worlds—the past, present, and future. Once each world is destroyed and turned into a single plane of existence, that is bliss."

I stared at the goddess, and a powerful internal force swirled at the base of my bones. As the transformative energy continued to course through my chakras, I closed my eyes and for the first time ever experienced perfect stillness.

It was like I was swept up into the stars.

The drumbeat slowed, matching the rhythm of my heart.

I had no idea how long I was standing there, but as I glided off the temple floor, I could feel my whole body begin to tingle.

Before leaving the temple, I stopped at a giant bronze statue of Ganesh, which had been watching over me the entire time.

Ganesh immediately captured my imagination. He is the elephant deity; he is the lord of success and destroyer of evil and obstacles. Ganesh's head symbolizes the Atman or the soul, which is the ultimate reality of human existence. Ganesh has eight arms, and in his upper right hand he holds a goad or axe, which helps to rid the path of obstacles. The noose in his left hand is to pull him to the highest goal.

One thing I've grown to love about Ganesh since that day is that he not only removes obstacles but also places them in his own path, for his own growth. This idea resonates with me. I think of the death-defying bus rides, the back-and-forth breakups with Naomi, getting stranded in Siberia. It makes me decide to get a tattoo of Ganesh while I'm in Thailand, as a tribute to that momentous day and to what Ganesh and obstacles have come to mean to me since. I've kept a picture of Ganesh in my journal and I even took it to a few tattoo parlors in London, but getting it done in England felt out of place.

Electromagnetic coils buzz. A needle digs into my skin, and black ink squirts across my forearm like a Jackson Pollock painting. I want to look tough, so I pretend like I don't even notice what's happening. Thankfully, Phuket is about the easiest place on the planet to get distracted. Across the street, big shiny silver letters spell out Patong Beach. I've walked down from my secluded hotel at the southern end of the croissant shaped beach to the bustling Bangla Road. At night neon lights illuminate this section of the small city and party people in search of loud music and cheap drinks clog its closed roads. The end of the afternoons are much more relaxing than the evenings and I set my eyes between the swaying palm trees that divide the street from the sand.

A woman is getting strapped into a colorful rainbow parachute, and there's about fifty yards of rope between her and the speedboat.

As the needle cuts into my arm for a second time, she starts running down the beach. Just as she's about to hit the ocean's edge, she gets sucked up into Phuket's pink sunset like a modern-day Mary Poppins. The boat twists and twirls around the bay for a few minutes while a handful of bronzed Thai men sell coconuts on the beach beneath her.

The smell of spicy pad Thai from the restaurant next door rolls through the inside of the tattoo parlor like a rogue wave. After four hours, Ukrit finally squirts disinfectant on my arm for the last time. He wipes away the excess ink and I look down at the tattoo that now takes up my entire left forearm.

I guess it's fitting that I decided to get this tattoo today because just this morning I was dealt yet another massive blow in my quest to make it around the world without a single airline flight. Just after breakfast, I received an email from Julie, my contact at Freighter Expeditions, telling me that the cargo ship that was supposed to take me from Singapore to Fremantle next month had been sold to another shipping company, and all future voyages of the MS *Victory* had been cancelled, effective immediately. This means my journey is at a halt. The MS *Victory* was the only option I'd found that could take me from Southeast Asia to Australia.

But instead of letting this Impossible Idea get the better of me once again, I clicked the email closed and smiled. I've been down this road before. It's just another obstacle that Ganesh and I will have to cut down and then pull ourselves past.

I am not worried. The blade on my axe is as sharp as it's ever been.

* * *

The only option on such short notice for getting to Australia without flying, I discover, is by cruise ship. After a fourteen-day trip around Southeast Asia, the *Sun Princess* will dock in Fremantle, near Perth. While I'm happy to have found an answer to my dilemma, that answer is three times the price that the MS *Victory* was. I try to make sure I get my money's worth by bellying up to the buffet as often as my insides will allow.

Even though this is the type of touristy travel I've purposely avoided thus far, it's kind of nice to take my hands off the reins and let the ship do all the steering. Life on board the *Sun Princess* tends to move a bit slower than the blistering pace I travel at. There are no crazy belly flop or bikini contests, and nobody's shot-gunning beers by the pool. This isn't that kind of cruise. The wildest thing I've seen so far are the daily Zumba dance classes that happen at noon around the lip of the pool. The cruise director puts a funny-looking bleached-blond wig on, and the DJ plays all the horrible hits from the 1990s that should have stayed in the 1990s. When he blasts "Who Let the Dogs Out," that's usually the cue that gets the conga line going.

When we arrive in Bali, I set the timer on my phone for six hours as I plant one foot firmly on Tanjung Benoa's floating dock. Four rows of Balinese dancers and drummers are in the midst of the *Panyembrahma*, a traditional welcome performance. The women are wrapped in stunning pink-and-gold–patterned sarongs and carrying silver dishes filled with flowers and incense. They're moving in unison to traditional gamelan music that the men seated behind them are creating from just two instruments, hand-played drums and metallophones (similar to xylophones).

There's a pushy, fanny pack–wearing Australian couple next to me and, with our cruise ship bobbing in the background, I must admit that it all feels a bit touristy. But for the moment, I'm just as much of a typical tourist as everyone else, so I lighten up and allow myself to soak in the festive atmosphere.

Everyone who hasn't prearranged an island tour is funneled through a weathered welcome center and into a big gravel parking lot. I push through a pack of friendly, but hungry, Balinese taxi drivers who are ready to swarm anyone that looks in their general direction, letting all the other tourists get swallowed up first.

Once I get about fifty yards away, I turn back and wave over one of the drivers that's lingering on the outskirts of the mob.

"I need to get to Ubud to meet a friend. How much?"

"It's very, very, very far," says the man.

I playfully roll my eyes and say, "I've been to Ubud before, and it's not that far. So how much is it really?"

"It's very, very, very far."

I let out a little laugh; this is beautiful Bali, after all—palm trees and a relaxing breeze surround us. "Okay, so how much is it to go very, very, very far?"

"Twenty dollars."

I look down at my phone; we've only been given six hours on the island. I decide not to haggle but instead ask him to hurry.

We head north in his beat-up Pontiac Sunfire through Denpasar, which is the capital of Bali, and then we cut through a dense maze of roads, the tropical overgrowth threatening to take over each one. When I see a pet store offering holistic healing for animals, it hits me that I'm back in Bali. It is truly one of my favorite places on earth.

The streets on the way to Ubud are about as confusing as they come. Each one looks nearly identical to the last, and most are lined with fresh fruit stands, herbal medicine shops, and open-air stalls selling statues. I'm not exaggerating when I say that Bali offers an endless supply of statues. With tourism being one of the main forms of income for Balinese families, you're never more than a few feet from Buddha, Ganesh, Shiva, and all the other Hindu gods carved into granite, tropical teakwood, or anything else people can get their hands on.

Within the hour, my driver drops me off at the entrance of the Monkey Forest in Ubud. I get out and pay him in US dollars while monkeys bark and screech at one another in the background.

The Ubud Monkey Forest follows a traditional philosophy that most of the island of Bali subscribes to. The Hindu principal *Tri Hita Karana* translates as, "Three causes of well-being," which seeks to make people live in harmony with each other, nature, and the Supreme God. Accordingly, the Monkey Forest has a philosophical goal of creating peace and harmony for all its visitors. The monkeys are free to come and go as they please and are not kept in cages or assigned viewing areas. The last time I was here, one snuck up behind me and climbed onto my shoulders. I'd be lying if I said I wasn't scared to death when I first felt his palms patter across my back.

When I think of Ubud, though, I don't think of monkeys, I think of expats. More specifically, I think of Western women with nose rings and dreadlocks. I've only been here for five minutes, and I must have already seen ten women fitting that description. This hippie haven seems to attract every free-spirited, yoga-loving, clean-eating, inner peace–seeking person on the planet. I've never been able to tell if people here are running away from their problems or running toward life's deepest answers.

Ubud is a draw in part because it's the cultural heartbeat of Bali, and it's as far away from the beach and party scene of Kuta as one could get. Ubud is surrounded by mountains and defined by the terraced rice paddies that are etched into the sides of those mountains. They look like stairs built for men ten times my size, and I could be content if that's all I ever had to look at the rest of this lifetime. Balinese traditions are still very much alive in the center of the island. Sacred temples and cultural heritage sites can be found around every bend in its rain-forested roads, and the galleries in the center of town are filled to the brim with colorful local art. Last time I was here, I took a vinyasa yoga class at the Yoga Barn, an open-air studio with panoramic views of a rice field. This is definitely the part of the island where people come to exhale, and if anyone were to attain eternal peace, I wouldn't be surprised if this is where they found it.

I glance at the time on my phone. My Balinese buddy Dek should already be here, but there's no sign of him. I can't call him because I don't have cell service in Indonesia, so I duck into a café and order a coffee that comes with a piece of dark Balinese chocolate so I can gain access to their Wi-Fi.

Bali's climate is perfect for growing coffee and chocolate. Local farmers are organized in a system called Subak Abian, and they grow most of Bali's coffee. Subak Abian subscribes to the same Hindu philosophy as the Monkey Forest, the *Tri Hita Karana*. This means that the coffee is grown organically, specifically with "happiness with the environment" in mind. There is also an interesting and unexpected twist to coffee in Bali.

Kopi Luwak, which is the type of coffee I just ordered, is brewed from beans that have been passed through the digestive system of a civet—a raccoon-like creature. The enzymes inside the civet's stomach remove the bitterness from the beans and create this wonderfully smooth and sweet coffee.

By the time I'm halfway finished with mine, I finally get through to Dek, who tells me that he's at a wedding and that he will be here soon.

I'm reminded that I'm in Bali and that I need to relax. People don't move at my antsy Western pace here, and almost every day has some sort of important religious ceremony tied to it. Every time I've talked to Dek since we met, he's either been coming from or going to a temple for some kind of ceremony.

I originally met Dek through a woman I went to grad school with. I was halfway through my three-month leave of absence and had four days in Bali. Twenty-five-year-old Dek, who was just starting his own tour company, agreed to show me the sights around Ubud at a discounted rate. I was one of his first clients, but it's impossible for anyone to meet Dek and not immediately forget that he's running a business. He's tall, tan, and the sweetest of souls.

My favorite memory of Dek is when he took me to Goa Gajah, also called the Elephant Cave. The façade of the cave is a rock wall carved with demons that are said to ward off evil spirits, and it looks like a setting straight out of the movie *Tomb Raider*. At the time, I was a little stressed out because I wasn't sure what I was going to do after my leave of absence and was burning through my life savings like it was going out of style.

I was just starting to realize that I couldn't return to my stale corporate job, but I also didn't have the faintest clue about what else I could do with my life. After we left the Elephant Cave, which is a meditation cave that has no relationship with actual elephants, we were walking alongside a small stream that ran up against a beautiful rice paddy. As Dek strolled a few steps ahead of me, he unselfconsciously began singing to himself.

The island breeze carried his brilliant Balinese accent up and over the rice field and back to me. He was singing the same lyrics over and over, one of Bob Marley's most famous lines, telling us not to worry because everything would be all right.

Those lyrics whittled their way into my psyche, and I stopped stressing about what I was going to do after my leave of absence ended.

Ever since then, I've not only believed in those words but felt like I understand their very essence. Even though I've obviously worried my fair share since that day, I've never strayed far from the last part of that verse, *that every little thing is* in fact *gonna be all right.*

So today, I want to repay the favor to Dek. I want to create a two-minute film of the tour Dek offers in hopes that it will lead to more business for him and his family. And I want to create a short film of beautiful Bali just for me. I want to get back to filming and photographing today in a way that nourishes my soul. I don't want to do it for likes on social media or in exchange for a place to stay; I want to do it because it makes me feel good.

Just as I finish the last sip of my coffee, Dek pulls up alongside me in a white minivan with a small red-and-white Indonesian flag hanging from the rearview mirror. I've made a handful of new friends since I began traveling, but there is something special to be said for seeing an old one.

I hop in and tell Dek that it looks like he has actually gotten younger since I saw him last, which is God's honest truth. After we stop laughing, I ask him to take me to the fountain of youth he's found here in Bali instead of the agenda we've already mapped out.

We're retracing our route from five years ago, and as Dek drives us through back roads that are overflowing with every shade of green the earth has on offer, I stick my GoPro camera to his dashboard and begin filming.

My thoughts return to the last time I was here. Had you handed me a DSLR camera and a GoPro and asked me to document Dek's tour, I'd have looked at you like you had ten heads. But now I'm at ease with my equipment and confident in my abilities. Creativity isn't inborn like I'd always assumed; it's more like a muscle. And just like doing reps at the gym to strengthen my biceps and triceps, curling my camera up to my eyes every day is doing the same to my artistic abilities. Inspiration feels like it's everywhere, and my eyes seem to envelop every inch of my surroundings now. And just like Johnny promised way back in my beginner photography class, all I see are possibilities. I'm finally feeling as though I'm able to express myself in all the ways I'd initially set out to do. Even writing has become easier.

At the Elephant Cave some fifteen minutes later, Dek and I work our way down a series of steps to the bathing pools that were built in the ninth century. Five Hindu statues holding vases act as waterspouts and fountains, which fill the stone pools in the courtyard with fresh water. Directly behind the pools is the entrance of the Elephant Cave. I unfold my tripod next to a patch of neon-green moss, feeling as though I've finally found my formula.

CHAPTER 11
AUSTRALIA

AUSTRALIA

"For my part, I travel not to go anywhere, but to go.
I travel for travel's sake. The great affair is to move."

— *Robert Louis Stevenson*

MUSIC HAS NEVER REALLY BEEN my thing, but Nina Simone's voice is running through me like a river as I wheel Timberland through Perth's Langley Park. She tells the birds and the sun in the sky that they know how she feels.

I call out over my earbuds, "Yesss! I know that feeling too!"

It's late afternoon in Perth, Australia's largest city on the west coast, and it's the end of the workweek. The temperature's inviting, and the air tastes like candy. Langley Park is a long walk; its football field-size lawn separates the city's shiny skyline from the sea and symmetrically spaced palm and pine trees line its perimeter. The birds, the sun, the sky, and the breeze are all showing off today as if they know I'm listening to a song that just mentioned them. One spotted dove in particular catches my eye; it glides by close enough that I could reach up and catch it if I wanted to. The city itself was rated the seventh best city in the world to live in by CNN this year, which actually seems like an insult now that I'm here. Perth is perfect, and even though it's technically fall here, it's one of those

Indian summer afternoons that feels like the evening won't show up until just seconds before the end of time.

As Nina Simone gracefully eases into the chorus and then hammers home the last line of it over the brass section that's backing her up, I can't help but sing along like I'm alone in the shower about a new dawn and a new day and a new life.

By the time I make it halfway up Hill Street, the smile on my face says it all. At the heights of my journey, I've been happy—really happy— but never like this.

After a left onto Hay Street, I prop Timberland up next to me and wait at the Red CAT bus stop. I need to head west around Saint Mary's Cathedral and then a few blocks north to Northbridge, which is the cultural hub of the city. The Alex Hotel, which is hosting me for a weekend's stay, is a luxury hotel with views of the stunning glass façade of the State Theatre Centre of Western Australia.

This will be the fourth hotel in a row that has agreed not only to a complimentary room but also to the three hundred dollar fee I've decided to set for my film and photography work. I've already got more hotels lined up across Australia that have agreed to this same deal, which means that by the end of May, I should turn my first real profit as a traveling photographer and filmmaker.

I'm also more at peace about my relationship with Naomi. Ever since that final soul-cleansing good-bye in a Thailand bathroom, there's been no more checking of emails, hoping for signs, or wishing for her to meet up with me. All the sadness of our breakup has been vacuumed out of me as if Hoover created a special attachment specifically for my heart, and I feel ready to love again. And here's the kicker: because of this new inner peace, I've been able to attract other women into my life for the first time in what feels like forever. I even have a date tonight with a tall beautiful blond Australian girl named Samantha, who's taking me to a "footy" game.

I'm now free from the psychological grip my past relationship had on me, and I'm unconcerned for what the future holds for my finances because I've got a pocket full of cash for the first time since I left for Africa. This leaves only one place to be. I've been sucked through that beautiful wormhole that's known as the present. Eckhart Tolle wrote, "When you honor, acknowledge, and fully accept your present reality—where you are, who you are, what you are doing right now—when you fully accept what you have got, you are grateful for what you have got, grateful for what *is*, grateful for Being. Gratitude for the present moment and fullness of *life now* is true prosperity."

The odds have been stacked against me since day one—a writer who couldn't write, a photographer who didn't own a camera, a world-traveling wannabe who had miles of credit card debt—yet here I am. Or here *we* are, my dreams and I, still going strong. We've finally arrived at the only destination we've ever wanted to get to: the present.

* * *

Samantha is perfect on paper. She's a beautiful blonde with legs that go on for days. Her mom is South African and her dad is Australian, so her accent alone makes my knees weak. She has a good job, she's intelligent, and I can tell by the way she treats people that she'll be a really great mother one day. She's exactly the kind of woman that any man would be chomping at the bit take home to meet his own mother, and as an added bonus, she's really interested in everything I'm doing.

But here's the problem with paper. I don't live on it. My old life, the one I grew to detest, sounded pretty good on paper too.

Samantha, like my old life, has everything I'm supposed to want, but as much as I want to fall for her, I can't. That spark, that fire that I need, the one that's fueling my journey around the world, just isn't there for me. And that's making things really difficult right now. As she drives us through Perth's symmetrical streets and past the entrance gate of Kings Park, I can tell she's falling for me—or at least for the idea of me.

Now, I don't think I'm anything all that special, but to her, I'm a tall, dark, and handsome stranger who's swooped into town at exactly the right time in her life. I've also got that mysterious starving artist thing going for me right now; I have long, wild hair and a new tattoo, and I arrived in Australia on a ship, having chased my passions halfway around the world. Just the other day, as we were sipping coffees on Hay Street, she leaned into me and blushed as she confided, "I've been praying for someone like you to come to town and sweep me off my feet the past few weeks."

Over the past few days, she has taken me to a "footy" game at the Subiaco Oval, where we sipped wine in the stands and cuddled underneath a blanket while laughing about not understanding the rules of the game, and to Cottesloe Beach, where we enjoyed a long walk and took funny pictures of one other taking pictures at the end of the pier. Tonight she's taking me on a moonlit walk through Kings Park, which looks out over the entire city.

After Samantha puts her car in park, we walk alongside the botanical gardens and down to the scenic viewing area, which has panoramic views of the Swan River and the city's shimmering skyline. We're the only ones here, and it's as romantic as you can imagine.

As we wander under the stars, I can feel her energy wishing for one of two things: either for me to tell her I'm going to stay forever or for me to ask her to travel the rest of the way around the world with me. With Perth twinkling behind us, I can feel the flames from her fire. Her eyes want more, but as I look back at her, it hits me that I have an important decision to make.

Do I disappoint her now or later?

* * *

Two days later, I wheel Timberland out into the hallway and then shuffle back into my hotel room and run through my normal routine. Before I leave a hotel, I check all the outlets, all the dresser drawers, and then the closets one last time. I own so few things that I can't afford to lose anything, not even a single sock. Once I'm confident that I've left nothing behind, I head for the elevator.

Samantha just texted to let me know she's double-parked outside the Alex Hotel's entrance. Since buses don't travel across the Outback, she's taking me to the East Perth Terminal this morning, where I'll begin a forty-eight-hour train journey on the mighty Indian Pacific to Adelaide, a warm coastal city in southern Australia. Once I arrive, I'll hop off and save a couple of bucks by switching back to my normal mode of transportation before moving on to Melbourne.

The Indian Pacific railroad runs the entire width of the continent, from Perth to Sydney, and has the longest straight stretch of track in the world. Back in 1917—when the first eastbound passenger train, the Transcontinental Express, made the journey—passengers were required to change trains at least five times. It wasn't until 1969 that an uninterrupted stretch of tracks was completed.

The Australian landscape is said to be so remarkable that even though

I don't have enough discretionary income for a cabin with a bed, and even after my horrible experience on the Trans-Siberian Railway, I'm excited. We'll cross the Nullarbor Plain, which is considered a quintessential experience of the Australian Outback. It's a barren, far-reaching frontier, and I've been told by the staff here at the Alex Hotel that it's dotted with gold mines and ghost towns.

As I push the down arrow for the elevator, I take a deep breath to steady myself. I still haven't found a way to tell Samantha that I just want to be friends. It's safe to say that I've officially been leading her on the past few days, but each time I gather up the courage, she looks at me with those big blue ocean eyes of hers, and I freeze.

Bing.

The elevator doors swoosh open, and I make my way inside the empty box.

As the fluorescent lights in the elevator hum and I hit the button for the lobby, I get an unexpected feeling. It's a feeling that I'm not alone, like someone else has stepped inside the elevator with me. I spin 360 degrees just to make sure no one else is here.

The elevator slides down past the third floor, then the second. The feeling intensifies, and my palms begin to sweat. My heart flutters, and I quickly realize what's happening. Although I can't see her, she *is* in fact here.

She's here. Oh my God, she's finally here!

The woman's presence feels so good, so euphoric that I can't help but close my eyes and try to soak it all in.

An ancient world map appears on the inside of my closed eyelids. It reminds me of the map explorers used in the 1500s—roughly drawn, with slightly misshapen continents. North America is far too oval, and Africa is way west of where it really should be.

On my next inhale, two pulsating red dots show up on the map, each at opposite ends. Then, those two dots zig and zag their way across the continents and oceans between them. A trail of stardust follows.

As the dots make their way toward Australia, I hear her voice echo inside the empty chambers of my chest. Besides the time I heard God's voice in Siberia, this is the clearest, crispest communication of my life. As we exchange a kind of transcendental internal dialogue, I can feel her presence spread out across my chest and then down my arms like roots taking to soil. Time slows.

I welcome this new soul into my being like a child seeing Santa Claus. "Oh my God, it's you, it's finally you!" Without an ounce of doubt, I blurt out, "I've been dreaming of you my whole life!"

"I know, me too!" she says. "We've traveled a long way, and we are so close to finally meeting."

I feel myself descending deeper and deeper into this mysterious and mesmerizing love, one that I didn't know actually existed until a moment ago.

I didn't know it was possible to fall in love with someone you've never met, never seen a picture of, and never spoken to, but—incredibly—that's what's happening.

This isn't what I envisioned love would look like, but having been on the road for so long, I can compare this feeling to what it's like when you slip into your own sheets for the first time after a long summer abroad. It's that moment when you finally return home and let your whole body relax so it can sink deep down into the mattress that's known every nook and cranny of your body for the past fifteen years. That is what's happening right now; her entire soul is descending into mine, and mine into hers.

As she sinks deeper into my being, we both say the same thing: "I've thought about you for so long—I've always known you were out there."

Her voice is so crystal clear inside me that I'm overwhelmed by our ability to communicate.

The elevator cushions to a stop at the ground floor, and before the doors open, she says, "It's been a long time, baby, but I'll see you soon."

The elevator doors open just as my eyes do. I walk out, feet barely touching the floor, thank the front desk staff for all of their help with the photos I did this week, and then slide Timberland into the trunk of Samantha's car. As she pulls away from the curb, I can't help but turn my head toward the window. My reflection is as happy as it's ever been.

Holy shit! I just met my soul mate in an empty Australian elevator.

* * *

I finally understand what the phrase *silence is deafening* means.

Samantha and I are the only two people on the platform, and my train car feels miles away. Normally this would have had all the makings of a romantic good-bye. I'd pull her in close and promise to see her again soon, and we'd seal it with a passionate kiss the second before the train pulled away. But this will not be a romantic good-bye.

The only sound I hear is the clicking of Samantha's high heels tapping down the platform like wrecking ball–sized raindrops against a windowpane.

I've officially run out of things to say. With each step, the lump of guilt in my throat grows larger. Samantha is quiet too, but for a much different reason. She's sad I'm leaving, fearful that she'll never see me again.

Every time I look over at her, the tears she's fighting back crawl closer to the edges of her eyes.

I'm in a real pickle. Not only do I need to be fair to Samantha and end things with her right now, but I should probably also tell her that I met someone else, which is going to sound bat-shit crazy when I try to explain to her that I have no idea who the woman is.

The farther down the platform we get, the quieter it grows.

How am I going to get myself out of this mess?

When we finally get to car 11, it's time. I set my bags down on the platform and take both of her hands in mine. Then, just as I'm about to lay it all out there, she asks the closest conductor, "Can I board the train with him?"

There's no way on earth he'll say yes.

"Sure, just make sure you get off when the whistle blows," he calls back.

I give him a sideways glance. *Thanks, buddy, you just made this that much harder than it already is.*

I wheel Timberland onto the train and down the aisle to seat R, and then I lift it up to the storage space above my seat. The cabin isn't even a quarter full. Not many people are choosing to travel across Australia by train anymore since all economy class seating has been removed from the Indian Pacific. The Australian government cut over nine million dollars in funding that subsidized the travel costs of pensioners, veterans, and seniors. Fares have quadrupled, even for backpackers like me. It would have been far cheaper for me to fly across the country, but that's the last thing I'm worried about right now.

Samantha helps me settle into my seat like she's tucking me into bed.

She wants to make sure I have all the snacks and supplies I'll need. She even bought me a special travel pillow.

Why does she have to be so sweet?

Samantha sits in the empty seat next to me and then leans in to speak. "I haven't been able to trust anyone with my heart since my divorce, until now. Thank you, Eric, thank you."

She kisses my cheek.

I can't do this to her.

Having been through my own heartbreak this past year, which is nothing compared to what's she's gone through with her former high school sweetheart, I can empathize with how she feels. It's not easy to open up your heart and allow love to come in after it's been broken. As I look over at those baby blue eyes of hers, I just can't find a way to get the words out.

Why can't I just be happy with her? I'm thirty-five years old, with yet another perfect woman in front of me, and all I want to do is end things. Seriously, what the hell is wrong with me?

I clear my throat. "Samantha, there's something I need to tell you."

She cuts me off. "Please don't go. You can get off the train and stay with me. Or better yet, I'll see if I can still buy a ticket and come with you to Adelaide!"

I take both her hands in mine. "Samantha, I really have something I should say." I take a long pause and then gather up the courage to rip off the Band-Aid. "I think it's best if we—"

The trains whistle blows three times like a trumpet, drowning out my voice.

My head dips.

The conductor sidles down the aisle and politely asks Samantha to leave.

As we pull away moments later, I press my hand up against the window and watch tears fall from her eyes. My world begins to move; hers is set to remain the same.

* * *

"I've been on a double cheeseburger kick lately."

"Yeah, mate, that sounds pretty darn good right about now," James says. He's as thin as the rails we've been riding on and a bit disheveled; he appears to be in his early thirties, his hair is a mess, and his beard is unkempt. He's always reading the same *Field & Stream* magazine when I walk past him on my way to the bathroom.

"I overheard the conductor say that there's a McDonald's open until midnight a few blocks away," I say.

"Mind if I join you?" he asks. "I didn't eat lunch or dinner."

I decide that it would be nice to share a meal with a stranger for a change. "Not at all."

"Well, we better hurry then, mate, because we sure don't want to get stranded out here."

"Yeah, I missed my train in Siberia once by a full twelve hours."

I can laugh about that now. I guess it's true what they say, and time has healed that wound.

James and I cut through the empty Kalgoorlie train station and toward the Golden Arches. Their yellow light shimmers over the tiny town like a halo. Kalgoorlie Courthouse clock tower rises high in the center of town, and the saloon-like exterior of the Exchange Hotel is a reminder of when business boomed here in the early 1900s. The facades of some of the buildings make me feel like I've stepped onto the set of a John Wayne movie. The streets all run to right angles and the perfect grid is easy enough to navigate without worry. This is the first of two stops the Indian Pacific makes on the way to Adelaide, and we have about forty-five minutes to stretch our legs or walk to the only place that's open at this hour. You can find a McDonald's in 118 countries around the world, and as embarrassing as it is to admit this, I still seek them out on a nearly weekly basis.

It's a cool, crisp, moonless night, and there aren't any signs of life out here. Kalgoorlie, founded during a nineteenth-century gold rush, is about eleven hours and 370 miles east of Perth. The population once exceeded two hundred thousand but dwindled to about thirty thousand once the mines dried up.

"You said you went to Siberia once?"

After I share some of my escapades around the world, James says, "This is actually the first time I've been away from Adelaide."

"You mean like your first time to Perth?"

"No, I mean I have never left my hometown, mate. I've never traveled more than twenty miles away from Adelaide."

"You're joking!" The thought of never leaving my hometown blows my mind. "Oh my God, we're complete opposites, then!"

I can't even comprehend what my life would look like had I never left my hometown of Coopersburg, Pennsylvania. Fascinated, I ask him why he's chosen to stay in just one place his whole life.

"I'm afraid of flying, but I also just never felt the need to go anywhere."

"You mean you've never wanted to see anything else? What about Sydney or Melbourne or Moscow?"

"I'm pretty content where I live. Adelaide has everything I need. You'll see once we get there."

The last time I "settled down" was back in London, and that was for a whopping total of ten weeks. Looking over at James, I realize that what I've really grown to love about travel is its movement. To wander, to watch the world go by, and to see the sun rise in one place and set in another.

"So what made you want to go to Perth?"

James jumps at the chance to answer. "Well, it was for a woman."

We both smile and then laugh. "Of course! I should have known!"

There is no greater bond between men from Sudan to Siberia, Allentown to Adelaide than when they discuss women. The second a woman is introduced into the conversation, it creates an instant camaraderie. The conversation usually starts with a sigh and ends with a laugh, or starts with a laugh and ends with a sigh.

James swings the door to McDonald's open, and I follow him through. The smell from an overworked deep fryer is both gross and intoxicating. It's nearly midnight, and the place is empty. The sole employee is at the register, and he looks more than ready to shut up shop and go home. He's not exactly thrilled to see us, so I apologetically tell him, "The food on the train was overpriced and awful."

Our only other stop over the next thirty hours is Cook, an uninhabited ghost town in the Outback, so this is our last chance to fill up on food.

After James and I get our orders, we make our way over to a plastic, teal-colored table and sit in a pair of plastic purple seats. As he unwraps his burger, he tells me that he hasn't worked in two years. It's really hard for him to find a job in Adelaide. He tells me that he used his unemployment check to pay for his ticket to Perth and that he only has a few dollars left until the end of the month.

"So this girl must be pretty special, then. How did you meet—was she visiting Adelaide?"

"Actually, we met online. This was the first time I met her in person. I took the train out to Perth two weeks ago."

"Wow, that's one hell of a first date. Where did you stay?"

"I stayed with her and her kids. She lives with her parents."

I start giggling. "So let me get this straight—for a first date, not only did you leave your hometown for the first time ever, but you spent nearly two weeks living with her and her entire family?"

"Yep."

I cringe as I ask, "How was it?"

James beams. "It was great—I can't wait to go back."

I shake my head in disbelief. But this is why I travel—to move, and then to sit and share a cheeseburger at midnight with someone who's completely different from me.

The conversation is similar to others that I've had with people on the road. We share bigger secrets or deeper fears with each other than we do with our closest friends. Perhaps it's because we both know that we won't run into each other again. I won't be at their local supermarket next Tuesday, and he won't be at my favorite coffee shop a week from Wednesday. But for the moment, our journey becomes a shared one, the cheeseburger our soul food.

James suddenly stops midbite. He peels the burger bun back and starts scraping off the onions. He looks over at me and says, "I hate onions."

I laugh. "Me too, my friend—maybe we're not so different after all."

CHAPTER 12
AUSTRALIA

AUSTRALIA

"How often have you sailed in my dreams. And now you have come in my awakening, which is my deeper dream."

— Kahlil Gibran

I PURPOSELY LAG A FEW FEET behind the group. I want to see if she'll notice that I'm gone and turn around to look for me. If she does, it will give me another chance to look into her eyes, to confirm everything.

I wholeheartedly agree with William Shakespeare: eyes *are* the windows to our soul.

Come on, turn around.

Flinders Street Station floods the street with people who are all headed to the same game. The black-and-yellow flags from Richmond Tigers fans mix with the red and white of Sydney Swans like a Turkish bazaar. A group of beer-guzzling fans cut in front of me, and I fall a little farther behind than I wanted to, but my plan remains the same. If she turns around, my heart just might explode.

Come on, turn around.

I can see the back of her head, her long dark hair tied up into a beautifully messy bun, and it's a bobbing silhouette against the Melbourne night. It's Saturday evening, and we're on our way to the Melbourne Cricket

Ground. We're a few minutes late, but I couldn't care less. The only thing that matters is Shiya. I'd give anything for a look, even just a glance.

Come on, turn around.

#

This morning, as I was eating breakfast in the communal breakfast area at Space Hotel, she sat down at the opposite end of the table. She was wearing a long black tank top decorated with the New Zealand silver fern, so I mistakenly assumed she was a Kiwi. Only later would I find out that she's actually Moroccan. Her dark hair and dark eyes blended with her tank top, yet still she glowed.

As she spread strawberry jam across her rye toast, I was immediately drawn in. There was something intoxicatingly mysterious about her, but at the same time she also felt familiar. It was as though I recognized her but just couldn't place where we had crossed paths.

I was dying to start up a conversation with her, but . . . I'm shy. Really, really shy. So I'm thankful for Harold, the good-natured Englishman with the motor mouth who sat down between us. I overheard him ask Shiya and her friend Jolene if they wanted to go to the AFL game later at the Melbourne Cricket Ground. As they were discussing details of the game, the tickets, and how they would get there, I saw an opening, so I went for it.

"Actually, if you guys want, we could all go together. I have some friends who live here, and they told me about a way to get really cheap tickets. If you go online to the Richmond Tigers website, you can buy a children's ticket for nine dollars. I think the cheapest adult ticket is like twenty-five."

Shiya said, "But we're not children—won't we get caught?"

I knew that if I even looked in her direction, I'd blush. So I turned to Harold to explain. "My friend said they do it every weekend and that when they scan your ticket at the stadium, they don't check to see what kind of ticket it actually is. And then once you're inside, you can just sit in any of the open seats. The stadium seats like over a hundred thousand people, and it's hardly ever full."

Everyone at the table was traveling on a tight budget, so they all liked the sound of this, and we quickly exchanged our contact information. Later that morning, Harold set up a group chat on WhatsApp that for some reason included a picture of him on a sailboat. Throughout the afternoon, we all texted back and forth and agreed to meet in the Blue Moon Bar that's adjacent to our hotel.

Lore and I showed up first, a few minutes before six; she's a pretty Belgian woman who Harold also invited (I'm starting to like this guy more and more). We got to know one another over frosty pints of Carlton Draught while we waited for everyone else. She told me about how she's been couch surfing in Melbourne for the past few weeks.

In theory, couch surfing is a great idea—someone will list their home or apartment online and offer up their couch or extra bedroom for free to someone who's traveling on an extremely tight budget. In practice, however, it can be confused with online dating. Lore said that she keeps having to leave each place in a hurry because the guy whose couch she's staying on sees the site more as a way to meet women and he ends up wanting more by the second or third night.

Harold sent a message saying that he was still sailing and he'd just meet us at the stadium. Shiya replied saying that she and Jolene were running late as well, and that Lore and I should leave for the game without them.

After reading the texts, Lore lifted her head out of her phone and looked over at me. "Well, let's go then, Eric."

But before I agreed to head for the door, my intuition jumped in and told me not to leave just yet. Intuition is a funny thing. My mind always pictures the long steel honing rod chefs use to sharpen their knives. Back in the midst of my corporate career, my intuition was like a dull blade, often indecisive and barely strong enough to cut through warm butter. I blame this on never being offered up any opportunities to test and strengthen my intuition. But the more I've listened to my intuition out here on the road, the sharper it's become.

I was able to convince Lore to stay for another round of beers by offering to pay for them, and just as we were taking our last sips, a breathless Shiya ran into the bar.

"I'm so sorry we're late. We were out in St. Kilda all day and got lost on the way back. I have to run up to my room and get changed, so I'm going to need another ten minutes or so."

I replied with, "Okay, sure, no problem."

"But you guys can go now if you want to."

Lore looked over at me. She was ready to leave twenty minutes ago. "I feel bad for Harold," she said. "He is going to be at the game all alone. I'm going to go now—Eric, are you coming with me?"

I looked over at Shiya. She had a tiny scar just below her eye on her left cheek; it was the most adorable thing I'd ever seen. After a second or two I, gathered up the courage to lift my gaze slightly higher so I could look into her almond-shaped eyes for the first time. They were beautiful and bottomless, and they took me down a rabbit hole. There was so much swirling behind them, so many layers, so many lifetimes, and it was somewhere in that free fall that it hit me: I knew where I'd met this woman before.

She's the one! She's the soul I met in the empty elevator in Perth!

As my heart was thumping through my shirt, Lore took her last sip of beer and slid her purse over her shoulder. Then she asked again, "Eric, are you ready to go?"

The question became so utterly absurd it was as unbearable as nails against a chalkboard. *Go? No, I won't go, are you crazy? I'll wait for Shiya in this bar forever if I have to!*

When I failed to respond for a second time, Lore added, "Eric, earth to Eric, are you coming with me?"

I reluctantly broke Shiya's seducing spell and turned toward Lore, but since I couldn't announce to everyone in earshot what I was thinking, I tried to play it cool. "I don't mind waiting—I'll just have another beer."

Shiya quickly changed into jeans and a light blue oversized sweater and we piled into a tram that dropped us off at Flinders Street Station.

\#

Come on, turn around.

By the time Shiya and Jolene get to the corner where St. Paul's Cathedral sits, I start to lose hope. This is a crazy idea anyway; it's so childish. It's such an utterly ridiculous way to see if she likes me.

Just because she is not turning around doesn't mean that she's not into me.

Right?

Who knows?

I don't. So I panic.

Come on, turn around.

As the crosswalk fills with people, I start wondering if maybe my dreams are making me delirious, and my mind is just playing tricks on me. What makes me think I actually had a transcendental conversation with another soul in an empty elevator, or that Shiya is The One? What are the odds of that?

The last thing I need right now is a relationship. In three weeks' time, I'll board a cargo ship and spend a month at sea crossing the Pacific Ocean. And I'm obviously not very good at relationships to begin with; it was only this afternoon that I found the courage to email Samantha and tell her that I just want to be friends.

How could I be so S-T-U-P-I . . .

Before my thoughts can put the D on the end of *stupid*, Shiya's black bun swivels. She turns in my direction, and her eyes scan the crowd in front of me.

A little to the left!

Then her whole body turns back toward me.

Look up!

Her eyes dart past me.

Look back!

She does.

A little more to the right!

Boom!

Our eyes meet in the middle of Melbourne.

The streets clear and the buildings get whisked away like it's a scene change at a Broadway play. Her eyes smile, widen, and invite me in. A hush falls over us, and we become the only two people on the planet. If only for a millisecond, time stops. Not kinda, sorta stops, but actually stops.

The earth dissolves around her, and we shed our skins just like we did in that empty elevator in Perth a week ago. We're no longer people; we're just souls—two white-hot, scintillating souls who have known one another for what feels like forever. My soul leaps to hers and hers to mine.

I've always questioned what a successful journey around the world would look like. Would it mean that I traveled across a certain number of countries? Would it mean that I wrote a certain number of stories on my travel blog? Filmed a certain number of episodes? Had one of my photos published by a major magazine? Amassed a hundred thousand followers on social media? Made a certain amount of money along the way?

Success for me isn't any of those things. It is *this*. This shared moment with Shiya that is so perfect that if I took my last breath right here and right now, it wouldn't much matter.

Time speeds back to normal, and Cupid plucks at his bow. He fires from one of the nearby rooftops, and as his arrow spirals toward me, I spread my arms out wide and make myself an even bigger target. On the tram ride over here a few minutes ago, Shiya told me her middle name, which in Arabic means "arrow." And that couldn't be more fitting because she has just landed squarely in the center of my soul.

* * *

I can't take my eyes off Shiya even though Melbourne's flickering like candlelight just outside the window of my hotel room. It's midnight, and we're eight floors up and smack-dab in the middle of the CBD (Central Business District). Across the street is the Old Melbourne Gaol Museum, which is said to be haunted. Directly behind the museum is the city's most impressive row of glass skyscrapers, all lined up and shimmering the moon's own light back to it.

I gently brush Shiya's long dark hair back and out of her eyes. Then I run my fingers through every inch of it, all the while hoping to never reach the end. My hands were created for this purpose.

Everything is perfect.

"I wouldn't want to be anywhere else in the world with anyone else," I tell her.

We've just returned from our first date. We had dinner and then played a few games of pool at an Irish pub. I don't think either of us wanted the night to end, so as cheesy as it sounds, I invited her up to my room to listen to music. I would have just as easily agreed to watch paint dry if that's what she wanted.

The longest ten minutes of my life came at her expense earlier tonight. She texted me just before we were about to meet in the lobby, saying that an iron had burnt a hole in her dress and that she needed to find something else to wear.

At dinner, we crossed the t's and dotted the i's on the basics.

She lives in the Netherlands with her mother, stepfather, two younger sisters, and two brothers, and she just finished her master's degree in business. And while she's only twenty-four years old, she's an old soul, so the eleven-year gap between us hasn't even entered my mind.

She's at a crossroads in her life, questioning everything, and she's in the midst of a three-month backpacking trip with her friend Jolene in search of answers. They started in New Zealand and then flew to Australia and drove along its eastern coastline, often sleeping in the rental car. Next, they're off to Thailand.

I like that she's traveling and roughing it by sleeping in cars. I like that she's questioning everything. She has this rare magic in her, though I don't think she quite knows it yet. She could do anything she wanted in this world—I'm absolutely sure of it. She's Moroccan and mysterious. She's sultry but shy. There's a fire smoldering just behind her eyes, and I have a feeling that no matter how well I get to know her, she'll always retain some of that mystery, but that's exactly the kind of thing I'm attracted to.

She wears huge silver rings on her fingers that she got in Marrakesh a few years ago; I've never seen anything like them. Every time she moves, she dazzles. She's unlike anyone I've ever met.

I wouldn't be the least bit surprised if one day she makes headlines because she's summoned dragons from the sky. At dinner, I just kept blurting out, "You're special," to which she would reply, "Everyone's special."

I love the arch in her lips. It's intoxicating. I'd do anything to kiss them.

I sit up and rearrange the pillows on my bed so I can make up an excuse to scoot a little closer to her. As I do, I think about leaning in for a kiss. I'd trade all my travels for just one. Shiya rests her head on my chest and then bats the lashes around her bottomless eyes at me. I melt into the mattress. We get so close that I can feel her exhale on my neck. Just as I build up the courage to lean in even closer, she whispers, "This is kind of embarrassing, but I have to tell you something."

I promise her that she can tell me anything.

Her cheeks grow rosy red. "Well, the thing is . . ."

My heart falls to the floor as her voice trails off. I brace myself for the worst by cycling through all the terrible things she might tell me. She's married, or she has a boyfriend back at home, or she just got out of a long relationship and isn't quite ready to meet someone new just yet.

How could a woman this incredible be single?

While I wait for her to break the news, I gaze at the adorable scar below her left eye. Then at three tiny birthmarks on her neck; they've become my constellations in her celestial sphere.

After a deep breath, she says, "Okay, so here it is, I've never . . ." After another a long pause, she nervously adds, "I've never kissed anyone before."

My mind goes blank like someone pulled its plug.

"I know to most people a kiss is just a kiss, but to me it means so much more, and I've never found the right man to share something so special with. I've tried to be open and tried to get to know the guys I was interested in, but no one's ever made me feel like I could share that side of myself."

Shiya goes on to remind me of her religion and her beliefs. She's Muslim, and she finds it important to share such deep experiences with someone she truly wants to be intimate with. I know from our conversation at dinner that religion plays a big role in her life; she tries to follow the Quran as closely as she can. However, during this transitional phase of her life, she's seeing her religion in somewhat of a new light. She tells me she respects and appreciates its rules but that it's been harder to follow them as closely as she once did.

As she sits up on the bed, she says, "My religion inspires me, but I am also exploring other ways to answer some questions about how I want to live my life."

The more she shares, the faster I fall for her.

Shiya adds, "I've been traveling with three books in my backpack, and I read from them every night before bed. They have really helped open me up to new ideas."

I tell her that's exactly what I did when I took my three-month leave of absence to travel around the world five years ago. I tell her how much the three books I kept at the bottom of my backpack set me on course to do what I'm doing now.

I ask, "What's one of the books in your backpack?"

"Eckhart Tolle's *The Power of Now*."

"Oh, wow, I had that one with me too. It taught me so much about how to tap into my true self. What's another one?"

"I also have this book called *The Alchemist*. Have you ever heard of it?"

"Oh my God, me too. I read that from cover to cover on a flight from Thailand to India five years ago! It's my favorite book of all time! Sometimes I feel like I'm Santiago! Okay, there is no way we could have taken the same three books with us. What's the third?"

"*The Power of Intention*, by Dr. Wayne Dyer."

I'm flabbergasted, literally flabbergasted.

Had I crossed Africa one day quicker or one day slower, I would have missed Shiya. Had I not missed my train in Siberia and been forced to wait for five days for the next one, I would have missed Shiya. Had the cargo ship I was initially ticketed to take from Singapore to Freemantle not been unexpectedly sold to another company, forcing me to find another way, I would have missed Shiya.

The list of these "could have beens" is endless, so it is with full confidence that I look over and say, "We were destined to meet."

Shiya looks back and smiles.

As she puts her head back on my chest, I have no doubt that I could lie here forever with her. Every time she looks at me, I can't stop the same line from spilling out of my mouth over and over: "You're beautiful, you're beautiful, you are so beautiful."

I tell her how much I respect her religious beliefs and that I can understand what she's going through. "I was at a similar crossroads five years ago, which eventually led to me finding and following my dreams. It's scary, but it's also a beautiful thing."

"You know what I said earlier about never kissing anyone?"

"Yeah," I say with a sigh, "but I've tried to put kissing you out of my mind because of just how badly I want to."

Shiya slides closer and moves within an inch of my face. Her energy is unlike anything I've felt before. She's like a lioness with a pride to protect. "I want to kiss you," she says softly. Then, as a strand of her long dark hair falls in front of her face, she asks, "Will you be my first kiss?"

I thought I was passionate about filming, photography, writing, and traveling, but all that all seems inconsequential right now. But what if I screw things up? What if it's awkward and doesn't feel right? What if our lips don't fit together like the rest of us does?

None of that really matters. All that matters is the little cocoon we've created around ourselves in the here and now. Zombies could be walking the streets of Melbourne for all we know. It's like we're on a deserted island on a deserted planet.

"I only want to do this if it feels right," I say.

I look deep into her eyes and feel the power that's hidden just behind them.

"It feels right," she says.

I reach over to Shiya and gently brush her hair back. It confirms our connection.

My hands cup her face, and our lips touch. The world flickers and then dims. We disappear into the haze where two destined souls go when they finally come together and connect. That place doesn't have a name; it's not somewhere you can point to on a map, and you can't *try* to get *there*. It's just this little sliver of space where time stands still and all is right.

It's love.

In this space, we share more than a kiss. We share our biggest dreams and deepest fears, and when we finally resurface, I have no idea how long we've spent *there*.

Shiya lets me know that she's getting sleepy and that she should probably go back to her room because she has a full morning of sightseeing planned with Jolene tomorrow, to which she invites me along.

I'm tired too, but I don't want her to go. And even though I couldn't care less about what time it is, my intuition perks up yet again. Somehow, I have a deep need to know.

I ask Shiya.

She stretches across my chest so she can see the alarm clock on my nightstand.

"It's 4:44."

* * *

I can unequivocally say that I've never met anyone like Shiya, but this is exactly what I do. I fall in love fast, throw all my logs onto the fire without thinking. I start with a massive four-alarm blaze and then work backward. Love has to be instantaneous; I'll even go so far as to say that it has to be love at first sight. I need the butterflies, the sweaty palms, and the skipping heartbeat the first second I lay eyes on someone or I know that it won't work—like with Samantha. This was also one of the things that held me back when it came to my relationship with Naomi. I didn't have that initial spark. We started out as friends, and it slowly evolved into a relationship. No matter how many logs I carried to the campsite in Africa, I just couldn't fan the flames into a full-fledged blaze.

Right before she leaves for her flight to Thailand, Shiya and I sip cappuccinos in one of my favorite cobblestone laneways, and I bring up the idea of visiting her in Amsterdam one day. She looks hesitant.

"I'm not sure if people in my community will be open to the idea of us hanging out together."

There's a certain freedom found when traveling, especially backpacking the way she is, but I know that when she gets a moment alone to sit and think about *us,* she'll inevitably picture her normal life back in Amsterdam. And that no matter how many angles she looked at that life from, I am always going to be the square peg.

In the days after she leaves, we exchange texts that are playful and short. I call her my *lil cous cous* because it's the only thing I could think of that's Moroccan, and we fill each other in on how our day is going whenever we both have Wi-Fi. When she tells me about the scorpion she ate on Koh San Road the day after she got there, I tell her I'll never kiss her again. I'm kidding, of course. Regardless of what we're talking about, we always end each string of texts with the same smiling emoji, the one with the little red hearts for eyes.

It's as I'm about to put the final touches on my packing routine and head to the bus station that I receive a long text from Thailand.

My heart sinks. I know what's coming.

I know she's given in to her fears.

She meticulously lists all the reasons why we can't be together. She explains that she hadn't thought things through and that she went with the flow while she was here in Melbourne with me because it felt so good at the time. And that things just went way too fast.

She also says she has no clue what she really wants and that it's not fair to me to try and build something together when she really needs to be figuring her own self out first. She goes on to say that she's so confused that even the crossroads have crossroads. She also cites the impossible distance between us. Finally, she gets to the thing I knew would be our unraveling: I'm not a Muslim. Her beliefs won't allow her to be with someone outside the religion, and the repercussions of a relationship with someone like me could be deep and long lasting for her family and friends. She could even be shunned by her community.

She ends the text by saying how much she cares for me and that it's just all too overwhelming at the moment, but she wants to remain friends and keep in touch.

Even though things were magical here in Melbourne, I'd be lying if I didn't admit I half expected this kind of text from her. We had only been together for ninety-six hours, though it felt like ages because of the depth of our connection. I was dizzy with ecstasy. We created our own world, and my heart was ricocheting off the walls, but I forgot to measure the risks, take a close look at the reality. I just assumed that we were on the brink of a love so deep that we'd glide past every obstacle thrown our way.

When I initially read Shiya's text, the thought of converting to Islam crosses my mind, but what would I be converting from? I grew up Christian, have a tattoo of a Hindu god, and have spent an equal amount of time in mosques and synagogues over the past few years, but at the moment I don't subscribe to any one religion. If anything, I'm a little bit of everything.

Throughout my journey, I've grown to trust God—to really trust every single thing that's come my way. And while I'm heartbroken over the fact that Shiya doesn't want to be with me, I'm also at peace with it. *Everything happens for a good reason, even the bad.* While on the surface this is awful, I don't know what's happening below the surface. I can't see the gears turning, levers being pulled, or doors opening behind the scenes. I've learned to put all my faith in the process because I don't know what kind of breakthrough this will lead to.

Knowing all of this doesn't make much difference in the moment, though. I'm still human, and heartbreak will always be heartbreak. Reading her text was far harder than I thought it would be. I desperately wanted to be with her.

My mind spinning with all of my confused thoughts, I somehow get myself to the bus station and on board the right bus. As my Greyhound bus merges on the M31 North, a bone-deep desire to return to the cocoon we created back at our hotel floods my body. It's a swell of emotions that pushes tears up against the rims of my eyes. I well and truly had it all.

I was creating, taking photos, making films, writing stories, traveling, making money, meeting like-minded people, and falling fast in love. And damn, it was great.

As the smokestacks on Melbourne's west side slowly fade out of view, I begin to fall apart.

I just wasn't enough for her.

CHAPTER 13
AUSTRALIA

AUSTRALIA

"If you follow your bliss, you will always
have your bliss, money or not.
If you follow money, you may lose it,
and you will have nothing."

— *Joseph Campbell*

I T'S FUNNY HOW LIFE WORKS. Just as I was falling apart over Shiya and beginning to lose all the ground I've gained, Adam and Joseph entered my life. Joseph, a stocky twenty-three-year-old African American, was waiting for me outside the Canberra bus station. He was sent by Adam, a white, middle-aged Australian family man, who emailed me, "Joseph told me he will be wearing a do-rag when he picks you up, but what that is exactly, I do not know."

They couldn't be more opposite of one another if they tried. Adam's the owner of Canberra Central, the hostel that's agreed to my exchange this week, and Joseph is his right-hand man. Joseph gets a free bunk and a small paycheck, and in return he checks in the guests, cleans the rooms, and does the little things like pick people up at the bus station. He's around my age and grew up on the mean streets of North Philadelphia, the part of the city with the highest rate of violent crime. His family moved around a lot when he was a kid, but he often found himself living in neighborhoods plagued by the same things: crime, drugs, and economic inequality.

After high school, Joseph enlisted in the military, where he served two tours of duty in Iraq. He was eventually forced to retire because of posttraumatic stress disorder. The combat toll still haunts him to this day, and he's not shy when talking about it. Before we even pulled away from the bus station, he said, "Whatever you do, don't sneak up on me or make any loud sounds around me."

He quickly added that he would be filling out an absentee ballot for Donald Trump in the fall because he desperately wants his veterans benefits increased. I wouldn't fault you for assuming that Joseph must be a tough guy with a mean streak, but this bowling ball of a man is exactly the opposite.

He's outgoing, fun, and funny, but he's also kind of a nerd. Instead of turning to the streets as a teenager, he turned to cartoons. He's a walking encyclopedia of all things superhero, and *The Big Bang Theory* is his favorite TV show. He's constantly quoting Sheldon like he knows him personally, and when he picked me up at the bus station he was wearing his favorite SpongeBob sweat pants (and do-rag).

Then there's Adam. He's a mountain man with a permanent five o'clock shadow. He's into camping and hiking and, like most Australians I've met, has a really dry sense of humor. He'd vote for anyone other than Trump if he could vote in our election, and he's always playfully pressing Joseph's buttons because of it. Adam recently spent every dollar he had to purchase the failing Canberra Central hostel, and he's doing everything he can think of to turn it around. The place was a known haven for meth users and prostitutes before he took over, but he said it's got "good bones."

Adam knows he's going to have to get creative to attract business because Canberra doesn't get much tourist traffic. "They usually go from Sydney to Melbourne or vice versa, often skipping over this amazing part of the country," Adam told me my first day here.

His hands are calloused from all the work he puts into remodeling the place, and his expression is a cross between exhausted and optimistic. He works six days a week at the hostel and then the seventh as a carpenter just so he can scrape together enough money to put food on the table for his family. One might expect Adam to be stressed to the gills—the stereotypical grizzled handyman who grunts instead of talks. But, like Joseph, he is the opposite of what I was expecting.

As different as Joseph and Adam are from one another, they do have one thing in common: they have hearts of gold. There is just something special about the way the two of them comically clash, and our chop-busting conversations around the hostel this week have helped me heal.

The plan while I'm here is to take photos and create a film of Canberra Central in exchange for a room. On top of that, I've struck a deal with Adam, who is starting a tour company called Backroads Adventure Tours. When he was telling me about it the day I arrived, a light bulb went off, and I came up with the idea that I could film one of the hikes his tour company will offer in exchange for a fee (like what professional travel filmmakers normally do).

I was stoked when Adam gobbled up my offer. When the dust settled a few minutes later, we agreed on a three-day hike to Budawang National Park next week. The film I'll create will be played on a loop in the lobby of Canberra Central to encourage guests to stay a few extra days and sign up for the hike. The other part of our deal was that I'd recommend the hike to the people following my journey online, which has recently ballooned to over a hundred thousand travel-minded followers across my social media accounts.

The arrangement is ideal for both of us. Adam's getting a film at half the price he would normally pay, and he's also getting to test out the route and terrain with Joseph and me as his guinea pigs. And for me, this is as good as it gets!

* * *

Just as I'm about to fall asleep in my bunk my third night in Canberra, Adam sends me a string of text messages asking me if we can bump our hiking trip. According to the forecast, a storm is about to move in, but if we leave in just a few hours, at 3:00 a.m., we might be able to avoid the rain altogether.

Before I can type out my reply, he also gives me the option of cancelling the hiking trip altogether. I cringe. There is a zero percent chance that I would ever cancel the hike. This is my first shot at a real payday since I got my final paycheck from my corporate consulting job nearly two years ago. Sure, I've made some money along the way, but nothing this substantial. I can't pass up this amount of money, regardless of the circumstances. Plus, I made it to the top of Mount Kilimanjaro once. Nothing can be harder than that. *Right?*

I remember when I showed up in Tanzania and met my guide, Festo, at the basecamp in Arusha, the first question he asked was, "Have you ever done any hiking before?"

After I said, "No," he asked, "Have you ever gone camping before?"

I said no a second time. I had never spent so much as a single night inside a tent.

"You do realize this is the tallest free-standing mountain in the world, don't you?" he asked.

But that's how I do things; I just throw myself off the cliff and learn later whether I'll fly or fall. There is a drawback to my strategy, however: I often find myself flapping furiously in the wind, which is exactly what happened the second Festo and I took our first steps down Mount Kilimanjaro's Marangu trail.

The seven days that followed were hell, but ultimately, after one of the most mentally challenging and physically demanding days of my life, I managed to will myself to the summit. The altitude, lack of sleep, and bodily exhaustion (all things I hadn't prepped for) had taken a toll—I could barely see straight—but I certainly learned a lot about myself.

After fumbling around in the dark driveway of Canberra Central, I throw my backpack atop a pile of backpacks in Adam's Land Rover. I packed super light; my toothbrush, deodorant, extra shirt, and socks make up the contents of my bag. I've also got my camera and tripod with me, but I set that between my legs just in case I want to film something out the window on the way. As I settle in next to Adam up front, Joseph slams the rear hatch shut and then hops in the back.

The old four-cylinder diesel engine knocks when it starts, and Adam calls out, "Settle in, boys, it's about four hours to Budawang National Park. We'll stop just after sunrise for some breakfast."

Joseph grumpily yells, "I still don't understand why we have to leave at three in the morning, but wake me up when we stop for breakfast. I want a sausage roll."

The smile on my face is as wide as the night is dark. Even though I didn't sleep a wink last night, this doesn't feel like work. This is a road trip with friends that I'm actually getting paid to go on. It's yet another layer of my dreams manifested.

A few hours into the drive, I ask Adam to pull over as hints of lavender begin to creep across the predawn sky. We're the only car in sight, and once he yanks the emergency brake up, I run across the road and unfold my tripod in front of the mountain pass. I've seen a lot of beautiful sunrises around the world, and this one is right up there with the best of them. This utterly ridiculous blue hue begins to emanate from the sun once it hits the horizon. Then in a flash, it's purple, then pink, and then every blinding shade of orange imaginable.

Frost has coated the grass and it's chilly out, but I don't feel the cold because I'm so locked in to what I'm trying to capture. I call Adam over so he can get in position for the shot I want. "Lean up against the hood and look off into the distance."

Not long after we pile back into the truck, we stop at a little hole-in-the-wall place for breakfast. Everyone wakes up as we sip perfectly brewed coffee and shovel delicious sausage rolls into our mouths. We arrive at the entrance to the Budawang National Park around eight. Adam drives us a few miles down a dirt road and then parks alongside an empty picnic area. We hop out, excited to start our adventure. Adam's so nice and so kind that he ran out and bought me all the gear I'll need for the hike, and he hands me a shopping bag full of stuff like it's Christmas morning.

I slide my right arm into the jacket first, but I can't even get it past my elbow. Something isn't right. I slip it off and hold it up to my eye.

"Um, Adam, I think this is a small." Then I jokingly say, "You do realize I'm like twice the size of a normal human being?"

"No, it can't be. I remember it was on the rack that was labeled extra-extra-large, and the hanger said XXL."

We both reach for the tag that's still hanging inside the jacket. "Yep, it's a small. It must have been in the wrong section. Happens to me all the time."

I think of the line Chris Farley made famous during a *Saturday Night Live* skit, and I start laughing hysterically. I try to put the jacket on again, and then I dance around Joseph as he and I recite Farley's line over and over: "Fat guy in a little coat, fat guy in a little coat."

Adam laughs along but feels terrible and apologizes profusely. I tell him that it's not a big deal and toss it back into the truck. "The sun is out, and it looks like it's going to be a beautiful day. I can't imagine I'll need it."

I reach for the wool hat next and try to slide it over my head, but that doesn't fit either. It looks like a yarmulke on my head. I laugh again as Adam starts getting mad at himself.

"At least the tags are still on them so you can get your money back," I say.

I toss the hat on top of the jacket and then hold up the pair of humongous sweat pants and say, "At least these will fit."

"What about the boots? They are the biggest ones we've got in Canberra. They've got to fit."

I unlace the boots and sit on a mossy stump nearby and slide them over my socks. They are really tight. I stand up and walk around in circles like I'm testing them out inside a Foot Locker and say, "I think they will loosen up over the next three days. I'm a size fourteen and these are a twelve, but it's not like I need them forever."

I throw the sneakers I was wearing on top of everything else in the trunk, put my backpack on, and start heading toward the trailhead. Adam calls me back.

"Eric, where are you going? You need your backpack."

"I've got mine on"—I turn to show him—"see?"

Adam and Joseph start laughing at me. Adam then pulls a third backpack out of the trunk. "It's got your tent, your sleeping bag, your food, kerosene for the gas stove," and then he rattles off about twenty-five other camping-related items I've never even heard of.

"That thing looks like we're going hiking for three years, not three days."

I unload my backpack into the one Adam's given me and then hitch it up onto my shoulders.

"This can't be right—how much does this beast weigh?"

"It's about thirteen kilos, which to you Americans is close to thirty pounds."

I stagger backward. "And I have to carry this for three days? I thought Joseph was going to carry some of my camping stuff so I could focus on filming?"

"He is. He's carrying some of your food and your flashlight. We gave you the lightest pack."

I'm feeling less exuberant than I was three minutes ago. Nothing fits, and this beastly backpack won't rest right on my shoulders. "I can barely stand straight, and these nylon straps are going to rub my shoulders raw."

Before we get even ten feet down the trail, a sinking feeling hits me. It's the same one I got at the base of Mount Kilimanjaro.

I'm in over my head.

In my excitement for the big payday at the end of the hike, I forgot to ask Adam anything about the hike itself. I don't know a single thing about the trail. I have no idea about the most basic things like our food and water situation. Hell, I don't even know where we're trying to hike to.

Mud sprays from my boots and up the back of my jeans as we begin an arduous climb through a damp Australian rain forest. It's hard for me to enjoy the sun ricocheting off the rocks because I'm holding my camera and tripod out in front of me, which is roughly another ten pounds of gear. Each time I move my arms, it feels like I'm curling a tiny dumbbell. I'm wheezing and sweating, and Adam, who's worried it still might rain today, is moving at a blistering pace.

I look over at Joseph; he seems to be doing fine, but he's a solider, for God's sake.

Adam's original plan initially included three more hikers from a club he's a part of in Canberra. They were going to be the "models" in the film, but since we had to leave early to beat the rain, none of them could make it. At the time, it didn't seem like a big deal, but now I feel its consequences. I have to run ahead, set my camera up, and then run back and walk alongside Joseph and Adam so I can fill out the shots. The back and forth, up and down, wears me out, and I quickly realize that this is not what I had signed up for.

About an hour in, we cross a small stream, which means that we're all but out of the rain forest portion of the hike. Adam shifts into fifth gear and leads us north. As we begin to walk through dense brush I start feeling my frustrations. The green shrubs are scrunched together tightly and they're just tall enough that it makes seeing anything beyond them all but impossible. Every twenty steps or so a rogue tree branch arches over the faint trail. Adam and Joseph zip under the branches with ease, but because of my height I need to find a creative way under them. That's no easy task with this thirty-pound beast on my back and my camera and tripod in my hands.

We're climbing steadily uphill on a winding, overgrown path, broken up only by the occasional downhill switchback where each time I take a downward step, my toes smash into the front of the too-small boot, which has absolutely zero give.

By midday, I'm streaming sweat and beginning to show signs of cracking.

"Adam, there is no way I can keep this pace up. We haven't taken a break for hours. If you're going to take *regular* people like me on this hike, you have to go slower and give them a chance to rest every once in a while. I'm in decent shape, but you're killing me out here."

Adam apologizes and jots down my advice on the notepad he's been carrying. Joseph and I are the guinea pigs here. Adam hasn't actually taken anyone on this hike before, and it's only his second time ever on this trail.

"I have to sit down and rest for a few minutes," I say.

I take my backpack off and lean against the smooth side of a boulder. After I drink the last of my water, I poke at the toe of my boot. "My toes are killing me."

Adam reaches for the tip of my boot, and then in the same second it dawns on us what the problem is.

"Oh my God, I'm so sorry," he says.

"You bought me steel-tip boots! These are for construction workers, not hikers."

Adam apologizes yet again. "I didn't think to look closely at the actual boot. I just bought the biggest ones."

I'm afraid to take them off because I doubt I'd be able to get them back on. "I'd give anything for my sneakers right now, but they're back at the truck five hours behind us."

"Well, we're almost halfway to the campsite, but I'd be happy to turn around if you want to."

Quitting now means I won't have enough footage for the film, which means I won't get paid. I grind my teeth and say, "I think I can keep going. It can't get any worse—my toes are already numb."

I stand up and dust myself off, bracing myself to endure the beastly backpack and steel-tip boots for the next long stretch of trail.

Seconds later, in the midst of my next awkward lunge under a low-hanging tree branch, I hear an awful sound like someone ripping a giant piece of paper in half and feel a cool breeze on the back of my legs.

The entire back side of my only pair of jeans has just split right down the middle. It's like someone fired a cannonball directly through them. Instead of stopping to change into the sweat pants Adam bought me and risk my toes swelling up once my boots are off, I decide to continue on with my entire ass exposed.

My dream project has quickly become a nightmare.

What else could go wrong?

#

Over the next two hours, I hike in silence as the same question keeps bubbling up in my mind. *Why am I really on this hike?*

When I strip away all the bullshit and answer honestly, I don't like what I find.

I hate hiking. I'm not an outdoorsman in any way, shape, or form. Kilimanjaro was pure hell, and I just remembered something I'd forgotten about it. Once I finished the hike and made it back to the base camp in Arusha, I donated all my hiking gear to Festo's team of porters because I swore I'd never hike so much as a single step ever again.

If I actually hate hiking, *then why am I really doing this?*

And that's when the real answer hits me. The money made me do it. This hike isn't any better than my old corporate consulting job. I'm slogging through the day like I used to way back then; it's just a different kind of slogging.

When I realize that I've sold out, my thoughts start spiraling.

This isn't the pot of gold I thought it was, and if this isn't what I want to do with my life, then what the hell is?

When the answer doesn't come, I feel as lost as I've ever been.

The hiking becomes too challenging to keep dwelling on such a monumental question, and I have to brace myself for each step because the higher we climb, the steeper the trail becomes. My energy begins to dip, which makes the backpack that much more mammoth.

Joseph and I have been reminiscing about Philadelphia all morning. In particular its food. I went to Saint Joseph's University for graduate school, so I lived in the city for two years. We've been debating age-old questions like Pat's or Geno's? Whiz or without? But the big problem with all this cheesesteak talk is that it's making me hungry. Really hungry.

Around three in the afternoon, when I'm on the verge of losing my mind, I call out, "At what point do we stop for lunch, and where do we get more water because I'm starving and dying of thirst?"

I can tell by the look on Adam's face that I'm not going to like his answer.

"Well, all of the food we brought is dry food, so we need to add water to it to cook it, but we don't have enough water left. By the time we find a water source, set up the stove, and cook the food, it might take an hour or two, and the campsite is just three more hours away."

I unravel. I take off my backpack and throw it like a shot put as far as I can.

"It's three o'clock! We ate breakfast at six this morning, and I haven't had anything to eat since! If you're going to take people on a hike that's this damn challenging, you have to give them a lunch break! I would have packed a sandwich or ordered extra sausage rolls this morning if I had known this. My blood sugar is low, Adam!"

I hold out my hand, and it's shaking like a leaf.

Before Adam can reply, I continue my rant. "I don't know how I'm going to hike for three more hours! My toes are killing me—they have got to be bleeding inside these damn boots, and I've got blisters the size of basketballs on my heels."

I punt my empty water bottle down the trail. "And what about water? I haven't had any all afternoon—this is inhumane!"

Joseph shakes his water bottle; he has less than a quarter left in his, and Adam the same.

"I understand your frustration, mate. There is a water source near the campsite. The one I was planning on filling our bottles up at this afternoon was all dried up when we walked past it."

Adam walks down the trail, picks up my water bottle, and then pours all his water into it. Joseph does the same, and with nothing else left to say or do, we get back on the trail.

These acts of kindness cause me to come to my senses a few minutes later, and I apologize. "I'm sorry, but this isn't what I thought it would be, and I've realized that I'm only doing this for the money. I'm just pissed off at myself."

The next two hours are a slow and silent march.

As the sun starts dipping toward the tree-covered horizon, I can barely get one foot in front of the other. I'm scared to see the state of my feet if we ever actually reach the campsite. They are going to have to be pried out of these boots.

All three of us are spent and, as morale takes one final dip, Joseph takes a misstep and falls. As he's sliding down the gravel trail on his stomach, I reach out for him, and we hook arms. I help him back to his feet, but his whole right side is cut and bruised from the fall.

The hike has humbled us all.

"We are the Bad News Fucking Bears of the hiking world," I scream out.

Adam chuckles and adds, "Even as a group, we are still a couple cards short of a full deck."

Two hours later and four hours behind schedule, we make it to the last stretch of trail. We've now been hiking for eleven straight hours in the hot sun with no food or water.

I look up at a never-ending stone staircase that Mother Nature has carved into the top of the mountain. Adam says, "This is called the stairway to heaven."

Joseph glances at Adam. "More like stairway to hell."

I chime in. "You mean after climbing nearly four thousand feet into the sky, you've saved the hardest part for last?"

Adam, forever the optimist, says, "The good news is, it only takes a half hour, and at the top is our water source and campsite."

The rocks look like they go on forever. "I can't even see where it ends."

Joseph has somehow regained his good spirits. He points to outer space and says, "I think up there."

I'm really not in the mood for jokes.

Today was supposed to be my dream day, but it's turning out to be one of the most awful things I've ever experienced.

As I'm looking up into the sky, I see Shiya's almond-shaped eyes in the clouds. I haven't been able to get her out of my head. I keep replaying the moment our eyes first locked, and I've been missing her like crazy. It's hard enough to climb a mountain normally, and here I am doing it with a heart that's breaking.

She's the one, I know it. I don't understand why she's running from that!

Throughout the course of my travels around the world, I've become the definition of resilient. When there is no way, I've found a way. If I'm going to transform my life and make it around the world without flying, I'm the one that has to do it. No one can do it for me. I'm the one who has to muster up the creative confidence and self-belief, day after day.

I've weathered so many storms that my thinking's gradually changed from *why me* to *what's next?*

I haven't been embodying that mindset on this hike. Not yet. So I stop thinking, stop talking, and stop feeling—and I take off like a dart.

The lion inside is set loose. It roars through every fiber of my body, and I start running up the rocky stairwell. I move like I'm possessed; with each step I take, I gain more and more momentum.

I climb through the clouds and up and out of sight of Joseph and Adam. The pain is pushing me, and miraculously I get stronger and stronger the higher and harder I climb.

Soon I'm in a full-out sprint and moving so fast that I can barely see where to place my foot. I could go on like this forever.

By the time I make it to the top of the mountain, I'm panting and gasping for air.

It takes Adam and Joseph twenty minutes to catch up to me. They both say that they've never seen anyone move like that. I try to explain it to them as we pitch our tents and make dinner, but words are only able to gloss over what I was feeling.

"That stairway revealed something in me. Most of the best moments in my journey have come when I was about to break. The struggle is the thing that's saved me each and every time. That's where the greatest growth has been."

After dinner, the three of us sit around the campfire like we've known each other for twenty years, bonded by the hike from hell and all our collective mistakes during it. On a serious note, I lean over the fire and tell Adam that I hope he knows that on good faith I can't recommend this hike to anyone following my journey on social media just yet. Then, after a long pause, I say, "But I have zero doubt that you will get this right. You'll turn this into one of the best hikes in the world one day. You were right—it really is beautiful out here and well worth the visit. Though I can't recommend the hike just yet, I can recommend you without reservation."

Adam thanks me. "I'm sorry for today, but you are correct. I will work as hard as it takes in order to get today's tour right." His passion for hiking and getting his adventure tour company off the ground reminds me of my own journey.

Adam then says, "Well, I guess there's only one thing left to do. Let's take that picture of the stars you were talking about."

I let out an exhausted sigh while looking over the flames of the fire. "I don't know, Adam, this campsite is pretty comfortable right now."

It'd be easy to sit by the campfire and fall asleep. My toes seem to have been in a car crash; they are a black-and-blue mess. It looks like I'll lose a few toenails before all is said and done. I've been filming all day, and every muscle in my body aches. But then I think of what Roger Staubach once said: "There are no traffic jams along the extra mile."

I get up and gently squeeze my feet back into my boots, then grab my camera and tripod. It's about a ten-minute walk to a rocky cliff that reveals a monstrous rift valley.

For the past three years, my photography goal has been to take one creative photo every single day, which I then post across my social media accounts. But during that entire time, I've never once taken a photo of the stars. I've looked at cool photos of the night sky on Instagram and dreamt of being able to do it one day, but I've never tried. It always seemed too technical for me. You have to know how to do a long exposure, which I've never done. Plus, you have to be way out in the middle of nowhere.

"There isn't a single light for miles out here, so you have nothing to worry about tonight," says Adam.

"But I can't really see any stars. It doesn't look like there's that many out tonight," I say.

Adam agrees but then says, "Let's try it anyway. You never know."

"You're going to have to bear with me. We might have to do this photo like fifty times. I really don't know how to take this kind of shot."

I set up my tripod and camera on the cliff and then slow the shutter speed down to thirty, which means the shutter will stay open for thirty seconds.

I ask Adam to walk out to the crest of the ridge, turn his headlamp on, and look up toward the sky. It's so dark out here that I bump up the ISO to two thousand and then open the f-stop to 2.8 so I can let as much light in as possible. Even then I can't see anything on the LCD screen or through the viewfinder.

"I think it's too dark, Adam. I probably shouldn't tell you this, but for as often as I use my camera, I still don't quite know what I'm doing."

I tell Adam how important it is that he doesn't move, and then I focus on where I think his headlamp is and say, "Okay, stay still for the next thirty seconds."

I snap the shot, and while the camera does its thing, I stare at the only star my eye can see and replay the entire day from the sausage rolls to the setbacks.

Once the shutter snaps closed, I tell Adam that he can relax. I take the camera off the tripod and hold it in my hands.

Adam walks back and looks over my shoulder. "Okay, let's see what we got."

We turn our headlamps off, and I push play. The LCD screen lights up and glows across our pitch-black world.

I gasp.

"I don't even know what to say."

"Oh my God, you did it. What an incredible photo—that's the best shot I've ever seen!"

In my hands is the most beautiful photo I've ever taken. It looks like Adam's at the apex of the earth. The entire night sky is lit up by a cosmic blanket of stars that our naked eye couldn't see. At the edge of the cliff is Adam's silhouette, and the blue beam from his headlamp is shooting across the galaxy like it's a light saber. We can see every single star the galaxy has to offer and even the orange crevice where the Milky Way begins.

When the magnitude of the moment hits me, I have to stop and compose myself. I've been pushing myself just past my edge every day. Raising the bar in terms of my travels and transformation is often done behind the scenes. It's almost always done without encouragement or applause, but this symphony of stars is a reward of the highest order for all that self-discipline.

I'm holding the entire universe in my hands, and I can feel my tiny, but powerful, place in it.

CHAPTER 14
TAHITI
PACIFIC OCEAN

"A journey is a person in itself; no two are alike.
And all plans, safeguards, policing and coercion
are fruitless. We find after years of struggle that
we do not take a trip; a trip takes us."

— *John Steinbeck*

M Y VOYAGE ACROSS THE PACIFIC Ocean has already been delayed two days due to rough seas off the coast of Australia. So I can't imagine that the captain's willing to wait so much as a millisecond longer than he has to for me. It's been raining nonstop ever since I got to Sydney earlier this week, and I only found out a few hours ago that we were cleared to embark tonight. I have to board the MV *Caprice* at exactly 8:00 p.m.

It's taken me two months, hundreds of emails, three thousand dollars, and a pile of paperwork to book my ticket on the cargo ship. Cruise ships weren't really an option for this leg of my journey because they don't often sail directly across the Pacific Ocean at this time of year. Plus, their itineraries are usually loaded with island stops, which means it takes twice as long to arrive. Even if one did exist it would be well beyond my budget.

A cargo ship was my only option, but you can't just go down to the docks and ask one of the deckhands if you can hop aboard. I had to pass a physical within ninety days of sailing and purchase an insurance policy that would cover me in the event that I needed to be airlifted to safety from the middle of the Pacific Ocean should things go terribly wrong.

Now I just needed to find the damn ship.

I'm an ant in LEGOLAND. Sydney's Port Botany is gigantic. Just the container terminal itself sits on 160 acres, and it's littered with thousands of shipping containers that are stacked as high as the sky. I'm supposed to follow a road past gate thirty-seven, where I will see a sign that reads "crew drop-off and pickup point." At the end of that parking lot, I will see a green shed and chain-link fence. I'm supposed to press the button, and a security guard will come to the shed, check my passport, and give me a ride to the ship's gangway.

The sun has just gone down, and I'm lost in a maze. Even though I'm finally in a country where people speak English, of course there's no one around to ask for help. Fitting. Thankfully, just before I reach an epic level of panic, I see a small white sign with red letters across it that reads "gate 37." I follow the road alongside it and eventually wheel Timberland right up to the aforementioned green shed.

I'm buzzed through a gate in what might just be the most unofficial immigration process of all time. No one looks at my ticket or my bags or performs any type of security check. I simply tell the guard that I'm a passenger on the MV *Caprice*, and I'm taken straight to the ship on a green golf cart.

When we pull alongside the ship, I'm in awe of her size. At 228 meters long, 37 meters wide, and 57 meters high, she's an absolute monster. She's over two and a half football fields long. Her sides are painted red, but it's a worn and weathered red; *Hamburg Süd* is written across her midsection in white.

The first person I meet on board is Rajeev. He's the second officer. He leads me up the gangway and directly to my cabin. When I ask him, he tells me that he's from a small town in India, but he's noticeably frazzled, so he cuts our conversation short. "We're behind schedule because of the bad weather the past few days. I've got to get back out there and make sure all our cargo gets on board. There will be a briefing with the captain tomorrow morning after breakfast at your muster station. I will see you then."

I close the door to my cabin and have a look around. The room is nicer than I expected. It has a couch, a desk (with a broken chair), and a twin bed (with a rock-hard mattress). I have a private bathroom and a small porthole window that looks out over the back deck of the ship, where I can see the containers Rajeev mentioned getting hoisted on board by giant dockside cranes. The ten-ton containers look as light as LEGO blocks as they're sucked into the sky and then gently set down on the back of the boat. It's like they're building a small shipping city around me.

I take my first deep breath of the evening, and it's filled with relief for having made it on board in time. Then I begin the ritual of unpacking. As I stuff my socks into a dresser that's bolted to the floor, I repeat the words I've been telling myself for weeks now: *You can do this. A month at sea isn't so long.*

* * *

I learn Rajeev is originally from Bazpur, a tiny town in northeast India. He says it's about halfway between New Delhi and the border of Nepal, and then he pours us two cups of tea. I take a sip. It's warm and minty. Then I look out over the ocean. I've never seen it quite like this. It's a mesmerizing mix of stars and sea from up here.

We're alone in the bridge, which is perched eight stories above the main deck. It's as high as anyone can go on the ship, and the view out over the Pacific Ocean at this hour is perhaps the only good thing about being on this ship. Rajeev's the officer on watch until midnight. The captain's usually the one up here during the day and into the evening. The ship is on autopilot, so Rajeev's job is to keep an eye on the navigational equipment and run through a few routine safety checks.

Rajeev's been hardened by life at sea, like most men who make a living on the ocean. His eyes are bloodshot and exhausted, but beneath it all he's a sweet kid with a kind heart. He's twenty-five years old and stocky, and his accent is part Indian, part British. His first language is Hindi and he's Sikh, which is the most common religion in the Punjab region where he grew up. This would explain why he's the only one on board who's wearing a turban.

"Thanks for tea and for meeting with me," I say. "I wanted to find out more about what it's like to actually live and work on this ship. I have to tell you, I've only been on the ship for twenty-four hours, but its already starting to wear me down."

"This is the first time we have ever allowed passengers on any of the container ships I've worked on," he says. "But I must admit, we were all a little disappointed when we saw the three passengers. We were hoping at least one of you would be a woman."

"Yeah, Tim, Howard, and I are real eyesores." We both laugh. "But it must be awful out here on the ocean. It's just you and the nineteen other crewmembers. When's the last time you even saw a woman?"

"Maybe in port about two months ago. I didn't have a chance to get off the ship in Sydney because the bad weather put us so far behind schedule."

"You haven't seen a woman in two months! Do you get lonely out here on the ocean?"

"Terribly. I miss my family, and it's hard to keep in touch with friends. We have access to satellite internet, but it's expensive and also really slow, so it's almost impossible to keep in contact with anyone."

"What on earth made you want to work on a massive container ship like this?"

Rajeev answers after a slow sip of tea. "I thought this would be a great way to travel and to see the world, and I thought I could make a lot of money. I grew up in such a small town that there really weren't any jobs there. My brother, who is three years older than me, has become a farmer like my father, and that's what I would be doing if I weren't here now. They grow sugarcane, wheat, rice, and mangos, and fix tractors in their spare time."

"How did you get hired for this job?"

Rajeev explains that he spent one year at Indian Maritime University, which gave him the certification he needed to apply for an apprenticeship with the German shipping company Hamburg Süd. Once he got hired, he did two tours as an apprentice. The first was nine straight months at sea on a ship sailing from New York to Brazil. "It was exciting at first," he says.

He stopped in some major American cities like New York and Miami, places he'd only ever dreamt of visiting, and then places in the Caribbean like Negril and Freeport. But he's quick to tell me that it wasn't what he expected. He works fifteen hours a day for three weeks straight and gets only six hours of free time at every other port they stop at.

After his first contract was up, he went back to India for five months to recharge and get his mind right.

"Mentally, it really takes its toll on you out here. Each day at sea is identical—we do the same routine, see the same faces, and eat the same food," he says.

The second contract he signed on for took him from Brazil to Spain and Italy, Switzerland, Belgium, and back to India. That too was a nine-month contract, but by the end of it, he was just completely drained and started wondering if he could do it anymore. Even when the guys get a few hours in port, they don't really get to see anything. They usually have just enough time to take a taxi to a shopping center and stock up on toiletries and snacks and use the Wi-Fi at a cafe to call their families. "Even though I've been to many great places, it's like I've never truly been there," he says, his words reminding me of some of my own travels. Particularly after I left London in October and raced from Belgium to Berlin and then on to Prague all within a few days. I'd been given such a short window of time by the hotels I'd bartered with at each spot that by the time I'd finished the film and photos I'd promised them, the next bus I was ticketed for was ready to board.

Rajeev then dives deeper into the other reason he was drawn to this job. "I love money—I saw the flashy lifestyle people had in American movies when I was growing up, and my dream is to own a Rolls-Royce one day."

He thought he could make a lot of money doing this, but Rajeev shares with me that he was only making seven hundred dollars a month as an apprentice. When he got back to India after his second contract was up, he knew he needed to try something different. He went back to school so he could get the certification required to become a second officer.

By his third contract, his responsibilities had changed along with his title, but so did the stress. There was more pressure on him now: he had to answer directly to an unforgiving captain as they sailed from Japan to Korea and China. He was doing less of the grunt work but felt like he was living under a microscope. Even though he was finally making a little more money, he says, "I learned that money's only good when you're with your loved ones. When you have money and you're alone, it's of no use."

"Wise words," I say.

Rajeev then opens the lid on the darker side of life on the ship. "There's no way to get off the ship if you're unhappy. Let's say you're six months into your contract and want to quit. You can't because it's not like you can just get off at the next jetty with your luggage and take a flight home. Most of the crew are from third world countries and are poor and often underpaid. Usually they are sending their paychecks home to support their families, so they don't even have enough money to pay for a flight home. You need official clearance from the captain anyway if you want the company to give you your passport back and pay for your flight home. The captain is only going to give you that clearance if there's a good reason. Being homesick or overworked isn't going to get you home."

My eyes widen as he tells me that crew members sometimes go crazy. When they first join, they're happy and optimistic; then, around the three-month mark, they start to change. They become impulsive and don't remember how to react to simple situations. Often small disagreements turn into shouting matches and fistfights.

Some crewmembers want to get off the ship so bad that they cut their wrists and pretend to commit suicide in hopes of getting clearance to leave.

Rajeev says that there really isn't much camaraderie on board. He has only made two friends throughout all his tours because it's very macho on board and they are really not encouraged to talk about their feelings. "We have to keep our problems and sorrows to ourselves. The second you show weakness, the crew will turn on you, and you will become the butt of all the jokes. So most of the crew turns to drinking. In the little free time we have each night, you can bet that everyone is alone in his room drinking either beer or straight from a bottle of Jack Daniel's."

This is his fourth contract, and it might just be his last. "It's exhausting. We just sail back and forth from Australia to the United States. This has been the hardest route I've ever sailed because it's such a long stretch at sea. It's thirty days at sea, and we only make two quick pits stops along the way."

At the captain's briefing this morning, I learned that the ship stops in New Zealand and Tahiti for six hours to unload cargo. This news came as a welcome relief. Rajeev tells me that we will have a chance to get off and stretch our sea legs in Tahiti, but that's not for another ten days.

I take my last sip of tea and thank Rajeev for his time and the tea, and then I walk down a dimly lit stairwell followed by a long, gray, lifeless corridor. As I walk toward my cabin, it feels like I'm getting lost in the woods again. All the good vibes and positive energy that I'd built up as I crossed Australia are getting swept out to sea with each wave we leave in our wake.

I wonder where Shiya is and what she's doing. I wonder if I'll ever get the chance to see her again.

I take a long look at myself in the bathroom mirror, feeling the kind of deep loneliness that having the ocean on all sides of you provides. I decide to move my mattress to the floor so the swells we're sailing through won't have a chance to throw me out of bed and to the ground like they did last night.

Lying on the mattress, I feel the port side sinking low and the starboard side rocking high. Getting some solid shut-eye in these conditions is out of the question, and I can't help but curse my decision to spend a month on a freaking cargo ship. Just like the Trans-Siberian Railroad, this isn't nearly as much fun as I thought it would be. Looking for a distraction, I grab the only book I brought. I hold it up to my face and stare at its cover in the moonlight shining through my porthole. *Robinson Crusoe.*

Why on earth did I decide to bring a book that's about a shipwreck?

* * *

When we dock in Papeete, Tahiti, it is sensory overload. I don't know where to look first. It feels like I've just stepped inside a casino and blinking lights and alarm bells are going off all around me. My eyes are spinning like slot machines.

Tahiti is my oasis, my refuge from the dreary life I've been living at sea, the gray interior of the *Caprice* and the dark blue surface of the Pacific Ocean out of the ship's depressingly small porthole windows. Turquoise water sparkles like sequins for as far as my eyes can see. I try to focus on a Polynesian outrigger canoe as it gracefully glides by, but I'm distracted by the town center that's just outside the port's gates. It's buzzing with people, which also feels totally foreign. I've either been alone in my cabin or with the same five or six faces in the dining hall since we set sail.

When I lock eyes on Papeete's historic Catholic church, the Palace de Notre Dame, with its yellow façade and bright red steeple, I'm reminded of something the Polish cook said to me yesterday: "Tomorrow you will have a chance to wash your eyes."

I just kind of nodded along to be nice because I didn't exactly understand what he meant. But as I look at the lush hillside behind the church that leads to majestic Mont Orohena, the extinct volcano that sits smack-dab in the middle of tiny Tahiti, what he said begins to make perfect sense.

I'm dying to get as far away from the *Caprice* as possible, even if it's just for a couple of hours. The captain promised us six hours of freedom, but the Tahitian customs officers, the ones tasked with checking our passports so we can legally enter the country, are behind schedule and running late.

Papeete and its nearly fluorescent green palm trees are so close but yet so far away. Looking at them from the main deck but not having permission to get off and soak in the island's energy quickly turns anticipation into sheer torture.

I know it's cliché, but it's never been so true; the seconds tick by like minutes, and minutes feel like they last as long as days. I pace around the deck and look down at the gangway, dreaming of what it will be like to step foot on steady land again, to walk without wobbling. I envision sinking my teeth into a big fat Tahitian cheeseburger.

"We're losing valuable time!" I complain to Rajeev. "Where the hell are the Tahitian customs officers?"

"They're probably on island time," he says, meaning that everything moves a little slower here and there's absolutely nothing he or anyone can do about it.

I don't subscribe to island time—never have and probably never will. If anything, I like to be early to things. Instead of just lounging around on board the *Caprice*, I've tried to work myself into a productive routine. My goal has been to get up and eat breakfast by 10:00 a.m., which sounds easy enough, but the ship's rocking is so severe that I don't fall asleep until exhaustion takes over in the early hours of the morning. In addition, we're constantly moving the clocks ahead by one hour as we sail into a new time zone. My body clock is completely out of whack.

Yesterday we crossed the international date line, so instead of turning our clocks forward one hour like we had been doing, we had to turn them back twenty-three hours. This was a punch in the gut because it meant that the day at sea we had just lived didn't count. We actually had to live the same Thursday twice! Let me tell you, a day on the *Caprice* is not a day you'd ever want to redo.

When I asked the Chinese deckhand about crossing the international date line, he struggled to find the words he wanted in English and then shrugged and simply said, "Tomorrow is today again," which sums it up perfectly.

It was just another chance to repeat the same routine, which meant that after my breakfast, I went to the ship's tiny gym and tried to work out without sliding and slamming into the walls while we bobbed our way across the Pacific. Then I ate lunch and sat down at the desk in my cabin to write until it was time for dinner.

I will say that the lack of distractions has helped me tap into my creativity. There's no television, no Wi-Fi, and no one to talk to. The crew members are busy all day, and our language barriers prevent in-depth conversation. The two other civilians on board aren't much better.

I do my best to avoid Howard. Every conversation I have with the guy is about him. When I asked him a few days ago if he was interested in learning about anyone else, he said very matter-of-factly, "No. Most people are boring," and then proceeded to talk more about the sailboat he lives on in New Zealand as though my question wasn't meant to serve as a clue.

Tim's Australian and around my age. He has cool tattoos that run down his arms, and a big red hipster beard. He's planning to motorbike across the Americas, but getting a word out of him has been a chore. He's quiet and solemn and only grunts answers at me while we pick at our dinners in the dining hall. Despite that, we've agreed to partner up today and explore the island (if the customs officers ever actually show up). I still haven't had much more than a one-word conversation with the guy, but I'm hopeful Tahiti will change that.

Just as my pacing speeds up, a white car with the words "Police" painted on its roof pulls alongside the *Caprice*, and two husky officers with buzz cuts make their way up the gangway. Once we're cleared to leave, Tim sprints away from the ship like it's on fire, and I hobble along behind him. My toes are still pointed sideways from the steel-tip boots I wore on the hike two weeks ago. Running is out of the question for the foreseeable future.

Port Autonome sits out in the harbor of Nanuu Bay and away from the coastline of Papeete. If you were to draw the letter G, the port would be the last part of the G before you pick your pencil up, so just getting to its exit takes us about twenty minutes. To get to the town center, we have to walk around the humped back of the G, which is another mile or so. Everything seemed so close from the deck of the ship, but it quickly dawns on us that if we continue on foot, we're going to waste a precious thirty minutes on a boring and beat-up industrial road.

We decide to stick our thumbs out and hitch a ride with the next car that drives by, which happens to be the Tahitian customs officers who just granted us access to their island. They're driving back to their office and, thankfully, they stop and pick us up.

We can't help but giggle like schoolboys at our first sight of a woman. She's sitting behind the information desk, and the top button of her blouse is unbuttoned. We stare at her like we're in a trance. She has long curly brown hair and is wearing a white linen skirt, which makes her golden skin glow from the inside out. I look at Tim and shake my head slowly in disbelief. "I really don't know how those guys on the ship do it. They live on that thing for nine months at a time."

Tim nods in agreement.

We ask the woman for advice on where to go and what to see. As she unfolds a colorful tourist map, we tell her we only have about five hours and that we'd at least like to get to a nice beach. Tahiti at its widest is twenty-eight miles across, so I'm assuming that we should be able to find one relatively easily.

She takes a pen, circles a beach that's just outside Papeete on the map, and then says, *"Vingt minutes en taxi."*

Tim and I race across the street in an effort to find Wi-Fi before we venture out of the town center. I immediately understand what Rajeev meant when he said that he's been many places but has never really seen them. We sit inside a restaurant for nearly two hours eating cheeseburgers, answering emails, texting friends, and calling our families. With just over three hours left, we still haven't seen a single thing in Tahiti.

While we were waiting in the information office, I grabbed a brochure that explained a Tahitian term called "mana"—a kind of magical life force that permeates the island's mountain peaks, turquoise waters, and white sand beaches and connects all living things. Eventually, Tim and I pry ourselves away from our phones and take a taxi to the beach that was recommended, hoping to find some mana of our own.

Tahiti is surrounded by an almost continuous coral reef, which is one of the reasons the ocean water is so clear here. The reef creates a shallow pool around the island that gently flows right up to its white sandy beaches. Unfortunately, there's no mana to be had because we don't have enough time to enjoy it. All we have time for is a quick dip in the crystal-clear ocean water and a short walk along the surf before we have to head back to the town center. I'm constantly checking the time, worried we'll be late, which further prevents me from finding magic in the moment.

With forty-five minutes left, the taxi drops us off at a tiki bar just outside the port's entrance. Tim wants to soak up each second of freedom before we have to get back on the ship. Even though I'm nervous about it—one of my few travel anxieties is being stranded without my things—I agree, and we sit at a table outside on the patio and order a pitcher of Hinano beer, which is brewed on the island. It's a light, crisp lager that's perfect for our palm tree backdrop.

It isn't long before we order another and then another.

By our third pitcher, making it back on board the *Caprice* doesn't seem quite so important. I rock back on the edge of my chair and sip bliss-fully from my glass; it reaches every cell of my body like I've never had a beer before.

With five minutes to spare, we are settling our bill when a light bulb goes off in my head. I blurt out to Tim, "How amazing would it be if we could be drinking a few ice-cold beers as we sail away from Tahiti tonight?" Tim, the most enthusiastic I've ever seen him, loves this idea, so I run up to the bartender and ask if we could buy a case of beer. She tells me they only have their beer on tap. Disappointed but not totally defeated, I scan the bar for anything that will do the job. I think of dumping flowers out of a vase that's at the end of the bar, but that's too disgusting, even for me. Then my eyes settle on a case of San Pellegrino water. As I close in on the case, I realize that all the bottles are empty and just waiting to be recycled. Another light bulb goes off. "Perfect!" I yell out.

I quickly grab six bottles and ask the bartender if she will fill them up with beer. The second she puts the cap on the last one, Tim and I grab three bottles each and race out the door. We start running (and hobbling) back through the port.

Just as I'm about to panic, thinking that this beer run has caused us to miss our ship, Rajeev calls out our names. I turn around as the bottles clang together in my arms and look in the direction of his voice. It's a relief to see that he's fifty feet behind us with two other crewmembers.

A wry smile spreads across my face, and it hits me just how much fun all this is.

I crack open one of the Pellegrino bottles and take a long swig to celebrate my sudden relief from anxiety as I wait for Rajeev and the other crewmembers to catch up.

Between the pink Tahitian sunset that's just begun to sprawl across the sky and the buzz from the beer, I'm back to feeling light on my feet. As the five of us walk toward the *Caprice*, we pass around the bottle until it's gone, sharing stories about life that span all corners of the globe. We talk about our favorite music and sports teams and recount stories of girlfriends gone by.

At one point, I lag a few feet behind the group just so I can take in a sky that looks like Van Gogh's painted it. Pinks, purples, and every shade of orange swirl together like if *The Starry Night* was a sunset instead. Maybe I didn't feel the mana the moment I arrived or at the beach, but in this walk back to the ship—sharing a bottle of beer and swapping stories with an eclectic group of near-strangers from Australia, India, China, and the Philippines—I finally stop feeling estranged from other people and from myself. Maybe it's mana, but then again, maybe it's not.

Back on board, Tim and I drag our desk chairs and bottles of beer out onto the deck that's just below the bridge. The view from this high up is breathtaking. We can almost see the other side of the island. Tim brings out a small portable speaker and plugs it into his iPhone. Then he cranks up the volume on Bob Seger's "Against the Wind." As the sun dips below the horizon, I hang my legs over the edge of the deck so all that's below them is the ocean. I take a sip of beer and look down at my toes. They're covered with blisters and are so black and blue that they don't even look like toes, but it doesn't matter. I feel like I've been blessed beyond belief.

I could go back to my cabin and read more about Robinson Crusoe or stare at the ceiling from my bunk, but watching the lights flicker across Tahiti is too magical to turn away from. As the island shrinks in the distance and darkness descends, I realize that our next port of call is in my own country.

I can't see the United States, but I begin to feel it.

CHAPTER 15

UNITED STATES

NORTH AMERICA

"If you risk nothing, you risk everything."

— *Geena Davis*

EVER SINCE I SAILED UNDER the Golden Gate Bridge and arrived in Oakland last week, I've been searching for flights to Amsterdam. Shiya and I have been texting nonstop from the moment I got off the *Caprice*. Our conversations are so immediate, so connected that it doesn't feel like we are separated by a continent and a vast ocean. We've created our own intimate world of words.

I worked up the courage to tell her about the encounter I believed I'd had with her in the empty elevator, and she told me about the concept of twin flames, a connection even deeper and stronger than that of soul mates. Sometimes people are able to sense their twin flame before they actually meet them in person. It's known as "glimpsing" the one. That meeting in the elevator was not just a figment of my imagination; it was a precursor to our meeting one another.

I've also been checking ticket prices for her to fly to the United States, but she isn't working right now and money is tight. I've offered to pay for her flight, but she's graciously turned me down because she wouldn't be able to explain to her mother how she suddenly got the money for such a grandiose trip. The answer could never be, "From this random American man I met two months ago that you've never heard me talk about."

I've learned a lot about her mother's expectations. Shiya isn't to have an intimate relationship with any man, not just me, before marriage. And, of course, that marriage is to be to a Muslim man. Religion seems like it will always be the insurmountable obstacle of our love story. But doesn't love conquer all? It's said to move mountains, and it wouldn't be a cliché if it weren't true, right?

I know I'm guilty of being an overly idealistic thinker, but deep down I believe that one day it won't matter that I'm not a Muslim. I believe our love will overpower the avalanche of obstacles, and I will go to Amsterdam and sweep not just Shiya off her feet, but her mother, her brothers, her sisters, and all her friends too. I'll be so kind and charming and sincere that nothing else will matter once they see how well I treat her. I'll even learn to speak Dutch. I always fantasize that by the end of my trip, they'll all be begging me to stay.

But even if I did fly there, I wouldn't get to meet them. The whole thing would have to be done in secret.

I guess there is some good news. We've inched closer, revealed another layer of our complex selves to one another this week. And our yearning for one another crept up to an all-time high earlier this morning when she begged me to fly there for a long weekend. I texted back, *Ok, I'll do it!*, followed by the airplane emoji, the Dutch flag emoji, and the smiling emoji.

I bought a new T-shirt and a small bottle of cologne to make sure I looked and smelled my best. What I haven't bought yet is the ticket. But today I've made the decision that I'm actually going to do it. I've got to do it. I can't take it any longer. I have to see her.

The flight's a red-eye leaving tonight, which would give me just enough time to take the BART (Bay Area Rapid Transit) from my hotel here in Fisherman's Wharf to San Francisco International Airport. I've already entered my credit card information, and the flight to Amsterdam is all but booked. Just one more click and it's done.

The only thing that's holding me back are my dreams. My big fat stupid dreams that have never been so infuriating.

I'd do anything to see Shiya, but if I fly to Amsterdam to see her, then my dreams die at the airport.

I move my mouse ever so slightly. Its tiny white arrow tracks across the webpage until it hovers over *confirm purchase*.

I run my hands through my hair. It's just a short four-day trip to the Netherlands, and I'll be right back in the United States before I know it, before anyone would know it. I won't post any pictures online from Amsterdam, and I won't even text my friends about it or tell my parents next time we FaceTime. Only Shiya and I would ever know I flew there, and then I could just continue traveling around the world overland once I got back.

Even if someone did find out, isn't that like the most romantic thing ever, to give up my dreams for love?

Maybe love is just meant to be complicated, and that's actually what makes it great. Or maybe, as my mother likes to remind me, I'm the difficult one. The only thing stopping me from flying there is me.

I set my right hand back on the mouse and realize that even though we're an ocean apart, only a single centimeter separates us. All I have to do is press the right button. I run my index finger back and forth over the mouse's smooth plastic coating while I beat myself up over the decision. Every muscle in my body tenses.

I pull up the first picture we took together on my phone. It was the night we met in Melbourne. We look so happy.

I ask my dreams, "Why can't I just fly there and then fly right back?"

I already know the answer. If I fly to Amsterdam, my dreams won't be waiting for me at baggage claim when I get back.

I move my mouse an inch to the right and click my browser closed.

* * *

To get across the United States, and to all the remote hotels I'll be working with, is next to impossible using public transportation, so I'll need a car. Since I sold mine before I left for Africa, I buy a 2000 Mazda Millennia for $2,200 in Palm Springs that I'll sell once I get to Florida.

The cheap clunker turns out to be one headache after another, starting with dying on me the morning after I buy it. The mechanic says the reason is the car stereo was installed incorrectly, and fixing it means I'm out another two hundred and fifty bucks, but that's only the beginning.

Two days later, as I'm driving through the San Gorgonio Pass, which cuts through the massive San Bernardino Mountains to the north and the slightly smaller San Jacinto Mountains to the south, the air-conditioning gives out. A problem as it's 115 degrees, and I didn't think to pack extra water because it was only supposed to be a two-hour trip to Los Angeles, but I've survived worse.

A half mile later, all the dashboard lights flicker and shut off. There's no shoulder, not even an inch, so I can't pull over, and I'm at the very top of the pass, which is well over 2,500 feet above the valley below. Even if I could pull over, I still don't have a data plan for my cell phone, so calling for help isn't an option either. There's nothing to do but keep driving.

A half mile later, I watch the little white needle fling itself into the temperature gauge's red zone. I reach past the steering wheel and tap on the gauge repeatedly, hoping that somehow that's going to magically fix everything.

Smoke starts to pour through the air-conditioning ducts.

"No, no, no! This can't be happening!"

I give the car a little gas, but it barely accelerates. This section of the pass has so many sharp twists and turns that a car could easily come flying around the bend and crash into me. I panic and push the gas pedal all the way down until it touches the floor mat, but the car fails to respond. My hands start to shake, and I go into fight-or-flight mode. I'm all but coasting now.

"I never should have bought this lemon!"

If all this wasn't bad enough, even though I've paid for the car, I don't actually have any proof that I own it. Idan, the salesman I bought it from, still hasn't turned over the title to me like he promised. Whenever I try to reach him, he's nowhere to be found. I thought we had built a bond after I showed him the film I made in his hometown of Haifa, Israel, and we reminisced over how great the falafel is there. But I guess he's the stereotypical sleazy used car salesman after all.

About a mile down the road, the lights on the dashboard flicker and miraculously shoot back to life. I ease my foot down on the throttle and get the car moving close to thirty-five miles an hour. My forward momentum pushes the smoke from the engine up and over the windshield, and I pull my shirt over my face like I'm about to rob a bank as the smoke pours through every vent in the dashboard.

There's just enough juice to get me up and over the last hump in the San Gorgonio Pass. I can see what I think is an exit sign off in the distance.

I say a prayer as the inside of the car fills with more thick smoke: "Dear God, if you get me to the exit ramp, I'll never ask you for anything again."

Thirty seconds later, all the gauges go dead. The speedometer, temperature gauge, gas gauge, and the one that measures RPMs all fall to zero.

The pedals lock up, but there's just enough downward momentum from the backside of the mountain pass that I'm able to get the car to stutter and sputter its way into Moreno Valley.

The car rolls to a complete and utter stop at the foot of the exit ramp. I'm able to just barely steer it off the road and into the dead grass that runs alongside the highway. With my heart pounding, I rest my head on the steering wheel, thankful to still be alive but having no clue where I am or what to do.

Today was supposed to be special.

I was on my way to collect my college roommate, Jeff, at Union Station in Los Angeles. Sixteen years ago, we started a coast-to-coast tour of all thirty Major League baseball stadiums. We were going to finish that tour, and attend a Dodgers game tonight and the Angels game the day after tomorrow. Jeff flew all the way in from his home in South Carolina so we could finally get to our last two ballparks; if we miss the game tonight, who knows when we'd both be able to make it back to California again.

We've had so much fun going to all the stadiums together that when I woke up this morning and realized it was about to come to an end, it felt bittersweet, but now I'm just bitter. And I'm mad as hell at Idan. He promised me I'd have no problem getting across the country in this car, and I couldn't even get out of the county.

I look at my phone and see that it is almost 4:00 p.m.—just three hours until the first pitch. I've got to do something.

It's so hot outside the car that wavy lines appear to hover above the asphalt. I walk a mile to a pay phone to summon a tow truck, carrying my camera bag and wheeling Timberland because the driver's-side door handle snapped off in my hand yesterday and the car no longer locks properly.

The tow truck driver deposits both me and the car at Riverside County Collision. After his mechanic examines the car, Ali, the owner, walks into the waiting room of his shop. I feel like a patient at a hospital, waiting on an uncertain diagnosis. He says, as matter-of-factly as anyone has ever said anything in the history of mankind, "It's going to cost more to fix the engine than what the car's worth."

"I'm going to kill Idan! How on earth am I going to get across the country now?"

Before Ali can answer, I start babbling to him like he's a therapist. I tell him about how I've been hustled and that I've only driven the car about forty total miles since I bought it. I then go into my spiel about how I'm trying to make it around the world overland and that I'm supposed to be picking up my college roommate in LA right now.

Ali cuts me off. "Well, you could sell it for parts. That's really your only option. Maybe you can get a hundred bucks back."

With no other option, I call the local salvage yard and reluctantly make the deal. Just as I'm about to hang up, the voice on the other end tells me to leave the title and keys in the glove box. When I tell the voice that I still haven't gotten the title from the dealership, the voice says the deal's off and hangs up.

I look at Ali. "I can't believe this. Even the salvage yard won't take it."

His response is unforgiving. "Well, you gotta get that car out of here if you don't want us to fix it."

"How exactly do you want me to do that?"

Ali yells over to Juan, the mechanic who checked my car, and tells him to push it out into the street. I plead for Ali to let me leave it in his shop overnight until I can figure out a plan, but he won't budge.

"The car's dead, you don't have the money to get it fixed, you're not from around here, and you don't have the title. You could walk off this lot, and I'd never see you again. No way I'm keeping this car here overnight for you. An abandoned car fee is upward of five hundred dollars in California, and you're not sticking me with that."

I can't drive it, I can't sell it, I can't scrap it, and now I can't even park it.

I watch in confused disbelief as Juan and another mechanic push the car out of the shop's parking lot and into the middle of the cul-de-sac the shop shares with a few other businesses. Just as Juan is about to walk away, I blurt out, "Hey, Juan, you want to buy it for parts?"

Juan stops and looks up as sweat pours off both our faces. "How much?"

"A hundred bucks."

Juan circles the car. He actually kicks all four tires and then peeks in the driver's side window. "Looks like the stereo is new."

"Yep, brand new." *Please, please, please take this nightmare off my hands,* I think.

Juan wipes a blue bandana across his forehead. "I think I could rebuild the engine at home, but if not, I could always sell the tires and stereo. I'll give you fifty bucks for it."

I jump at the deal, but he too wants the title. I make the most sincere promise I've ever made, putting my hand to my heart as I say, "You have my word, if you buy this car, I'll mail you the title the second I get it from the dealership."

What follows is the ultimate sucker punch: the second Juan gives me the fifty bucks, I have to walk inside and pass it over to Ali because that's how much it cost for the diagnostic checkup.

Down and dispirited, I sit on a folding chair in the waiting room. First pitch is in two hours. I text Jeff and tell him about the ordeal, that I won't be able to make it to the game tonight and that our dream is dead, but that he should still go without me because he's flown all the way across the country for it.

My shoulders slump forward. Pounding my fist against my knee, I see the Ganesh tattoo on my forearm. Almost instantly I flip from defeated to determined. I'm not going to miss the game!

Think!

How can I get to the game?

The slogan "We'll Pick You Up" shoots across my brain like lightning.

After a quick online search and a phone call, Gerald's waiting outside Ali's shop to take me to the nearby Enterprise Rent-A-Car. Eighty dollars later, I'm behind the wheel of a brand-new, fully loaded Nissan Altima. I have the car for the next twenty-four hours, and I text Jeff to tell him that we might have a shot of making it after all. The only hurdle now is the legendary LA traffic.

I get on Interstate 10, where I'm weaving in and out of lanes like I'm Dale Earnhardt in his prime. The car drives like a dream, and I can't believe that within two hours of my car exploding on the side of the highway I'm racing across California again.

I keep waiting for a traffic jam, for the famous never-ending string of brake lights, but they never come, and within forty-five minutes I'm miraculously just outside LA.

The only time I actually have to brake is when I slow down to turn into Union Station. And the only time I stop is to let Jeff in.

I peel out as Jeff and I both scream, "Next stop, Dodger Stadium!"

A few hours later, with a Dodger dog in one hand and a beer in the other, we watch Yasmani Grandal, the Dodgers catcher, crush a four-seam fastball over the wall in right field. Jeff and I always root for the home team regardless of the city we're in and tonight's no different. We cheer and chug our beers, just like we did when we first started sixteen years ago.

* * *

Through a somewhat ironic twist of travel fate, I'm able to borrow a car temporarily. My mother had hip surgery, which meant that she'll be on her back and recovering over the next three months. Instead of just letting her car sit idle in their driveway, my parents have kindly offered to let me borrow it.

The car's a two-seater SLK Mercedes. It sounds plush, but it's fifteen years old with a crumbling interior. It's also tiny—so tiny I don't actually fit behind the steering wheel.

When the car was dropped off in the parking lot of the Quality Inn in Denver, I realized right away that it was going to be tricky. I had to take my sneakers off just so I could lose an inch of my length. Even then, my head was flush against the roof, and my legs were pretzeled under the steering wheel. The solution I eventually come up with is a complicated one. I extend my left leg all the way under the brake pedal, lean my torso across the center console, and rest my right elbow in the middle of the passenger seat. Contorting my body like that gives me just enough room to get my right foot on the gas pedal.

I'm only able to drive this awkwardly uncomfortable barefoot way for about an hour and a half at a time before I start cramping up and have to pull over and stretch for a few minutes. It's a one-man clown car, and you should see the looks I get when someone passes me on the highway or when I peel myself out of it at gas stations.

Although I've made it as far east as Denver, I decide to backtrack when I sign a month-long contract with GreenTree Hotels. They have four properties in Arizona and California and have hired me to create films and take photos for their website.

During this time, I call and email Idan repeatedly, but get no response. Call me crazy, but I think that when you sell a car to someone and it blows up less than forty miles from the dealership, the least you can do is apologize (even if you don't mean it).

But this feels more like a reflection of the United States than of Idan. The country is beginning to unravel at its seams this summer. Every time I turn on the news, I see an injustice more disgusting than the one reported the day before. Police brutality is at an all-time high, and it's being unfairly directed at African Americans. The Black Lives Matter movement, which has my support, is in full swing, but so too is the rise of disgusting hate groups. And that's not even mentioning all the ugliness that's surrounding Donald Trump and his bid to become our next president. I feel embarrassed to call this country my own.

Traveling around, I find myself surrounded by unhappy people with their heads always buried in their phones. I've felt more foreign here than almost anywhere else I've been during this journey. I don't remember it being like this two years ago, but maybe I'm just naïve and this whole shady used car situation has left me with my own partisan perspective. I start to wonder if anyone actually cares about anyone else anymore.

After six weeks of failing to get a response from Idan, a mysterious email pops up in my inbox that simply reads, "Call me immediately with regards to the 2000 Mazda Millenia, Kerri."

Who the hell is Kerri?

I dial the number and brace for the worst.

It turns out Kerri is in charge of pushing through all the legal paperwork at Idan's auto yard, and she's taken it upon herself to help.

She tells me that due to a used car–buying loophole, I miraculously might be able to get my twenty-two hundred dollars back. It turns out Idan never received the title from the Manheim Auction House, where he originally bought the car, because Tom, the previous owner, never turned it over like he was supposed to. Apparently there's some sort of time limit in California for how long someone has to turn the title over once they've sold their car at auction. Tom's about to exceed that limit.

Tom's been notified by the auction house that he needs to bring the title to them by 3:00 p.m. tomorrow, and now it's basically a race between

Tom and me. If he gets the title to the auction house on time, then he gets to keep the money he made from selling his car. If I can beat him there, then I'll be the one who gets the money in the form of an arbitration check. But here's the catch: I have to have the car with me.

"Where's the car, Eric?" Kerri asks.

"I have no idea. I sold it to a mechanic for fifty bucks the day the engine exploded."

Kerri lets out an exasperated sigh. "You've got to be kidding me."

"What was I supposed to do? The auto body shop I took it to pushed it out into the middle of the street. I had no choice."

"Can you get it back from the mechanic?"

"Oh, man, I have no clue. He told me that he was going to take the engine out and rebuild it. I know he was thinking of selling the tires too. Does the car need to be running for me to get my money back?"

"No, but the engine needs to be in the car, for God's sake. If you can get it to the auction house, find a woman who works there named Jessica. Tell her that you bought the car from Idan like that."

I could have been anywhere in the United States when Kerri emailed me, but this is the last week of my agreement with GreenTree Hotels, and it just so happened to bring me back out to the Los Angeles area because they had recently bought and rebranded the Old Pasadena Inn.

Which means I'm currently in Pasadena, within sixty miles of where this whole fiasco started.

Kerri gives me the address of the auction house in Anaheim and tells me that the decision is mine to make. She ends the call by saying that she's going to let Jessica know I'm coming tomorrow just in case I happen to show up.

After thanking Kerri profusely, I hang up and stare at the piece of paper I scribbled the auction house address on.

Do I try to get the car back from Juan and have it towed all the way to Anaheim without knowing if Tom's going to beat me there with the title? Or do I just swallow the twenty-two-hundred-dollar loss and move on?

I didn't come this far to suddenly play it safe. All the best moments of my journey have occurred when I push all my chips to the center of the table and go all in. Because even the times I've lost that hand and had to start back at scratch, I've gained more than I ever could have imagined.

Adrenaline fires from my glands. There's nothing like that initial rush of blood when you feel inspired. God damn, it feels good.

I crack an excited smile and call out to my empty room, "Tom, you better be one tough son of a bitch because the race is on, buddy boy!"

The next morning, I'm stuffed inside Mom's Mercedes, barreling toward the San Moreno Valley like a man on a mission.

When I pull into Ali's shop, Juan comes out of the garage to greet me. I was able to track him down last night and offered to buy the car back for four times what he paid me for it. He gives me a greasy handshake, and after I begrudgingly hand him two crisp one hundred-dollar bills, he writes the address of the car's location on the back of a cream-colored business card. I don't stick around for small talk. Instead, I frantically dial a tow company and arrange to have them meet me at the address Juan gave me and take off myself to find it.

I wind my mom's Mercedes through a few residential streets in Moreno Valley and eventually find the address Juan has given me. When I lock my eyes on the car from hell, it gets a sadistic smile out of me. I'd never thought in my wildest dreams or worst nightmares that I'd ever see this hunk of junk again, yet there it is. The sun's beating down on it in the driveway of a two-bedroom townhouse. I park alongside the curb while I wait.

The tow truck company I called said they'd have someone here in about an hour, but I'm desperate for them to show up sooner. Not only do I need to beat Tom to the auction house, but I can't tell you how awkward it feels to be shoeless and crammed inside a tiny clown car outside some stranger's home whose front door is propped wide open. I start to worry that Juan already sold the car to whoever lives here and is just hustling me out of an extra two hundred bucks. He knows that I still don't have any proof of ownership.

I wait anxiously. It's another god-awful triple-digit day in Moreno Valley. I turn on the radio to pass the time, but when I turn up the air-conditioning, it starts belting out wave after wave of hot air.

I get out and pop the hood open, but I have no idea what to look for. All I can do is slam the hood shut in frustration and stuff my long limbs back inside the car. I drive up and down the street a few times to make sure that the only thing that's given out is the air-conditioning. The car seems to be running okay, but there's a faint rattling sound that can't be good. After a few laps around the neighborhood, I pull back alongside the curb.

Two agonizing hours go by before the tow truck appears. I beg the driver, Anthony, who has a mullet and colorful tattoos up and down his arms, to get this thing the hell out of here as fast as humanly possible. I still haven't been able to tell if anyone knows I'm here to remove a nearly two-ton car from their driveway.

Thirty minutes later, I'm following Anthony west on I-215 while keeping my eyes locked on my Mazda, which is bobbing back and forth like a buoy on the back of his truck. All the while I've got my fingers crossed (literally) in hopes that my mom's car gets me all the way to Anaheim today.

We drive through Riverside and then Corona, but right around Anaheim Hills we hit midafternoon traffic and slow to a standstill. I begin to bake inside the unair-conditioned car. As I melt through my seat, my legs start twitching and cramping. I'm long overdue for a stretch break. I'm overheating and exhausted, but I can't allow myself to pull over.

Usually I find the lesson from hard times like this in hindsight. I only really enjoy those challenges when I'm looking back on them. But today I can appreciate it as it's happening.

This feels like a new level of awareness.

With my legs tangled around the pedals and sweat cascading off my body, I embrace everything about the awful situation and remind myself that this is exactly what I need. The pain becomes pleasure, and I begin to feel a swell of thankfulness.

By the time Anthony and I are outside the front gate of the Manheim Auction House, I have less than twenty minutes to drop the car off and find Jessica. But the property is so big and so confusing that neither of us has any idea where to take the car. Plus, there are more security checkpoints here than at Fort Knox.

I ditch my mom's car in the visitor parking lot and hop in with Anthony to expedite the process. Even with the personal growth I've attained today, I can unequivocally state that I still want my money back. Even more so than before.

Every guy we drive past on our way to Gate A looks like Tom. There's Tom with tan khaki pants on and a blue button-down shirt. There's Tom wearing stonewashed jeans and an Anaheim Angels ball cap.

This place is crawling with Toms!

I look over at Anthony. "Do you think we can make it in time?"

"I don't know, man. I hope so, for your sake."

When we show up at the Jefferson Gate five minutes later, we're told by the guard that we're going to have to make a space because there are no spaces left. Thousands of cars are nearly piled on top of one another from one side of the chain-linked perimeter to the other.

With ten minutes left, Anthony and I wedge the car into half a space. I wave over to the guard for approval. It's good enough for him, so he slaps a bright orange sticker on the driver's side window and then gives me a form to take up front.

Anthony's job is officially done, but I beg him to drive me back to the main entrance of the auction house office so I can find Jessica. There's no way I'll make it if I have to walk that far.

He agrees and then distracts me from my jangling nerves during the ride back over by telling me about his life as a tow truck driver. He shares horrible stories about all the times he's seen dead bodies at accident sites. As nice—if somewhat creepy—as Anthony is, I'm ready to be done with his morbid stories by the time we get to the front of the auction house. The guard at the main gate stops us and won't allow the tow truck inside the visitor's parking area. So Anthony drops me off about fifty yards shy of the building's entrance.

The clock on his dash reads 2:55 p.m. I take off in a full sprint after thanking him for his help. On my way to the front doors, I run past a guy who is leaving with a wide smile on his face. It's Tom. It has to be Tom. I shoot him an evil look.

When I push open the doors and clear security, it's exactly 3:00 p.m., and it feels like I've blown my chance. Thankfully there's still one person at the claims counter. Wheezing for air and drenched in sweat, I ask for Jessica.

"I'm Jessica," says the woman. "You must be Eric. Kerri mentioned you might be coming by today."

As I try to catch my breath, I say, "Did Tom beat me here with the title?"

She smiles. "He didn't show up today. Looks like you'll get your refund."

CHAPTER 16
UNITED STATES
NORTH AMERICA

"I wanted to teach people how to dream a bigger dream."

— *Phil Alden Robinson, director of* Field of Dreams

J UST AFTER RAY KINSELLA MOWS down all his crops to build a baseball field in the middle of his Iowa farm, he smiles and says to his wife, "I have just created something totally illogical—am I completely nuts?"

Later that same night as he looks out his bedroom window at the empty baseball field, he whispers to himself, "Something's gonna happen out there—I can feel it."

I'm on my way to Chicago, but I've made a detour because I always promised myself that I'd get to the place they filmed *Field of Dreams* one day.

I pull down a long, dirt Dyersville driveway, and the first thing I see is the instantly recognizable Kinsella family farmhouse where Kevin Costner, playing Ray, said those lines. The baseball field carved into an Iowa cornfield back in 1989 is still here, and it's become a popular tourist attraction. Nearly two million visitors have turned up at the farm over the years.

The softly undulating, crop-covered hills here are a stark contrast to the landscape I've been driving through the last two weeks. My favorite stretch of scenery (to date), was when I left Sedona at sunrise. The way the light reflected off the desert town's gigantic red rocks gave me a new appreciation for earth's architect. Just an hour later, the caked desert gave way to Coconino National Forest and the winding road took me towards the highest point in Arizona. It felt like I'd suddenly landed on another planet, and I couldn't help but stop and look out over the sea of ponderosa pines that filled the canyon I'd just threaded through.

That afternoon I unpacked my lunch in Horseshoe Bend's dusty parking lot and finished off an apple as I hiked to the east rim of the Grand Canyon. I got onto my stomach and inched to the edge so I could hang my camera over and snap an unobstructed shot of the U-shaped river. Utah's red rock formations were equally impressive, and the baked brown and yellow landscape changed one final time when I drove to the top of Big Cottonwood Canyon to Solitude Ski Resort in the Wasatch Mountains. I'd reached an elevation of nearly 8,000 feet by afternoon's end and the meadowed mountains surrounding me rose to snowcapped peaks.

I continued eastward, driving for thirteen hours yesterday, all the way from the west side of Wyoming to the east side of South Dakota. Now my left arm dangles out the window of my mother's car against the warm Midwest air, and when I see the baseball diamond, it becomes impossible not to smile. The grass has just been cut, and the air smells like late September.

When the producers of the movie were scouting farms in Iowa and came across the farm where the Lansing family had lived since 1906, they simply went up and knocked on the front door and pitched the idea. The Lansings replied, "Sure, we like baseball." Even though the Lansing family sold the property in 2011, it still remains open to the public. It's free to visit, and you're even allowed to come and play catch if you want to.

Stepping on to any movie set feels surreal, and this is no different. It's like I've been transported back to a much simpler time. A father is pitching underhanded to his young son in the infield, and a few people are strolling across the outfield in pairs. There's a bright red barn behind the farmhouse, and the sun is hovering just above the left-field cornstalks. Everything feels so mystical under the bright blue sky that I'm half expecting to hear the same mysterious whisper Ray heard.

"If you build it, he will come."

In the movie, Ray maintains a steadfast belief that this completely useless baseball field in the middle of his Dyersville farm does in fact have a purpose. He refuses to stop believing in it. That's the thing I've always loved and related to about Ray. He did things without a clear understanding of why he was doing them.

At the beginning of my journey, I often found myself having to trust my gut just like Ray. When he cut down his cash-yielding crops, the whole town ridiculed him, and while no one ridiculed me for my decision to do what I'm doing, no one could really see what I wanted to create for myself. When I told my cousin that I was going to write about my inner journey around the world, she replied, "Don't you think that's a bit conceited?"

I do feel a bit self-absorbed holding my camera up to my face in public to get certain shots as well as the number of times I mention myself in my stories. But my point is that I couldn't put everything I was hoping to become into words because, like Ray, it was something I just felt.

In the movie, nearly a year goes by before the ghost of Shoeless Joe Jackson shows up on Ray's infield lawn. Ray walks out to meet him and pitches him a few balls, which Shoeless Joe belts high and deep into the cornfield. At the end of each day, Shoeless Joe walks across the outfield and back into the cornstalks until he slowly fades away. Eventually, more ballplayers from the early 1900s begin to manifest out of thin air, and they spend their afternoons playing on the field where I'm now standing.

I kick off my flip-flops and toss them behind first base, then I walk around the grass just behind the infield. The soft sod underneath my bare feet feels like medicine after being crammed inside my mother's tiny car all day.

As I close in on the pitcher's mound, the urge to take just one swing fills every pore of my body. I have a funny feeling that one swing's all it will take to hit one deep into the cornfield just like Shoeless Joe. I'm not saying this because I'm good at baseball but because this place has so much pixie dust in its cornstalks that the ball would surely jump off my bat even if I swing and miss by a mile.

I ask the father who's pitching to his young son if he'll take a second to toss me one. He agrees, and so I grab a wooden bat that's propped up against the backstop and dig my toes into the dirt around home plate. I think of the irony as I take a couple warm-up swings. I didn't plan to be shoeless.

Shoeless Joe got his nickname because he had blisters on his feet from a new pair of cleats. His feet hurt so much that he decided to take his cleats off before he went up to bat in a game in Greenville, South Carolina. The story goes that a heckling fan noticed this and, as Jackson was running to third base in his socks, the fan shouted, "You shoeless son of a gun."

I tap my bat on home plate and then look at my bare feet, still bruised and battered from the hiking boots that were too small in Australia. Then I close my eyes and envision the ball sailing out into the Dyersville cornfield. It's 281 feet to left field, 314 to center, and 262 to right field, which is just a shade smaller than most Major League Baseball stadiums.

"Okay, I'm ready, go ahead," I call out.

As the man starts his windup, I raise my right arm up and cock the bat back.

I can't believe I'm about to hit a home run at the famous Field of Dreams.

As the ball comes toward me, I can see the red seams of the baseball like time's strength has been sapped. I twist my hips back and hitch my shoulders up, and as the ball crosses the front of the plate, I close my eyes and uncoil my body as fast as humanly possible.

With my eyes closed, the beautiful crack of the bat is amplified. You can only get this thunderous sound when using a wooden bat. The crack is like music to my ears.

It feels like I've sent the ball flying, but before I can open my eyes and watch it land in the cornfield, I start thinking about whether I should jokingly jog around the bases to celebrate or if I should just do some sort of silly home run dance around home plate.

I open my eyes and look up into the late afternoon sky. The sun is just about to set in the west. I try to track the baseball as it sails away, but I don't see it.

Maybe I've hit it so hard that it's already landed in the cornfield.

It takes a second for it to dawn on me to look down. The ball is rolling slowly toward second base. It stops before it even clears the infield grass.

I shrug my shoulders and laugh as I sarcastically say to the pitcher, "Even though I'm shoeless, I guess I'm no Shoeless Joe."

Act three of the movie begins when Ray hears a third message from the same mysterious voice. This time the voice tells him to "Go the distance." As I walk across the outfield grass toward the towering cornstalks,

I replay that line over and over. It starts swirling through me. Even after having traveled over forty thousand miles across the surface of the globe, and with another twenty-five thousand miles to go across North and South America and the Atlantic Ocean, some part of my being feels that I won't have gone far enough.

As I stand face-to-face with the magical cornstalks, it dawns on me that I've always left one entire continent off the list. I've never thought to include Antarctica because getting there overland just seemed too far-fetched, too implausible. No one goes to Antarctica anyway.

Whenever I've seen Antarctica on TV or in magazines, I've only ever seen research teams of scientists or those *National Geographic* explorer types there.

I look down a row of cornstalks and ask them, "Is Antarctica even open to the public?"

I hope for an answer; after all, I am thirty-six, the same age as Ray, and it's also around the same time of the year and same hour of the day when he heard the mysterious voice for the first time.

But no answers come.

I don't know the first thing about how one would get to Antarctica without flying. Then there's getting a visa. Antarctica isn't even a country, it's a continent, and so where would I even have to go to apply for one? Still, I've got to get to Antarctica one way or another or this circumnavigation of the globe won't ever fully feel right.

I take a big step forward until I'm within arm's reach of a dangling cornhusk. Eye-to-eye with the outfield wall.

I peer through the towering green stalks and wonder what would happen if I walked through them.

"Am I going to melt into you and disappear like Shoeless Joe?" I ask them.

I grin because I know that I won't, but it does feel sort of heavenly out here. The sun has just passed the horizon, and it's creating a majestic golden glow across all of Iowa. Everyone who was milling around the field has piled back in their cars and headed home. I'm the only one still here. Fireflies begin to pop out of the dusk like tiny fireworks, and it reminds me of when I would collect them in mason jars in my grandmother's backyard years and years ago.

I run my fingers along one of the stalks and then stick my right arm into the cornfield. I pull it out quickly to make sure it hasn't disappeared, which, of course, it hasn't.

I take one full step in the cornfield; then I jump back out. I feel like I'm five again.

I take a deep breath. On my exhale, I charge in, and a few of the taller stalks brush against my face. I shield my eyes with my arms as I keep walking deeper and deeper.

By about my seventh or eighth step, I hear a voice.

I kid you not! I hear a freaking voice!

My heart skips not just one but two beats. I can't quite make out what the voice is saying, but I'm one hundred percent sure that the word begins with a Z.

This is incredible; I'm going to hear the voice just like Ray!

The Z sound intensifies, and as I cup my ear and lean deeper into the cornfield, I whisper, "What do you want to tell me?"

I feel a sharp prick inside my ear.

I swat at my ear a few times, and that's when I realize that the voice I'm hearing isn't a voice at all. It's a BEE!

It's a big, bright, yellow-and-black-striped bumblebee! I'd seen a few buzzing about in the outfield earlier, and now one's flown directly into my ear and gotten lodged in there!

I run back out of the cornstalks and across center field while slapping at my ear like a maniac. I grab the bottom of my earlobe and try to shake it loose, but the bee's so plump with nectar that it won't budge.

The buzz intensifies and turns into one long zzzzzzzzzz sound.

I take my index finger and scoop it deep inside my ear, which does the trick and sends the sumo-sized bee floating away. I survey the damage done to my ear, and I'm thankful when I realize that I'm completely fine.

As I stand alone in center field, I smile. I can legitimately say that when I walked into those magical movie cornfields, something spoke to me.

I heard a voice out in those cornstalks! So what if it was just a bee.

At the beginning of the movie, when Ray's explaining the voice to his wife, he says, "When primal forces of nature tell you to do something, the prudent thing is not to quibble over details."

I'm not going to quibble over the details about the voice I heard. All I will say is that maybe I'm no Shoeless Joe Jackson and maybe I'm not meant to hit home runs into this Iowa cornfield like he did. But maybe, just maybe, I've got a little Ray Kinsella magic in me after all.

Go the distance I shall.

* * *

My drive from Chicago to Pittsburgh helps shift my thoughts away from the mini depression I've fallen into over the fact that none of the ships that sail to Antarctica have taken me up on my film and photography offer. But instead of thinking about the penguins and orca whales I was hoping to see, the whole thing has reminded me about the worst part of traveling alone.

I never have anyone to commiserate with.

Just once I'd like to be able to share something with someone, so it will be good to drown my Antarctic sorrows over a few beers with one of my best buds this weekend.

The last time I came to visit Justin, he lived on the other side of Pittsburgh, in Wexford to be exact. His second daughter, Ella, had just been born and his first daughter, Livia, had just turned two. His new neighborhood in Peter's Township is quite impressive, and his house is picture perfect. It looks like one of those model homes that every American family aspires to have one day. The only thing missing is the white picket fence.

He told me not to honk the horn or ring the doorbell when I arrive because his daughters might be sleeping, so he bounds out of his front door to greet me the second my headlights hit his house. He's six foot two and slender, and his dark hair has receded since my last visit four years ago, which will surely be a target of mine for some good-natured ribbing this weekend.

Justin's been a constant cog in my inner circle for over twenty years now. He's actually the only person I've texted with every single day during my travels (Wi-Fi permitting), and ironically we rarely talk about my travels. It's usually dumb off-the-cuff stuff that helps me take my mind off the stresses of my journey. When we give each other a big bear hug on his front lawn, it hits me how important all those seemingly inconsequential texts have been along the way. He kept me sane in Sudan and reeled me in in Russia when things seemed destined to completely fall apart.

Justin and I met way back in 1994 at an AAU basketball team tryout. About thirty kids showed up at the barnlike East Side Youth Center in

Allentown for the tryout from twenty area high schools. Neither Justin nor I made the team, but fortunately for us, the coaches decided to start a second team called the Wolfpack with all the players that were not good enough to get selected for the Blue Devils.

We were terrible. We were the castoffs, the Bad News Bears of basketball. We even had a player we affectionately called "Stone Hands" because he couldn't even catch the most basic of bounce passes. Looking back on it now, I almost think that the coaches of the Blue Devils put the Wolfpack together for their own amusement. During our first season, we were completely overmatched by every other team we came up against, but whether we lost by seventy points or seven, I loved every minute of it. I loved the instant camaraderie we formed as oddball teammates and playing practical jokes with my new and goofy friends in the bleachers in between games.

Our bond has been brotherly ever since, and I am not surprised in the least that Justin has gone on to become a husband and a father, and I have not. Despite our solid friendship, it's comical how different we are. As he takes me on a tour of his new house, I can't imagine living in the suburbs of Pittsburgh and having a mortgage, a wife, and two kids. And surely he cringes at the idea of living on the road and out of a backpack like me.

I wander, he plans; I spend, he saves; he's Catholic, I'm anything but; he's clean-shaven, and my hair's nearly half way down my back now. He's a numbers guy and I'm an ideas guy, but we've always bonded over a ballgame and a beer, which he pours me once we get down into his basement.

He's created the perfect man cave down here. There's a fully stocked bar, a pool table, and two rows of movie theater–style seats that face a monstrous TV. He even has a pop-a-shot basketball arcade game. As we sip our beers, it's not like we need to catch up because we text every day, but I fill him in on the whole Antarctica thing and share my disappointment about not being able to go. I tell him, "I broke one of my golden travel rules and used Google to find out how to get to Antarctica, and then I emailed all the companies that sail that far south, but none of them have responded." I take a big swig of beer and add, "It's actually going to be impossible for me to get there."

"Well, it's only been a week since you emailed them—give it some more time, bro."

Suddenly feeling stressed out, I say, "There will always be a big hole in my story for the rest of my life. Whenever I tell people that I once traveled around the entire world without flying, they'll all say, 'Even Antarctica?' I'll have to reply, 'Well, no, not Antarctica.'"

"Can you pay for a ticket?"

"I can't afford it—the cheapest ticket is close to ten thousand dollars."

The basement door creaks open, and Justin's wife calls down to him, "The girls just got out of the bath and it's time to put them to bed—can you come up and help me?"

Before Justin runs upstairs, he gives me the password for the Wi-Fi. I haven't been online all day, and I should probably check my email because I'm headed to Toronto once the weekend ends. I emailed one hundred hotels there before I left Chicago this morning, and I'm hoping that one has already replied by now.

I scroll through my emails and delete the junk mail I've gotten since the last time I logged in. I don't see any responses from Toronto hotels yet. However, as I get to the last email in my inbox, I see that the subject line reads: *Re: Antarctica.*

Before I let myself get too excited, I remind myself of the staggering odds against one of these cruise companies actually accepting my offer. There are only twelve companies in total that sail there. I'm sure it's just going to be a short email that ends with the words, "Thank you for your proposal, but we are not interested at this time." In order for me to get just one hotel to agree to my offer, I usually have to email around fifty to sixty, so I've gotten countless similar emails from around the world.

But I still race to open the email.

Eric, we like your proposal, and we would like to accept your offer.

My brain is so confused that instead of yelling out *yes, yes, yes*, I call out *no, no, no, this can't be true* to the empty basement. As I read on, the next line says, *Antarpply Expeditions would like to offer you a twin cabin on our voyage—Weddell Sea Quest, January 10–21, free of charge.*

I scream out, "FREE OF CHARGE!"

A feeling crashes over me, unlike anything I've ever encountered. The energy inside my body starts pulsating like giant waves during a winter swell.

My knees go weak, and I have to lean against the bar.

I reread the email a second and third time. I want to make sure that this email is in fact real and not some cruel and twisted practical joke. Once I confirm that I read everything correctly, it hits me that I will actually be going to Antarctica.

I stand there dumbstruck, truly dumbstruck.

Not only does it mean I'm going to get to Antarctica, but it means that I'll now have the chance to complete my dream of making it around the entire world and across all seven continents entirely by land and sea. This email has to go down as the most miraculous news of my life.

Once I get my wits about me, I run upstairs into the living room. This is the first time in all my travels that I've had good news to share and someone to share it with.

I look down the hallway and directly into the bedroom of one of Justin's daughters. Her door is slightly open, and there's my buddy of nearly twenty-four years, tucking his daughter into her pink princess sheets.

It brings a hush over me. Neither of them knows I'm there, so I just quietly watch one of life's most precious moments. The sound of laughter drifts out of the room, and he hands her a teddy bear and then kisses her on her forehead. It's really a thing of beauty. I don't exactly know if and when I'll ever have kids of my own, but watching him, so selfless with his time and energy, is inspiring.

As I stand there, I think back to the reason we met. We were the castoffs, the ones who were deemed not good enough to make the first team when we were fourteen, but I can't help but swell with pride for both of us. He's living out his calling here in Pittsburgh, raising a beautiful family, and now I've got the chance to continue living out mine in, of all places, Antarctica.

* * *

When I'd initially bought my refurbished Canon camera, just a few blocks from my parents' place, I couldn't figure out how to record video on it. In my first video, the old me says, "I don't even know if it's on," and my face is completely out of focus, as is everything in the background. Since then, I've vastly improved, creating videos and photos for over 130 hotels in 30 countries around the world. I feel like a true professional, and my creativity has just about come full circle. Geographically, I've almost come full circle too. After traveling as far north as Toronto and then snug against the eastern seaboard as I moved south, I've been staying with my parents in Port Saint Lucie, Florida, just like I did before flying to South Africa to start this whole journey. And just like last time, they've cleared their schedules to see me off.

After we laugh some more at that very first video I made, it's time for me to pack up my camera and computer and start the next long leg of my journey. The Celebrity cruise I'll be boarding later today at Port Everglades will make stops in Colombia, Panama, Ecuador, Peru, and Chile. I'll disembark on Christmas Eve in Valparaiso, Chile. That section of the journey will be easy, but after that I'll have just sixteen days to make it 2,500 backbreaking miles by bus across rough and often unpaved roads to Ushuaia (pronounced Oosh-why-a). Antarpply Expedition's cruise departs for Antarctica from the southernmost city in Argentina, and I'll have to race across South America if I want to make it to the port in time.

After lifting Timberland into the trunk, my dad slams it shut, and then we arrange ourselves just like we did the day I left for Africa. My dad's driving, my mom's perched in the seat behind him, and I'm riding shotgun. I can't think of a better way to honor the way they raised me than to follow my deepest dreams, but I also know that this journey has been pretty rough on my parents. Not only did I put myself through all those often dangerous bus rides, but I put them through it as well. My father has felt every bump in the road, and my mother has chewed all her nails to nubs by now.

Over the two years I've been gone, I've missed every birthday, holiday, and special event imaginable, while all of my younger cousins got married and popped out enough kids to field a little league baseball team of their own. My parents are my biggest cheerleaders, but I'm sure they'd much rather see me settle down and start a family than head to South America today.

Both my mother and father had serious operations this spring and summer while I was bobbing across the Pacific and then traipsing through the US. I wasn't there for them. Their recoveries were long and agonizing, and all that they had was each other. My dad, who had a knee replaced, had to hobble around the house to help my mother, who had hip surgery, and vice versa. They were housebound for months, and when I'd call to check up on them, it sounded like they'd been clawing at the walls.

I never wished for a brother or sister while growing up, but now that I'm older, I think it would have been nice to have one, even if all that sibling did was take the attention away during my absence. My parents never even hinted once that they thought my traveling was a bad thing, but as time keeps ticking by, the questions about grandkids are getting louder and louder. I always reply, "One day."

But that *one day* is starting to feel like it's never going to come. When I was in my twenties, I thought I'd want kids by the time I was thirty, and then when I was thirty, I assumed I'd want them by thirty-five. I turned thirty-six this summer, and the desire to have a child still hasn't surfaced. The older I've gotten, the more unimaginable it's starting to feel.

My friends with children always tell me that I'm only able to travel the way I do because I don't have kids, but I'd like to think that I'd still be out here trying to make my way around the world even if I had a child (and they'd be right here alongside me). I'd rather let my child see my struggles and just how hard I'm fighting for my dreams than hide all that good stuff. I imagine that kind of openness would bring us closer together as a family. But what do I know about parenting? Everything seems so much easier when it's only imagined.

Even though I may not know anything about parenting, I can say one thing definitively about parents: I've been blessed with the best. As my dad drives past the line of swaying palm trees and pulls through the main gate at Port Everglades, I am flooded with gratitude for their support. This journey would be a hell of a lot harder if I didn't have it. I hug my parents good-bye and have a hard time letting go, just like I did when we were in Greece.

While the determination and faith my parents passed down to me have been my strongest weapons, that camera I initially didn't know how to work has turned out to be my most important tool. It's allowed me to barter my way around the world, even to Antarctica; more importantly, it's helped me to express a side of myself I never knew existed.

CHAPTER 17
CHILE – ARGENTINA
SOUTH AMERICA

"Ushuaia, end of the world, beginning of everything."

— *town motto of Ushuaia*

I T'S CHRISTMAS EVE, AND VALPARAÍSO, Chile, reminds me of a Lite-Brite. The city's colorful colonial houses are stacked on top of one another, and they rise up a series of steep hills that cup the bay like an ancient Roman amphitheater. I love when things take me by surprise just like this. I guess that's the beauty of not using a guidebook or looking things up online before I arrive at my destination.

Nicknamed the "Jewel of the Pacific," Valparaíso was declared a world heritage site in 2003, but for as much as there is to see here, I feel like I don't have a second to spare, and once the *Infinity* settles into her spot at port, I race toward the ship's gangway.

I've got to cover over 2,500 miles by bus in sixteen days, zigzagging between Chile and Argentina to make it to Ushuaia, at the southernmost tip of Argentina, in time for the cruise to Antarctica. I'll be making my way through Patagonia, an isolated region dominated by the mighty and monstrous Andes Mountains. The tiny towns that dot its countryside are few and far between, and I've heard from other travelers that many of the roads will be as arduous as the African ones I know all too well.

It's easy to see how this whole thing could get derailed for someone with even the most precise travel plans. And my travel plans (as per usual) are anything but precise. The margin for error is so small that if anything should go wrong, there's a good chance that I won't make it to Ushuaia in time. As nice as Antarpply Expeditions has been to me, they've made it very clear that there isn't a backup cruise should I miss this one. All their other cruises for the rest of the season are fully booked up. I max out all the Spanish I know asking the first police officer I see outside the port where the *estación de autobús* is. I quickly follow the direction he points and after stopping and asking someone inside a small bodega the same question, I eventually find Avenue Pedro Montt and then Terminal Rodoviário Valparaiso. I buy the first ticket available through a tiny window that's got metal bars separating the saleswoman and me. By 2:15 p.m., I'm on the bus to Santiago, Chile's capital and largest city.

It's a straight shot, just two hours southeast, and I've got a seat with decent legroom in the first row of the bus. There's an elderly man across the aisle from me; he's bald but a wispy white beard covers much of his face. It feels far too warm for the frumpy blue sports jacket he's wearing and when I snap a selfie that includes him he scowls. Chile Route 68 will see us all the way to Santiago and the bus bends around rolling hills and low rising slopes when we pass by the royal blue top of Peñuelas Lake.

Just before dusk descends, I meet Ignacio, the owner of the charming six-room Providencia Bed and Breakfast. He welcomes me warmly, and we wish each other a Merry Christmas. I thank him for accepting my offer and agreeing to host me for two days in exchange for the photos I'll take. He leads me up the steps to the living room and lobby, which is where I wait as he runs to the kitchen to get me a cold glass of water. If I had to guess, I'd say Ignacio is in his late forties; his hair is a mix of salt and pepper, and it gives him that distinguished-gentleman look that's hard to attain.

When Ignacio returns, I get right down to business so I can plan the time I'll need for the work. "What type of photos would you like me to do for you?"

It takes him a few seconds to translate my English to Spanish and then his Spanish thoughts back again. "I just want the photos from the sky," he says. He waves his hands in circles and then finds the word he's looking for. "Drone," he blurts out.

I'm completely caught off guard by his request because I've never done drone photos for a hotel. I tell him, "There must be some mistake."

Just as the words come out of my mouth, I realize that the mistake is mine.

I remember that when I emailed the hotels and hostels in Santiago, I had added that I could do drone photos in exchange for a room. When I was in Florida, I decided to buy a drone to enhance a film I was making for my parents' country club. The video footage of the lakes and rivers that cut through the club's sprawling golf course added incredible drama to the film, and instead of returning the drone to Best Buy like I'd planned, I decided to keep it because I thought it would increase the likelihood of hotels accepting my offer moving forward. But when I was packing up Timberland for South America, I realized that I didn't have enough room for the drone, so I left it behind with my parents.

I sheepishly say, "I don't have the drone with me although my email did promise drone photography in exchange for a room. I screwed up, and I'm sorry."

Ignacio, rightfully so, is skeptical of my explanation. I can tell that he thinks that I never had a drone to begin with and just used it to reel him in. I've heard from many hotels that travel photographers and bloggers like me often fail to do all the wonderful work that they've promised.

The language barrier isn't helping much either, and the more I talk in English, the more frustrated Ignacio becomes with me. I try to explain that I've worked with over a hundred and thirty hotels around the world and that I can do amazing photos and a wonderful film for him without the drone, but he isn't buying it. He skeptically says, "But you promised a drone," and I keep saying, "I know, and I'm so sorry, I didn't have enough room in my bag."

I even unzip Timberland to show him that there isn't so much as a square inch to spare, but that seems to only infuriate him. I offer to do photos and a short film of the guest rooms, the exterior of the house, and the breakfast he offers his guests, but he turns it down. He's adamant that the only reason he accepted my offer was specifically for the drone photos. Ignacio says, "Instead of the two nights, I now can only offer you one. I will let you stay tonight, but only because it's Christmas Eve."

I stare out a wide-open bay window at a sea of thatched orange roofs. There's a vase with white and pink carnations on the windowsill. I could stay here for the one night and then try to find another place for tomorrow night, but the thought of staying for free without doing any work for him in return doesn't sit well with me. Plus, Ignacio thinks I'm lying, and I know that I won't be able to sleep a wink here.

I apologize to Ignacio, and we part ways without so much as a handshake. He's happy to see me traipse down the steps and out onto the street. I shuffle along, feeling defeated.

I'd spotted an open Starbucks on my way to the bed-and-breakfast, so I make my way back there to catch my breath and hopefully hatch a plan to barter with another hotel in Santiago. But by the time I order a coffee and get the Wi-Fi code to actually work, it's dark out, and I know that bartering isn't going to happen. Most families spend Christmas Eve together in Chile, and I know that no one's going to be checking their email for the rest of the night. The streets are completely empty, and all of the stores I just walked by were already closed. So I decide to search for a hostel online, which is painful when I see the prices for even the cheapest rooms, but I grit my teeth and settle on the Bellavista Hostel only because it's within walking distance. I hitch my camera bag up onto my shoulders and grab Timberland and begin the lonely process of making my way across the empty city on Christmas Eve.

* * *

All the buses that happen to be heading south are night buses that usually leave around midnight. I hate traveling that way. Not only do you miss out on seeing the landscape, but it's also damn near impossible to sleep. I don't fit in a normal bed, let alone a cramped South American bus seat that's built for someone a full foot shorter. Add in all the stops and starts and swaying from the uneven Patagonian roads, and it quickly becomes a punishing and sleepless affair.

After two nights in Santiago, I settle in for a twelve-hour bus ride to Pucón, then another twelve hours to Bariloche, which means crossing the Chilean-Argentinean border for the first time. A stray dog finds its way onto the bus at one of the rest stops and works its way to the back of the bus, providing some entertainment. But when the bus hits a rut in the road around 3:00 a.m. and I fall flat on my face in the aisle, my mood sours.

It isn't all bad. Bariloche is beautiful. The Alpine-esque village snakes around the sparkling southern shores of Nahuel Haupi Lake. It's located in the foothills of the Andes Mountains, so there's never a bad time to be here. It's summer at the moment and everyone has rolled out their beach blankets to sunbathe along the glacial lake's edge. I've been told that in winter it becomes Argentina's biggest draw because of the world-class skiing it offers; it's a Patagonian paradise.

I rent a bike and ride between cinnamon-colored trees whose twisted trunks are native to this region, stopping often to admire the views as I pedal my way around the southern rim of the lake. On New Year's Eve, I enjoy my first Argentinian *asado*. The Fortaleza Hostel, where I've bartered a room, has organized a huge barbeque for all their guests. There's beer, beef, pork, ribs, sausages, and blood sausages as far as the eye can see.

I leave shortly thereafter for Comodoro Rivadavia, which takes an excruciating twenty hours to get to. There aren't any places willing to barter with me in Comodoro Rivadavia, but even if there were, I don't have time take photos. So I schlep my things back and forth across the tiny town for hours in the rain looking for the cheapest room. Hotels and hostels are few and far between, and I eventually give up and spend the night in a bedbug-infested hostel in the shadows of the modern-gothic San Juan Bosco Cathedral. I later read one guidebook's assessment that this was the "ugliest cathedral you'll ever see," and I have to agree. The exterior looks like it was pieced together with green and brown bathroom tiles left over from a 1970s remodel. The two tones form a puke plaid color. At the top of the 151-foot external tower is a giant, hollow metal cross that looks like it was put together with wire hangers. Worst of all, the architect did all of this on purpose.

The very next night, I'm back in a cramped bus seat for twenty more hours, heading to the Argentinean outpost of Rio Gallegos.

For the last ten hours of the ride, I'm the only passenger on the bus, which just goes to show how far off the grid I'd gotten since leaving Santiago ten days prior. The countryside opens up, and we drive along a long, smooth patch of a highway that winds around a stretch of sea as brilliant as any I'd ever seen. There's something about the ocean that always helps me tap into another layer of myself, and I wish that part of the ride could extend on forever. Once we cut back inland, we witness something just as majestic—a pack of wild horses running alongside the road like we've been transplanted into the middle of a Budweiser commercial. Their long, flowing manes and gorgeous, black coats make them look like show ponies in the afternoon sunlight as they gallop together like gods.

Alpacas are everywhere, too, though some of them met an unfortunate fate. Hip-height barbwire fences run alongside the road, just like they do in Texas, but instead of tumbleweeds it's the skeletons of alpacas that were occasionally caught in them. My best guess is that they had tried to jump over the fence but didn't quite make it. In such isolated parts of southern Argentina, no one was there to help wriggle them loose.

The last leg to Ushuaia takes fourteen more tiresome hours, which drains what little life is left in me. I cross into Chile from Argentina and then back to Argentina again, which means confusing questions from immigrations officers that I have to navigate without knowing a lick of Spanish. But when I clear the last set of questions and cross back into Argentina for the final time, the pressure is finally off. I know then and there that I am going to make it to Ushuaia in time for my expedition to Antarctica.

The bus drives onto an industrial-looking ferryboat and crosses the Strait of Magellan. We're shuttled across the narrowest part of the Strait, but strong winds whip the water into whitecaps, slowing our progress. I then sit patiently for a few more hours as the bus chugs ever so slowly along the knife-edge of a cliff. I fight my fear of heights while we wind our way up the skyscraping Martial Mountains at sunset, and when I finally arrived at the bus station in the center of Ushuaia around 9:00 p.m., I nearly collapse.

I've arrived with two days to spare. "Spare" isn't really the right word. I need one day to run around town and rent the necessary clothes that are required for the harsh conditions in Antarctica and another to decompress and catch up on my sleep.

The past two weeks were equal to the most demanding stretch of overland travel I've ever endured. Spending seventy-five hours on a bus in one week is damn near insane, and it has me at my wits' end. Not to mention the toll it has taken on my body. Everything was so rushed, so unorganized, and so stressful that I've been eating like crap the entire way. I was grabbing greasy food from rest stops and gas stations, often eating massive amounts of slimy salami (the meat that's most readily available in Argentina) in one sitting. Whenever I missed a meal, I'd replace it with overly caffeinated energy drinks and bags of M&M's.

By the time I finally find the front door of the bed-and-breakfast I've bartered with, I don't know right from left and up from down. Tere answers the door and welcomes me in warmly. She's the owner, and I'm instantly caught off guard by her energy. She's as kind as anyone I've ever come across, but I can tell she's tough as nails too. She reminds me of my great-grandmother.

Tere is probably in her early eighties, and she's in her housecoat with her curly white hair in rollers. She speaks little English, but the bond between us is immediate—it's one of those unspoken things that I could never explain. Travelers often share stories of the times they didn't need a translator because they encountered a strange force that overrode the language barrier. I think this might just be that force.

Tere ushers me up to my room with the same grace my great-grand-mother possessed, and when she shows me how to work the shower in my room, she says something I know I'll never forget.

"Frío, agua from the glacier."

That's when it hits me. All the sacrifices, bumps in the road, and hard work it took to get to the southernmost city in South America in such a short amount of time suddenly fade away.

Holy shit! I think. *All that's left is Antarctica.*

CHAPTER 18
ANTARCTICA

ANTARCTICA

*"The most important thing in life is to learn how
to give out love, and to let it come in."*

— *Mitch Albom*

A S I MAKE THE SHORT walk to Puerto de Ushuaia to meet
Dolores, the marketing manager for Antarpply Expeditions, I'm
so flooded by happiness that I don't think my mood can get any
better. But when I step aboard the MV *Ushuaia*, I feel another surge of
joy.

I've boarded an hour before the other passengers so I can photograph
and film the cabins while they are still clean and empty. I stow Timberland
underneath my bed in my shared cabin and get right to work. The MV
Ushuaia is a modest ship. She's dark blue at the bottom and a weathered
white around her bow. She was built in 1970 and has enough room for
eighty-eight passengers and forty crewmembers. At 278 feet long and 51
feet wide, she's smaller than I was expecting. Of course, technically she's
more of a research ship than a fancy cruise ship.

She isn't full of bells and whistles because she was built for the harsh
Antarctic conditions we're sure to face over the next two weeks. There's a
basic dining room, an observation lounge that doubles as a lecture room, a
small bar, and a combination library and gift shop on the main deck. The

panorama deck stretches all the way around the main deck and houses orange life vessels on one side and black Zodiacs on the other. Since there aren't any ports in Antarctica, we'll use the Zodiacs, which are those cool little inflatable dinghies that zip across the water, to reach land once we get closer to the continent. Below deck is the infirmary, which I'm hoping to avoid.

Built originally for the National Oceanic and Atmospheric Administration (NOAA), the *Ushuaia* served twenty years under the name *The Researcher*. The NOAA used her to warn of dangerous weather, chart seas, and conduct research to improve the stewardship of the environment. From what I've read about her, it sounds like she's been a good servant, but she does have one accident on her resume that slightly concerns me. In 2008, she hit a rock in Wilhelmina Bay in Antarctica, and a Chilean Navy ship had to evacuate the hundred passengers and crew who were on board.

I'm sure we'll be fine, though. Our exact journey has been running regularly for years, and it's scheduled, weather-wise, during the best time of the year. Antarctica is in the midst of their austral summer, so temperatures shouldn't dip too far into the negatives like they do during its insanely frigid winters.

After the rest of the passengers board, the *Ushuaia*'s Argentinian captain quickly navigates us through the Beagle Channel and out to sea. Everyone is summoned to the observation lounge, where the expedition team introduces themselves. They seem like a kind-hearted but somewhat serious group. The team is made up of six Argentinians, who all either have or are pursuing their PhDs in marine biology. They're all wearing blue bubble vests with the words "Expedition Team" sewn into the back like letterman jackets, and they all have on the kind of cargo pants that have eight million tiny pockets. Besides keeping things in their pockets, they'll be tasked with important things like keeping us safe, guiding us once we reach land, and telling us about the plants and animals we'll see. A few of the team members mention that they'll also be conducting research along the way, which gives this trip a more scientific vibe than I'd expected.

The expedition leader, Julieta, goes over the rules on board, first in English and then Spanish. She covers simple things like always wear shoes while walking around the ship, and much more serious things, like what we can expect from the Drake Passage.

There's no way around the dangerous Drake if we want to get to Antarctica. It's the biological barrier where cold polar water sinks beneath the warmer northern waters. The positive is that this creates a surplus of nutrients like plankton and krill, which sustains the biodiversity of the region, but the negative is that this coming together of warm and cold waters creates the most dangerous and roughest sea in the entire world. Even Charles Darwin was sensationally seasick while rounding Cape Horn. I'm sure that the ship we're on has evolved compared to his, and that we'll be moving much faster and living in far greater comfort than he did in the mid-1800s, but at a minimum, Julieta tells us, it's going to take thirty-six hours to get across the Drake Passage.

After Julieta finishes her briefing, the two bartenders who have been standing by begin to fill empty champagne flutes that have suddenly appeared atop the bar. I grab a glass with my left hand because my camera is glued to my right hand. Julieta raises her glass towards all sixty of us and says, "To Antarctica!"

As I hold the flute up to my lips, I pause to think about all the effort and energy that's gone into every day of my travels and every moment of my transformation.

If this isn't the last bit of proof that anything and everything is in fact possible, then I don't know what is.

* * *

Peter Nichols wrote a book titled *A Voyage for Madmen*, which documents the story of nine sailors who raced around the globe in 1968. About Cape Horn, Nichols wrote, "None but the callowest sailor can pass Cape Horn without gratitude and trembling, without being acutely aware of its history, of all the ships, seamen, and civilian passengers, men, women, and children wrecked, smashed, and drowned there. Deaths often came at the end of weeks of the vilest discomfort and despair imaginable. For most sailors the Horn is their Everest."

To read about it is one thing, but to experience it firsthand is quite another. The Drake Passage is exactly what all those other sailors have warned about. We're delayed by a full day before we even enter the passage because the captain deems the seas too rough to proceed. Reports eventually filter down to the passengers that the waves in the passage are topping out at nearly ten meters.

The captain doesn't have much choice in the matter, so he drops the *Ushuaia*'s anchor, and we wait out the bad weather. Then we wait some more. We bob back and forth a little south of Cape Horn for what feels like forever. I've noticed that when you really want something and you're super close to getting it, waiting becomes that much more intolerable. It doesn't matter whether you're five or fifty. But while I'm willing to take a lot of risks, the one thing that I won't willingly step into the ring with is Mother Nature. She's got Hagler's chin, Tyson's uppercut, and Ali's speed and footwork. She is and will always be undefeated.

Our big break finally comes after twenty-four hours of worry and wonder. I was beginning to think that we'd never make it to Antarctica, but when the ship's intercom crackles to life, the mood on board quickly lifts. Julieta announces that we are finally going to attempt to cross the world's most dangerous stretch of sea and that we should all begin to mentally prepare ourselves for the rough road ahead. At minimum, we're warned, it's going to take at least a day and a half, but most likely two, to get safely to the other side.

Each cabin has been tailored for extreme weather. Everyone's bed has big, metal, cage-like bars on each side, which are meant to keep us from falling out at night. There are railings in all the hallways and inside each stairwell too. Everything in the dining hall and observation lounge is bolted down. But as we passengers quickly find out, the same can't be said for the human body's frail and fragile stomach.

Thankfully, I'm one of the three or four passengers to escape the death grip that seasickness takes on the ship once we enter Drake Passage. It ravages the ship relentlessly for nearly two straight days. The angry ocean makes merely walking around the ship nearly impossible, and every time we hit a whitecap, everything flies out of my closet and across my cabin, regardless of how much I had tried to secure everything.

I have no idea why I don't get sick. I took one of the seasickness pills that the onboard nurse passed out, but so did everyone else. From the sight of people, you'd think that the *Ushuaia* has turned into a floating quarantine center. Yellow faces, bloodshot eyes, and that *where's the closest toilet* look overtakes most people.

Everyone keeps to themselves. Because of my natural introvert nature and love for solitude, I hang out in the cabin I'm sharing with a perfume salesman from Prague. Yes, my roommate is a perfume salesman from

Prague. Even Dr. Seuss couldn't have dreamed up this unlikely pairing in his book *Oh, the Places You'll Go!*

Congratulations!

Today is your day.

You're off to Antarctica!

Hope you and the perfume salesman enjoy your stay!

#

At 7:30 a.m. on the fifth day of our journey, the ship's loudspeaker rips through our cabin and wakes me up. As the desire for more sleep fights for my attention, Julietta's voice crackles as she says, "Good morning, good morning, my dear passengers. I am happy to announce that we have cleared the Drake Passage, and we will be arriving at Half Moon Island shortly."

At breakfast, even the passengers who still look green around the gills after the rough passage are buzzing with excitement about our first trip in the Zodiacs. Back in my cabin, I stuff my long limbs into all the layers of clothes I rented back in Ushuaia. It takes me fifteen minutes to get dressed. I put on every layer I have with me, starting with a thermal top and stockings, followed by a sweatshirt and fleece-lined sweat pants, then a light jacket, two pairs of wool socks, and finally my waterproof ski jacket and pants. Since I haven't cut my hair in over two years, the gigantic size of my man bun means that I'll have to let my hair down if I want to get my wool hat past my ears. I'm so insulated that I can barely bend over to pull on the knee-high rubber boots the expedition team provided us with.

I bounce down the hallway and stairwell like the Michelin Man. An Antarctic blast of cool air slaps my face as I step into what I can only describe as a real-life snow globe. The breadth of the winter wonderland immediately sucks all the oxygen from my lungs. Snow is falling ever so gently, and a Godlike hush has fallen over everything. I've never felt so far away. I don't just mean far away from the places I once called home—like Pennsylvania and Miami Beach or even, most recently, Argentina—but just so far away from the world itself.

Everything is so peaceful and so calm here; even the ocean water, which tormented the ship for the past five days, is still and lake-like now. The *Ushuaia* is moored in the middle of the natural bay that the island's crescent-shaped shoreline creates, and I can see Half Moon Island off in the distance. The first Zodiac is sliding toward it, and the tiny waves it's leaving in its wake are rippling across eternity.

Technically, today's landing location is part of the South Shetland Islands and not Antarctica, but I'm not one to split hairs. This feels like Antarctica, and we're only seventy-five miles from it anyway. After a second Zodiac takes eight more passengers, I board the next one, and we bounce across the ocean like a perfectly skipped stone. With the wind whipping across my face, I quickly become the giddiest I've ever felt.

My excitement only builds as we close in on land. After I jump off the Zodiac, I spring into action. There's an incredibly photogenic old wooden whaling boat that had wrecked at the south end of the island, so I head toward that first. The cutest chinstrap penguins you've ever seen are waddling by in their tiny tuxedos, and as I crouch down to film them between the snowflakes, I'm just so thrilled that my *job* is to capture exactly this kind of thing.

Each step takes me deeper and deeper into my surroundings and also down the well of my own creativity. I'm finally feeling the way I'd always wanted to feel behind the camera. Not only am I creating content for myself and my travel blog out of my purest passions, but this is also actually considered *work*.

Half Moon Island is so different from anywhere else I've ever been. Here there are no throngs of tourists racing to and fro, trying to fit in as much sightseeing as possible before the itinerary calls them back to the bus.

This land is vast. Untouched.

After a short hike to the top of the island to look out over thousands of chinstrap penguins, I board the Zodiac for a second time, and it zips me across the bay to Cámara Base, a scientific research station nestled in the foothills near the Menguante Cove. It's Argentinian owned and only open during the summer season, which is when the research is conducted. The base is composed of four small brick buildings, which are surrounded by a couple of satellite towers. Most recently, a Colombian geologist was here mapping out the region with the use of drones.

After a few hours of exploring, I head back aboard the *Ushuaia*. I'm shocked by what I find. It's like a magician has been on board because the distance between the passengers has vanished. Buoyed by our first landing and awakened by the cold Antarctic air, a wave of camaraderie has ripped through the belly of the ship.

At lunch, the dining hall is transformed into a rowdy saloon where everyone is trading stories, not just of their morning but of their lives. I swear I can almost see it—this invisible thread weaving its way through us all as our spoons clang against the bottom of our bowls of vegetable stew.

My grandmother's favorite hobby has always been knitting. As a child, I would watch her knit for long periods of time. She'd sit at the end of her couch with a big ball of yarn in her lap, and she'd work two long knitting needles effortlessly together without looking. This lunch is like that. We're being pulled tightly together by something bigger than ourselves, knitted into something meaningful. Something important.

We're being made into something new. And we won't ever be the same again.

There's a reality show–worthy obstetrician named Jim, whose thick Scottish accent takes me an extra second to process. He's traveling with his smiley seventeen-year-old Australian daughter, Annika.

There's Maya. She's twenty-six years old and from San Francisco; she's kissed her job good-bye for six months so she can reassess the arc of her corporate career. Victor's here too; he's as cute as a button. He's seven years old and from São Paulo. He speaks three different languages and looks like a miniature version of Ricky Ricardo. He's come along with his Portuguese parents.

There's a big, barrel-chested Alaskan named Derrick who clears land-mines that have been long left behind from World War II in Palau, a tiny island in the middle of the Pacific Ocean. And there's a group of giggly college students. They're here as part of a study-abroad program from Seattle, and their professor-slash-chaperone has got his own interesting story to tell. He's been on a twenty-year quest to photograph every species of penguin in the wild, and he only has one left to capture with his camera.

The life-of-the-party award goes to three best friends from the United States who have spent the past ten years traveling the world as nurses, either saving lives or living theirs to the fullest. There's even a satellite phone–carrying, assault rifle–selling Russian on board whose chiseled chin and buzzed blond hair are nearly identical to that of Ivan Drago in *Rocky IV*.

Ed and Liz's story is as captivating as anyone's. They're a retired Kiwi couple who have traveled nearly ninety thousand miles around the Americas in a 1957 Mercedes-Benz over the past two years.

Each of the sixty people on board is more interesting than the next, and it's almost incomprehensible that I missed all these wonderful people our first five days at sea. I guess I was just so locked into my own dreams and so focused on getting to Antarctica that I put my blinders on.

I forgot to look up.

For many of these travelers, this will be their seventh and final continent, the last checkmark on their bucket list after years of wonderful wanderlust.

Many on board have saved this winter wonderland for last, so the energy that's buzzing around the ship's shared spaces is palpable. A genuine enthusiasm has emerged, and a more authentic side of each person has begun to show itself. I know this because I can feel it surfacing inside my own skin.

Once again, my travels have changed me.

Ever since Naomi left in Africa, I've been barreling down nearly every road this world has to offer, and I've been barreling down them alone. The deepest connection I share with another person on this planet exists only in the form of text messages with Shiya. While this journey has taught me wonderful things like perseverance and how to rely on myself, it's also built walls around me. Throw in the language barriers, the fact that I'm still a touch on the shy side, and that writers tend to be in search of solitude more than most, and it's like I've been traveling down a path of extreme isolation. Just last week, I was the only passenger on a bus for over ten hours.

These long stretches of isolation have taken their toll. At times, I've become too self-sufficient, which contributes to a social awkwardness. I find myself immediately plotting ways to escape conversations, which I'm sure doesn't go unnoticed. I don't care how much anyone likes their solitude—no one wants to feel like their energy and attention isn't appreciated.

But the affection from everyone on board is unconditional. It's hit me like a tidal wave and washed away all of the walls I've been building. We've made landings at Robert Point and Hydrurga Rocks, and we've sailed past the Weddell Sea's big, *National Geographic*–esque, tabular, blue icebergs together. We've taken Zodiac tours right up to the mammoth edge of those icebergs, and each landing has been more remarkable than the last. But it's not just the landscape that's affecting me. We've had late-night limbo contests and silly dance-offs; we've spotted whales out the ship's tiny portholes together and done celebratory shots of Jägermeister together. All of these unexpected experiences have opened me up more and more, and I'm feeling the most vulnerable I've been in years.

However, there's still one very important thing left to do: step foot on the actual continent of Antarctica.

We've been skirting around it because of the weather, but today's the day. Julieta woke us up through the ship's loudspeaker at 7:30 a.m. with the same line she always uses, "Good morning, good morning, my dear passengers." And then she announced that we'll be split into two groups of thirty. Group A will go on a two-hour Zodiac tour to see the lion seals lounging in Foyn Harbor, and group B will go directly to Orne Harbor and explore it on foot. Orne Harbor is where each group will step foot on the continent of Antarctica for the first time. After two hours, the groups will switch.

When the Zodiac tour I'm on in Foyn Harbor comes to an end and slides across the glass-like water toward Orne Harbor, I can feel my soul spilling out of my skin. Orne Harbor is hands-down the most beautiful place I've ever laid my eyes on. We've had extremely cold and cloudy days up until today, but the blue sky above is spotless. The sun is as bright as a beach day, and there isn't the faintest trace of a cloud anywhere. If you told me that the tops of the snow-covered jagged peaks that cup the mile-wide cove we've just pulled into were the fabled pearly gates, I'd believe you.

The closer we get to the landing spot, the wider my eyes become, and about a hundred yards out, my pulse quickens. As we wind through a cove and around a few small icebergs, group A comes into view. Some people are boarding the Zodiacs and pulling away to begin their tour of Foyn Harbor, but a few people are still scattered on a series of switchbacks that run up the side of the mountain that juts up from the base of the shoreline. Their red-and-yellow jackets pop against the bright white snow.

At the top of the mountain, I see the familiar pink jacket and white ski pants that Annika wears. I would tell you to keep an eye out for this girl one day and that she's going to be something special, but she already is.

She's only seventeen, but I've never seen anyone mix and mingle so genuinely and effortlessly with so many people of different ages, races, and backgrounds. She's just got "it," an indescribable magical quality so rare that mere words wouldn't do it justice. She's become like the little sister I never had. She's one of the brightest lights I've ever come across and aside from Shiya, she's quickly become the most important person I've met in my travels. As I watch her plop down in the snow, an incredible joy bursts across my chest. Rarely have I felt this kind of happiness for others, but I think this is a reflection of how much these people mean to me and how much I've grown since we left South America eight days ago.

I keep my eyes on Annika because I feel something special's about to happen. A second later, she lifts her black rubber boots up out of the snow and leans back with her legs pointed up toward the sun. Then she pulls her hands out of the snow and slides from the top of the mountain all the way down to the bottom on just the back of her ski pants. She bounces back and forth like a skier flying across moguls, and the widest smile I've ever seen rips across her rosy-red cheeks.

By the time I hop out of my Zodiac and officially step foot onto Antarctica, it's got to be nearly forty degrees out. Everyone in my group has peeled off their layers and thrown their jackets, hats, and gloves into a pile at the bottom of the mountain. I look over at Piero, standing beside me. "I can't believe I'm saying this," I tell him, "but I'm hot!" Piero is a sixty-something, lion-like lawyer with a thick Italian accent who has the uncanny ability to light up a room like no one I've ever seen. He happens to reside in Miami Beach now, just a few blocks away from my old apartment.

We hike up the same series of switchbacks I saw from my Zodiac, and I stop every fifty feet or so to film and photograph the view below. The higher I hike, the more majestic it becomes. The *Ushuaia* is moored in the middle of the cove, and a more photogenic sight I have not seen. The water is mirror still. I can't decide where to look first.

Thanks to the Antarctica Treaty of 1951, the land we're enjoying together will remain just that: a place to be together regardless of nationality. As of 2016, fifty-three countries have signed the treaty, which sets aside Antarctica as a scientific preserve and bans military activity on the entire continent. Ships carrying more than five hundred passengers are not permitted to land their passengers ashore in Antarctica, which will keep the number of visitors down. My favorite part of the treaty is a provision stating that Antarctica shall be used for peaceful purposes only. It's the only place in the world where there have been no wars and no bloodshed, and I can feel that goodness in its air. It is untouched and raw, and by the time I get to the crest of the ridge, I'm officially drunk on life.

I fall back into the soft snow next to Piero, and we look out over what feels like both the beginning and end of the world. The air is silent and still; there's barely a breeze. Thunder from a collapsing iceberg somewhere nearby breaks the silence, but only for a few seconds. A more impressive sound I have not heard. Our breaths are still heavy from the climb, but our bodies take on an incredible rhythm. Joseph Campbell wrote, "The goal of life is to make your heartbeat match the beat of the universe, to match your nature with Nature."

Piero and I are vibrating at a higher frequency, and I can feel it in every cell.

We've grown close over the past few days. Piero's become a mentor and offered advice in areas I've needed it.

After a few minutes, his Italian accent cuts across the cobalt sky. "Eric, everyone really likes you," he says with a smile.

I soak up what he says, wanting to absorb it fully because it's so rare that we as humans tell each other nice things like this out of the blue. I'm not quite sure if anyone's ever pulled me aside since I've started my journey, if ever in my entire life, to say such a simple but meaningful thing. Even my own mother told me I was a pill to be around during my time in Florida a little over a month ago, and she wasn't wrong. I was in a creative rut then, and when that happens I'm 100 percent closed off and prickly to the touch.

But this trip has changed me in a soul-deep way. Even my chemical composition feels different. I don't know exactly why Piero's chosen to tell me such a remarkable thing at the top of a mountain at the end of the earth, of all places, but where others would chalk this up to coincidence, I sense a deeper meaning.

I didn't know it, but I needed to hear these words. I take a pride and comfort in them.

Piero slaps my back and says, "I want a jumping picture." I'm not exactly sure what he means, so he stands up and shows me. He jumps in the air and kicks his legs back and throws his arms up toward the bright yellow sun. When he lands, he says, "When I'm at the top of my jump, you take the photo."

At first I scoff at the idea because it seems a bit touristy, and this has got to be the least touristy place on the planet. But out of the deep respect that I have for the man, I decide to play along. Plus, he's so enthusiastic that it's impossible to not get swept up in his energy. I bet he could sell ice to one of the seals down below.

I grab my camera and lie down in the snow on my stomach. Once I get my lens into focus, I tell Piero that I'm going to count backward from three and that when I say one, that's his cue to jump.

After he does, I pull the picture up on my camera's LCD screen so I can show him the photo. It's the same screen where I showed Adam the Milky Way in Australia and reviewed all those sunrises back in Miami Beach when I first started practicing photography. And now this, a *jumping photo* in Antarctica. Piero's ecstatic when he sees the photo. He's so thrilled by it that I decide that I need one of myself doing the same thing. But just as I'm about to set the timer on my camera, we hear the crunch of snow beneath rubber boots. Others have joined us.

Lili, a writer from Spain, Melle from France, and Carlyon, a thirty-something chiropractor from Australia with long strawberry-blond hair, have made it to the top of the ridge. This is that final nudge I need. The last reminder that I'm not alone and that moments like this are not only meant to be shared but made better by doing so.

I pull everyone into a huddle like a quarterback and tell them the plan for the group jumping picture. Then I prop my camera up in the snow and set its ten-second timer. Once it starts beeping, I run around to join the group.

The five of us count backward together like it's New Year's Eve and we're in the middle of Time Square. When we all scream "one," we jump toward the cloudless sky in unison. There's a hurricane in my heart as joy spreads across my face. My past, present, and future merge. This is bliss.

At the top of my jump, with my arms opened wide to the world, I learn my most important life lesson of all.

I learn how to let love in. Who would have thought that the coldest place on the planet would wind up being the warmest?

* * *

As the *Ushuaia* makes its way back into the Beagle Channel, I don't want things to end. I've truly had the time of my life. Besides more late-night limbo contests, there's been a delicious Argentinean *asado* out on the main deck one sunny Antarctic afternoon, a blood-orange sun that set behind a translucent blue glacier, and an endless supply of penguins, whales, and laughs. Over the course of our two weeks on board the *Ushuaia*, there were so many stupid and silly sophomoric jokes among us all that it felt more like we've been away at summer camp than braving the elements in Antarctica.

The group has taken on this incredible rhythm, and I've grown extremely close to everyone. In particular, Annika has come to mean so much to me that I'm not quite sure how I'm going to be able to say good-bye to her. We've had so much sibling-like fun together that I cannot physically walk over to her and say the word *good-bye*. I just can't. I know that if I do I'll end up standing in a puddle of tears.

I don't know how I'm going to adjust once we all disembark and go our separate ways. Everyone will either be leaving with someone or returning home, where they'll have their friends and family waiting for them. And I've got to reprise my old role and sink back into the skin of my solo traveling self, which feels like it won't fit anymore.

Even though I've reached Antarctica, my around-the-world journey isn't quite done yet. I've got to keep grinding and get all the way back to London if I want to officially complete my lap around the globe. Two days from now, I'll board a bus (by myself) and begin heading north back through Patagonia, then make my way to the northern Brazilian city of Natal to catch the cargo ship that will take me across the Atlantic Ocean. I know I have weeks of long, empty hours ahead of me—hours that will feel even emptier because I'm filled to the brim with this wonderfully shared experience.

I'd always imagined making exactly this kind of connection with people on my trip, but that was back before the difficulty of this journey fully set in. Each leg, regardless of whether it's a bus, boat, or train ride, has been so challenging that I've had to focus and commit to it in a way that I never could have anticipated. Whatever energy I have left has been dedicated to my creative endeavors, which means that I've subconsciously moved making connections to the back burner.

I met with Julieta late last night in the expedition team's modest office below the main deck, in a part of the ship I'd never been to, and showed her the film I'd been putting together for Antarpply Expeditions. I told her, "I'd really like to be able to share this with everyone on board. I've put my heart and soul into it, and I want them to see my finished work before we all go our separate ways."

I also asked her if I could show the film I'd created of my around-the-world travels, which is the one we're currently watching. I wanted everyone on board to see what it's taken for me to travel this far without flying, especially after having shared so much of myself with them these past two weeks. They've heard my stories, but I wanted them to see it firsthand.

Thankfully, Julieta was impressed with both films. She's a bit of a tough cookie, and so I held my breath as she watched them play on my laptop. She said that I could have about ten minutes at the beginning of the closing ceremony.

I get a little fidgety when people watch my work. It's like hearing the sound of your own voice for the first time in a long while. I don't know where to look, so I glance around the room and then up at the TV screen again. One of my favorite parts of the film is playing. About half of us stripped down to our bathing suits or boxers three days ago at Deception Island, and then we raced into the ice-cold water to complete the polar plunge.

What I'll miss the most besides the connections I've made is just how simple everything's become. Without access to modern technology, time has passed slowly and therefore beautifully. During our shared meals, no one was checking their phones at the table or posting selfies on their social media accounts. It was just good old-fashioned banter. I'm afraid that the second we return, I'll get swept right back up in the never-ending blitz social media puts on our senses. I don't want to run to the nearest Wi-Fi hot spot in Ushuaia like I've always done while traveling and reconnect with that world. It suddenly feels shallow and far less important. It's like we've stepped into a real-life snow globe whose plastic shell is protecting us from the ills of the outside world.

I want to hold on to this feeling for as long as I can.

The loud applause when the film ends brings tears to my eyes, and I have to cut short what I want to say to the group because my voice begins to crack. Kind words and high fives follow me back to my seat.

Once I sit down, it takes a second to compose myself before I can look up and around the room. Julieta begins the certificate ceremony, calling each passenger to the makeshift stage, where they're presented with an Antarctic Expedition Certificate signed by Captain Calle and given a rousing round of applause from their fellow passengers.

After the final name is called, the bartenders buzz through the lounge and deliver champagne flutes for one final toast.

I'd thought that the champagne toast the day we all boarded was one of the most special moments of my life. But thinking back on it, I remember that I didn't actually clink my glass with anyone else's. My shy side had gotten the better of me, and I did what I often do in those kinds of situations. I retreated into my own world and ignored everyone else.

Once everyone has a glass, Julieta says for the second time in two weeks, "To Antarctica!"

This time, I make sure I don't retreat. I dive headfirst into the experience. I make my way around the room and touch glasses with every single person that's been on the trip. I even interlock my arms with people, and we take silly sips together. As amazing as that first toast was two weeks ago, this one is shared, and though I still have miles to go yet, it feels like my Impossible Idea has finally come full circle.

EPILOGUE
ENGLAND
EUROPE

*"People are capable, at any time in their lives,
of doing what they dream of."*

— *Paul Coelho*

I T'S BEEN 1,074 DAYS SINCE I started my journey from Cape
Town, South Africa. I've circumnavigated the globe, ended one relationship, begun another, learned about the inner workings of myself,
heard the voice of God, jumped off the top of a party boat in Ha Long
Bay, sailed across the Pacific and Atlantic Oceans on cargo ships, and
slid down a mountain on my backside in Antarctica. I've traveled nearly
seventy thousand miles in total, but perhaps the most preposterous thing
of all is that I used public transportation almost exclusively to make my
way around the world. In forty-eight of the fifty countries I traveled across
(and even the oceans in between) I used the same method the locals did to
get to wherever they were going.

Last night, when I calculated up how much I'd bartered for in terms
of free lodging, meals, tours, and cruises over the course of my three
years, I nearly fell out of my chair. The final number was over a quarter
of a million dollars. I had $444.08 to my name the day I decided on my
dreams and was the only person in the beginner photography class at
Miami-Dade Community College who didn't own an actual camera. This

summer, I was able to attract some sponsorships, and my passions have finally yielded paychecks that I can be proud of.

I would be wrong to say I've done this all by myself, though. I've had divine help along the way. I've followed the signs and believed in the omens and let them guide me like the North Star does a sailor. I treated the trail of breadcrumbs as if they were clues instead of coincidences. So it was fitting to have gotten one last "God-wink" this morning.

As I was packing up Timberland for the last time, my hair, which I haven't cut this entire time, was still wet from showering, and it dangled in such a way that it left a huge heart-shaped wet spot just atop my heart. When I noticed it in the bathroom mirror, I got a lump in my throat. It's always been the little things that I've been most grateful for. It was just one final reminder that, even though my overland journey ends today, I need to continue to follow my heart. It does indeed know the way.

As I glide along the National Rail tracks across the green English countryside, I'm getting closer and closer to the end of my journey. I'm also, finally, getting closer to Shiya. While her family is in Morocco, she's flown to London and will be at Victoria Station to meet me. At the end of the Antarctica trip, I knew I needed to have the most important person I met along the way there with me at the end, and my connection to Shiya feels more important than ever. Our relationship is so full of obstacles that it feels like another version of my Impossible Idea. Why is it, I wonder, that the harder something is to gain, the more I want it? As the gap between Shiya and I closes, my palms begin to sweat. With each rolling hillside we rumble up and over, I feel her presence growing closer and closer.

Across the aisle is a British family of four. The mother is sipping tea out of a paper cup, the father is reading the *Daily Mail*, and their children are busy on their iPads. As we pull away from Barnham station, I chuckle as I think about my favorite seatmate of the entire trip. The bus Naomi and I were traveling on had stopped at a rural intersection in the middle of Mozambique when the man sitting beside me decided he had to have the bow and arrow that had just gone past the window. He leaned over me and called out to the owner of the bow and arrow, a skinny and shirtless man who looked like he had just gone hunting. They went back and forth, haggling in a language I couldn't understand, and then suddenly I was being handed the six-foot-long wooden bow and its three-foot-long, bloodstained arrows through the open bus window and passing them to my seatmate, like a sports fan passing a beer and a hot dog down the row at a ballgame.

I think about the many other seatmates I've sat shoulder-to-shoulder with over the weeks and months of my travels. Christians, Jews, Muslims, Buddhists, Hindus, hippies—all have extended their arms and helped me up. I'm a better man for it; it's easy to find tolerance for others when you're able to see how similar we all really are. However, my heart still hurts for the Syrian refugees I ran into. I don't think I'll ever let go of the look I saw in their eyes. I hope one day I'll be able to do more to help.

I can't stop my mind from pulling up the past. I go all the way back to Miami Beach, to the days when this Impossible Idea actually felt impossible. I think of the gigantic vision board I created in my living room. I had no phone, no guidebooks, no fancy backpack, and no background in any of the areas I pursued, but what I lacked only helped me learn that much more about myself. I wanted to pull off this Impossible Idea as much as anyone has ever wanted anything, and I willed myself past every single setback. I didn't leave my dreams at the bottom of a wishing well, and while chasing my dreams hasn't always been fun, it's always been worth it.

I owe much of this moment to Naomi, and I cannot thank her enough, truly. She was there for me during my most trying times. More importantly, however, she believed in me when I didn't believe in myself, and for that I'll forever be indebted to her. I reach my hand to my lips and blow a kiss to her. I have no doubt that it will make its way to her in India before the afternoon ends.

The train's brake pads hiss when we stop at Horsham station, and as we pick up a few more passengers and pull away, I think about the man I've become. I think about the creative transformation I've forced myself through. It's been as awkward as puberty at times, but I desperately wanted to shed the corporate shell I'd settled for, and I was going to stop at nothing to make sure I did just that. There's never been a plan B, and I've doubled down on my dreams countless times, investing more and more of myself into each and every step along the way. The longer I traveled, the more I started to realize that this journey is my life's work. And now that it's almost complete, my one wish is that I might somehow share this incredible experience with everyone. This is exactly what I plan on doing next.

Even though my journey will come to its conclusion this morning, completing a book about the entire experience is the thing that will bring my creativity full circle. So sometime over the next month or so, I'll head back to Miami Beach, use what little life savings I have left to find a cheap apartment, and turn all the stories I've been sharing on my travel blog into a book. I want everyone to see what I've seen and feel what I've felt. I want my trials and tribulations to inspire people to find, follow, and stick with their own dreams. I think the world needs that right now more than anything else.

When the train reaches Three Bridges station, a group of well-dressed and rowdy men pile into my compartment. It's only 9:32 a.m., but each one is holding a Heineken. I don't want to get caught staring at them, so I check my phone in hopes of snagging a Wi-Fi signal from the station while we're stopped at the platform. But nothing reaches me. I haven't been able to communicate with Shiya all morning. My right knee begins to bounce anxiously as I wonder if she made her flight. My stomach summersaults at the possibility of her backing out at the last minute. I worry that I'll never see her again.

The train makes quick stops at Gatwick Airport and then East Croydon. As the train rattles toward Clapham Junction, I see the triangular top of the Shard and then the rest of London's brilliantly balanced skyline. When I realize that, in just two more stops, this Impossible Idea will be a memory rather than a dream, my heart beats harder than ever before.

The train's intercom crackles five minutes later, and a pleasant British accent follows. "We are now approaching London Victoria station. Mind the gap."

Mind the gap reminds me of one of my favorite pieces of advice, related by Joseph Campbell: "A bit of advice was given to a young Native American at the time of his initiation: As you go the way of life, you will see a great chasm. Jump. It's not as wide as you think."

I've had to jump every single day for 1,074 straight days. The enormity of the experience ripples across my chest, and I see each of the seventy thousand miles I traveled across the surface of the earth all at once. I don't even try to stop the tears as they fill my eyes.

I've earned this elation, and it feels like I'm standing at the summit of every mountaintop the planet has to offer. The view from here is amazing, and I can't help but pump my fist, beat my chest with my closed fist, and whisper to myself, "OH MY GOD, I've done it!"

The train slows and then stops. I quickly wheel Timberland off.

I've met countless people of all different shapes, sizes, and colors in these past three years, but there's only one I want to see right now.

I scan the faces in the waiting crowd, anxiously looking for those almond-shaped eyes. And then . . . I see them.

I race down the platform toward Shiya. Her arms are open wide, and she's waving a black-and-white-checkered finish line flag. The words "You did it!" are written on it. Once I reach her, I drop all my things so I can do the one thing I've dreamt about every single day since I saw her last.

I cup her face with my hands and run my fingers through her long dark hair. She jumps into my arms, and I brush her hair gently away from her eyes.

I softly kiss her lips.

I don't know what the future holds for us—maybe everything or maybe nothing—but I know that in this moment, I feel like I am the person I set out to become. A person who can circumnavigate the globe, who can tap into a deep well of creativity, who can connect with people. This journey has given my life the meaning it was missing, and now that I'm back in London, I can finally separate the *im* from *impossible*.

I always knew this day would come as long as I didn't give up.

PHOTO GALLERY

Photo 1 – Miami Beach, Florida: Since I was working two jobs, I didn't have enough time in the day to practice photography. So I started waking up before the sun and biking to the beach in order to practice every morning. This was one of the first mornings I showed up, and I snapped this shot with my iPhone 4. Seeing the sunrise like this almost every morning gave me the confidence to leap.

Photo 2 – Cape Town, South Africa – Day 2: On my second day in Cape Town, I hiked to the top of Table Mountain. With all of Africa at my feet, the enormity of what I was trying to accomplish had set in.

Photo 3 – Tofo Beach, Mozambique – Day 84: They told us, "When a bus passes you, flag it down." After waiting alongside the road for thirty minutes, that's exactly what Naomi and I did. This was the first leg of our two-day, backbreaking journey to northern Mozambique.

Photo 4 – Mwanza, Malawi – Day 87: Once Naomi and I had finally cleared customs and immigration for both Mozambique and Malawi, we took this tin can bus the rest of the way to Blantyre. Fifteen people crammed into eight seats without any air-conditioning.

Photo 5 – Cape Maclear, Malawi – Day 100: While bartering with Chembe Eagles Nest Hotel for five days, I walked into the tiny village about a mile down the road. When I pulled my camera out, all the children gathered around to see what I was doing. It was a special moment.

Photo 6 – Lyantonde, Uganda – Day 190: While waiting for my passport to be returned to me in Uganda, I bartered my room and board with a family that owned a handful of hotels across the country. On the way from one hotel in Lyantonde to another one in Mbarara, I strapped my GoPro to the front bumper of the maintenance man's truck. As the staff at the Skyblue Motel gathered around, I explained that it was recording us.

Photo 7 – Nairobi, Kenya – Day 213: The conditions inside the dilapidated buses were always cramped and exhausting. This is what the inside of the bus looked like on my way back to Nairobi. The following morning, I began the most dangerous leg of my journey.

Photo 8 – Northern Kenya – Day 214: If you squint, you can see the decals that look like bullet holes. This was the final rest stop before arriving at the Kenya-Ethiopia border. This was the only bus I traveled on that had metal bars across each passenger's lap; the roads were unpaved and in such bad condition that the bars were needed to keep everyone from flying out of their seats.

Photo 9 – en route to Addis Ababa, Ethiopia – Day 216: I never like taking photos of strangers—it always makes me uncomfortable to stick my camera in someone's face—but when this man cracked a smile, I couldn't resist.

Photo 10 – Khartoum, Sudan – Day 239: Outside of Al Kabir Mosque, these men asked for a photo, and the shot quickly became my favorite photo I had taken to date. It's the same one I risked saving the next day when I was detained and questioned by three men for not having the proper photography permit.

Photo 11 – Athens, Greece – Day 308: Outside the Acropolis with my parents. When I posted this photo online, a friend commented, "It must be nice that your parents are paying for you to travel around the world." The contrast between that perception and reality only increased my financial anxiety.

Photo 12 – London, England – Day 400: I never went out of my way to take a photo—I didn't visit tourist attractions or plan where and when I was going to try and take a photo each day. But I always had one of my cameras with me and trusted that a creative shot or angle would show up, which is exactly what happened each and every day.

Photo 13 – somewhere in Mongolia – Day 446: Not only was the Trans-Siberian Railroad freezing (if you look closely you can see the tissue paper insulation around the window), but for some strange reason, the dining car was disconnected when we reached Mongolia. I had no food with me, and when we stopped in Mongolia, I ran off to buy as many cups of noodles as I could find on the platform. However, the Mongolian vendors wouldn't take my Russian money, and they couldn't understand that this was my only chance at having any food for the next two days. Out of desperation, I pressed about thirty dollars' worth of rubles into a woman's hand and ran off with the noodles.

Photo 14 – Beijing, China – Day 452: Every time I stepped outside in China, people wanted to take a photo with me, which was fun. It was when people would run up and scream and laugh in my face that it became the opposite of fun.

Photo 15 – Ha Long Bay, Vietnam – Day 489: The traditional Chinese junk boats, one of which I spent the night on while filming and participating in the booze cruise for Central Backpackers Hostel.

Photo 16 – Bali, Indonesia – Day 602: Dek and I pulled over on one of the roads through the rain forest on our way to the Elephant Cave to check my GoPro, which I had stuck to his dashboard. Turns out, it was on.

Photo 17 – Cook, Australia – Day 614: The Indian Pacific Railroad stretches across the Australian Outback, and the train I was on stopped for thirty minutes at an uninhabited ghost town so we could get off and explore its remains.

Photo 18 – Budawang National Park, Australia – Day 633: The first long exposure I ever tried turned out to be a photo and a moment that I'll never forget.

Photo 19 – San Francisco, California – Day 677: After a month on a cargo ship, I wanted nothing more than to get off said ship. But due to congestion at the Port of Oakland, we were delayed all afternoon. The Golden Gate Bridge felt like a finish line that I wasn't allowed to cross. However, the delay, like all my setbacks, turned out to be a good thing in the long run. It was at sunset that we finally sailed underneath the bridge, which made it that much more remarkable.

Photo 20 – Palm Springs, California – Day 688: In order to barter my way around the world, I would take photos and/or make a film for each hotel along the way. I always gave my all, whether I was working with a five-star hotel or a run-down hostel. This is a shot of me in action as I staged a shot for the Monkey Tree Hotel.

Photo 21 – San Moreno Valley, California – Day 730: The car from hell! I bought the car that once exploded on me back from the mechanic I had sold it to. I had it towed to the Manheim Auction House in hopes of getting my money back. All the while, I was racing Tom, the invisible man who had the car's title.

Photo 22 – Dyersville, Iowa – Day 745: I had always wanted to take just one swing at the famous Field of Dreams. If you look closely, you'll see I'm shoeless, but unlike Shoeless Joe, I didn't get the ball out of the infield.

Photo 23 – Chile-Argentina border crossing – Day 848: Lots of unspeakably long bus rides as I raced towards Ushuaia. Thankfully the beautiful Patagonian landscape helped take my mind off the grind of getting there in time for my expedition to Antarctica.

Photo 24 – en route to Ushuaia, Argentina – Day 857: I had gotten so far off the grid that I was the only passenger on the entire bus for the day.

Photo 25 – Orne Harbor, Antarctica – Day 868: To give the gigantic glaciers some perspective, I snapped a shot of a Zodiac between these two absolute beauties. The clear blue skies and nearly aqua-colored waters were something I never expected to come across in Antarctica.

Photo 26 – Orne Harbor, Antarctica – Day 868: At the end of the earth, I learned my greatest lesson. This will always be my favorite photo.

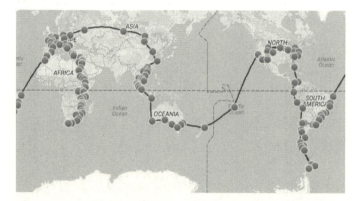

Photo 27 – London, England – Day 1,074: On my travel blog, I had an interactive map that I used to plot my route around the world. I was finally able to connect all the dots when I stepped back onto the same platform from where I'd departed London's Victoria station 736 days prior.

On June 24, 2020, Annika Ferry died in a tragic hiking accident in Australia. I cannot express how much of an impact she had on me. I was lucky enough to spend two weeks with her in Antarctica and then a few more days in London after my journey ended. In short, in all my travels, and in all my life, she was quite simply the most incredible human being I have ever crossed paths with.

Annika, I was in awe of you—this book is for you.

ACKNOWLEDGMENTS

Belief is a very powerful force, but so too is encouragement. I'm grateful to have parents that have supported me every step of the way. I love you both. When I came back from my three-month leave of absence in 2011, I wrote a fictional story about my travels. The writing was terrible, but a friend of mine took the time to help me with it. She got nothing in return. Had she told me the truth about how bad it was, I might have stopped writing altogether, but said it was good and that I should continue writing. That encouragement led to all this. I cannot thank you enough, Elizabeth.

Many others have helped along the way when it comes to my writing: Justin, Ben, Mary, Teresa, and Ned. A massive thanks to the editors that guided me through this process: Kristen Tate and Christina Boys. Kathryn Maus created the cover, which I love. I'd be remiss if I didn't mention the hotels that accepted my barter agreement along the way; each time a hotel allowed me to stay in exchange for my work, I was humbled in a way that's hard to explain. Often my eyes would well up when they returned my email because it meant that I could keep moving forward for free. I feel a deep sense of gratitude for each hotel I worked with; there are too many to name here, but the full list can be found on my website. I would also like to thank Monica for her support.

To the two women I've written about most in these pages—wow, what can I say?—you will always have a special place in my heart. While a thank you doesn't suffice, *thank you*. I feel blessed because of you and I appreciate you allowing me to share our story here.

Finally, to anyone who has read this book cover to cover, while I wrote it for me, I also wrote it for you. I hope in some small way my story has a ripple effect and it helps you find, follow, and stick with your deepest dreams.

CDXLIV

HELP SPREAD
THE WORD

If you enjoyed my book, please consider leaving a review on Amazon. Reviews are very important to independent authors and will help other readers find my book. Just a line or two would help enormously.

Follow me @traveltall, for updates on Instagram, Twitter, and Facebook. My website houses more content from my time on the road, so I would encourage you to visit www.traveltall.com. Or just reach out directly and send me an old-fashioned email: traveltall@yahoo.com.

ABOUT THE AUTHOR

Eric Giuliani was born and raised in Pennsylvania, but quickly realized that wanderlust was what made him tick. After stints in Hawaii, Seattle, and Miami, he set out on the around-the-world journey chronicled in his first book, *Sky's the Limit*. Eric's idea of a good time is catching a ball game with his buddies and swapping stories from the road with fellow travelers. He now spends his days photographing South Florida's coastline and thinking about how he wants to throw a dart at a map and go wherever it lands. At six feet ten inches tall, Eric is an expert at ducking through doorways. Find Eric on Instagram, Twitter, and Facebook @traveltall and visit his website traveltall.com for additional information about his around-the-world journey.

Made in the USA
Middletown, DE
12 March 2021

35361507R00165